THE KID CHRONICLES

HOPE PAGE

Published in the United States of America

ISBN 978-1-962110-20-4 (SC)

Hope Page Books
222 West 6th Street
Suite 400, San Pedro, CA, 90731
www.stellarliterary.com

Ordering Information and Rights Permission:

Quantity sales. Special discounts might be available on quantity purchases by corporations, associations, and others. For details, contact the publisher at the address above.

For Book Rights Adaptation and other Rights Permission. Call us at toll-free 1-888-945-8513 or send us an email at admin@stellarliterary.com.

Contents

First Saturday

Niko begrudgingly walks through the door of the First Steps program with his mother and is greeted by Ginelle Miller and Mallory Campbell. Ginelle reaches out to shake Niko's hand; she asks, "What's your name young man?"

Niko accepts her hand and answers, "My name is Niko."

Ginelle replies, "I'm Mrs. Miller and this is Mrs. Campbell." Mrs. Campbell shakes Niko's hand and invites him to sit down with the boys while Mrs. Miller talks to his mother. Mrs. Miller welcomes Niko's mother, Rita, to the program. Mrs. Miller leads a nervous Rita to the room full of mothers talking; Rita takes a seat in the circle.

Mrs. Campbell walks Niko to the room designated for the male participants. Niko sits in the circle of boys. Brad sits next to Niko. Stephanie sits next to Rita; Stephanie is just as nervous as Rita. Not knowing what to expect, Stephanie and Rita sit quietly waiting for the meeting to start. Niko and Brad sit quietly irritated.

Exactly at nine a.m., Mrs. Campbell stands at the center of the circle of boys and Mrs. Miller stands in the center of the circle of mothers. Mrs. Miller welcomes the mothers to the support group for mothers of boys who have exhibited aggressive or inappropriate response patterns at school. Mrs. Campbell welcomes the boys: Niko, Brad, Tucker, Mega, Lucas, Eli, Xander, Levi, Caleb and Jace to the court ordered First Steps program intended to get young, violent boys on track in school.

Mrs. Miller explains to the mothers that she has two goals to accomplish within the six-week program: "My first goal is to create connections between you and your son that will heal any hurts and repair broken bonds that have occurred over the years. My second goal is to give you tools to help you support yourself in troubling times. Just because we are mothers doesn't mean our needs shouldn't be met."

Mrs. Campbell asks the boys if they understood why they are here.

Xander shouts, "Because we don't know how to act."

Lucas raises his hand and says, "I have ADHD, and I do stupid stuff."

Tucker raises his hand. Mrs. Campbell points to him; he says, "Fighting!"

Eli says, "We broke a rule."

Mrs. Campbell listens to their answers. She says, "Boys, those are all great attempts to understand the true answer. Honestly, the real answer is more complicated than just you don't know how to act, you have ADHD, or you broke rules. It will take a lot of work to identify and address your personal struggles."

Mrs. Campbell explains, "The purpose of the program is for each of you to gain perspective on how your reactions affect other people. Hopefully, you will continue the journey after the program ends and do more work to address your specific needs."

Mega says, "We need to get out of here." The boys laugh.

Mrs. Campbell says, "See, right there. You dismissed me by making light of my point. That's why we are here to think about how we affect others before we act. Mega, not cool."

Mega says, "I apologize." Mrs. Campbell thanks him for his apology.

Mrs. Campbell asks for a volunteer to share the details of the event that resulted in your requirement to be here. All the boys are shamefully quiet until Niko says, "A boy was bullying my friend. He was hitting and smacking her, so I beat him up."

Xander says, "That's understandable!"

Mrs. Campbell asks, "Xander, do you think there were more options?"

Caleb says, "If you tell the teacher, people call you a snitch and think you're scared."

Lucas says, "The best way to stop a bully is to beat them up."

Mrs. Campbell says, "But, look where that got Niko, and how it inconvenienced his mother. You must think about how everyone is affected by what you do. Niko can you see how hard this has been on your mother?" Niko puts his head down and nods yes.

Mrs. Campbell asks, "Where does it end when we take vengeance in our own hand. Then someone comes back for you. It can be a never-ending cycle. The person you beat up has friends and family who don't want to see them hurt and may want to hurt you for what you did."

Jace says, "That's just how it is. You get everyone who crosses you until one day somebody gets you. You can't live where we live and not accept that chance."

Mrs. Campbell says, "Understandable, Jace, but if we live our whole life just to hurt people then we die, what's the meaning of life? Jace, it just can't be that simple."

Jace answers, "It's just the way it is."

Mrs. Campbell says, "I once knew a young man just like you all, always ready to fight for any reason. Very angry, very unhappy, all that fighting didn't make him happy, all that fighting made him angrier so much so that he almost lost his sanity. You all need to consider the long-term negative effects of putting out so much negative energy."

Eli replies, "You're talking about karma. My mother tells me that I bring bad karma to us."

Mrs. Campbell says, "Thanks for sharing, Eli. I want to share the story of the young man I mentioned to illustrate what your mother is telling you about karma."

The Apex Animal

The sun is sitting high in the bright, clear, blue sky illuminating the entire Apex. Summer fun fills the air as kids are laughing and playing. Some younger kids play in sprinklers in their front yard. The older boys on the block play basketball in the street. Some girls jump rope. Cars blast music riding up and down the street. The white box-shaped ice cream truck playing music is riding slowly through the neighborhood selling popsicles and soft-serve ice cream.

Aria James, a pretty, little girl who just turned six-years-old last month and preparing for the first grade, enjoys the summer day riding her bike. Aria dressed in white shorts, pink sandals, and a pink t-shirt has a huge, beautiful smile on her pretty face. Her hair fixed in long ponytails wrapped in pink and white hairbows and barrettes.

Aria James is known as Redbird throughout the Apex. There's a superstition that red birds are good luck. There's on old wise tale that says kiss at a red bird, and it will bring you love or something good will happen to you. Red birds represent passion, endurance, and strength because they are persistent and unyielding to environmental circumstances. Red birds are small, and the females are warm brown with a reddish hue, and that was fitting of Aria's personality and physical description.

Aria rides her pink and white bike up the walkway and right into Jesse James' toe. She looks at him and laughs. Jesse says, "Oh! Okay! You ran over my toe, Little Girl." He picks her up from her bike. He tickles her while he holds her in the air.

"I got you Big Brother," Aria says holding her stomach and giggling.

"You better watch your back, Little Sister," he says touching her nose. "I'm going to get you when you least expect it," he adds.

Aria laughs: "I love you, Big Brother!" she says.

"I love you, Sister," he says. Aria is the only person Jesse loves. As a child Jesse, cold and heartless, hated everyone and everything. One would think Jesse had a hard life, but his life was typical for someone in his working-class neighborhood.

Jesse was born socially awkward and very angry. He has always been a natural loner and a born fighter. Not a wizard with words, Jesse James is a master with his fists. Jesse had to fight early and often. He enjoyed fighting because fighting was easier than talking or feeling; he didn't start them, but he didn't run from them.

Jesse James grew up to be the most feared and most erratic agitator in the seven-square-mile neighborhood on the east side of Detroit known as the Apex. No one in the Apex ever called Jesse James by his given name. He has always been known as Blue Jay, mainly because he always seems sad. Many also noted that like the bird, Jesse James is intelligent, tricky, and aggressive.

Twenty-year-old Blue Jay loves his sister with all his heart. Aria never saw the angry, aggressive side of her brother. He is always so proud of everything she does. With Aria, Jesse James has always been kind and caring. While the world sees Blue Jay as a monster, Aria sees him as her loving big brother.

From the moment Redbird was born, Blue Jay loved her. She is his only friend. Blue Jay spoils Aria by giving her everything she wants when she wants it. Blue Jay has worked six days per week, eight hours each day since graduating from high school to make money to provide for Aria and her future.

Just after four p.m., Blue Jay sits Redbird on her bike. He bends down to her eye level and hugs her; he says, "I'll see you later, Redbird! Be careful Redbird!"

She replies, "You be careful, Big Brother."

He says, "I will Redbird," as he gets in his car sitting in the driveway. He starts the car, backs out of the driveway, and pulls off.

Redbird happily went on riding her bike up and down the block. Je`Lynn James, registered nurse, single mother, and only child of deceased parents, listens to the news on the television as she cooks and watches her daughter through the window with the biggest smile on her face.

Je`Lynn goes outside to get Redbird for dinner. Je`Lynn repeatedly calls for Aria, but there is no answer. Je`Lynn panics as she frantically calls her daughter's name. "Aria! Aria! Aria, baby come to mommy" Je'Lynn calls out with tears in her eyes.

Neighbors notice Je`Lynn is panicking and joins the search. "Redbird," the neighbors shout as they check the backyards and alleys.

Je`Lynn walks down the block screaming and shouting for her daughter. When she reaches the corner, and she sees Aria's bike lying on the curb with the back tire slowly spinning, Aria is nowhere in sight. Je`Lynn screams, "Call the police! Call the police!" The neighbors rush to her side, pulling out their phones to call 9-1-1 to report Aria missing. An eerie, aberrant feeling takes over a once pretty day in the Apex.

The spinning tire says something very ugly has just happened to Aria. Je`Lynn is distraught at the possibilities of what could have happened to Aria. Je`Lynn knows what happens to little girls that are kidnapped, most don't come home. Je`Lynn's entire body is weak; her heart and mind race with thoughts that are unspeakable. Je`Lynn is out of her mind with fear and anxiety.

By the time police arrives on the scene, Je`Lynn is uncontrollably hyper ventilating on the curb where her daughter's bike lays. The neighbors stand around Je`Lynn watching her in sorrow as they strategize what to do next. Mrs. Sawyer, Je`Lynn's neighbor of twenty-four years, does most of the talking to the police.

Brucille Liggett, who lives across the street, goes into Je`lynn's house to get several pictures of Aria to give to the police. Brucille and Je`Lynn have been good friends for more than twenty years.

Je`Lynn had no family in Detroit, so her neighbors and her kids were all she had outside of her career as a beloved nurse. The residents of the eleven hundred block of Mansfield Street are very close and always look out for each other.

In this moment, the neighbors are extremely concerned and distraught about Aria. The police try to keep everyone calm as they gather information from the adrenaline-laced crowd.

The police organize the neighbors to search the surrounding area. Uniformed officers lead one group west, another group walks east, the third group goes south, and the last group searches north of the James' home. Each group searches every garage, vacant home, alley, dumpster, car, pile of trash, and backyard.

When the detectives arrive on the scene, they walk up and down the streets of the Apex questioning everyone who walks or drives through the haunting streets of the Apex. Two K-9 units search vacant houses and dumpsters in the alley. The police ask every neighbor if they saw any strange or suspicious vehicles or persons in the neighborhood at the time of the disappearance of Aria "Redbird" James. Not one neighbor admits to seeing anything of importance.

The mystery of the disappearance of Aria "Redbird" James has the entire Apex on pins and needles when it broke on the six o'clock news.

After a few hours with no leads, the detectives widen the search to cover the entire Apex. The neighbors and police search beyond sunset. When the night falls completely over the Apex, Blue Jay arrives home. He has no clue what is going on at his house. He couldn't find his charger and his phone died while he was at work. Panicked by the sight of police surrounding his house, he belligerently shouts when the police stop him from turning the corner.

He hops out the car, screaming at the police demanding to know what was going on at his house. Just as the police are about to restrain Blue Jay, Mr. Woodland yells, "Your little sister is missing." Blue Jay runs home leaving his running car at the corner.

As soon as he reaches the porch, he hears Detective Mosley telling Je`Lynn that a young girl's body fitting the description of Aria was found in an abandon home just outside the Apex; he says, "We need you to look at a picture..." Je`Lynn faints falling into her caring neighbors' arms before Det. Mosley could finish the sentence, so Mrs. Sawyer kneeling and holding Je`Lynn looks at the picture nodding her head saying yes that is her.

Mrs. Sawyer tries to hold it together, but the tears and emotions burst out of her. Jesse "Blue Jay" James is infuriated as he looks unsympathetically at his mother; Jesse snatches the phone from Det. Mosley's hand. When he comprehends the image, he screams and falls to his knees sobbing, "She should have been outside watching her."

What was originally a missing child case is now a rape and murder of a minor case, so the attitude and the approach of the detectives have completely changed.

Everyone who was once a potential witness is now a potential suspect. EVERYONE, especially Blue Jay who is a known terrorist in the Apex.

All the residents of Mansfield Street are suspects because they had opportunity. The intensity of the scene increases as the questions aim to narrow the whereabouts of every neighbor at the time of the crime. While the detectives canvas the block questioning every neighbor and resident on the block where Aria James' body was found, the crime scene investigators process Aria's body and the abandoned house.

Blue Jay's swinging emotions range from despair to rage. While the detectives try to get the details of his actions and whereabouts throughout the day, he demands to know where Aria was found. He repeatedly yells, "Stop, asking me questions and tell me who took my sister. I want to know who touched my sister right now." They can't calm him down on the scene, so they take him to the precinct.

At the precinct, Blue Jay is authentically overcome with grief, so the detectives give him some time to gather himself. They watch him in the interrogation room via the secret cameras planted around the room. A river of tears flows as he screams his pain. He is shocked and bewildered. He finally gathers himself enough to give the detectives his supervisor's name and number at the factory. They call his supervisor to confirm he was at work the entire evening. The detectives' emotions conform from suspicion of him to pity for him.

Blue Jay says his sister was the only person on earth that he loved and the only person on earth that truly loved him. Jesse James swears, "As long as the sky is blue, the oceans' water flow, and the grass is green, I will love my sister and never hurt her." With more than seventy-five years of hunting and interrogating murderers between the four detectives working the homicide case. The detectives believe him with their heads and guts. They express their deepest sympathy, conclude the interview, and offer to take him home.

Home...what is home for Jesse "Blue Jay" James? A place where he resides with a mother he hates, and a mother who hates him. Without Aria, that house is no longer a home. The last person he wants to see is her. He blames her. If only she wasn't in the house cooking. If only she had been outside watching over Redbird as she rode her bike.

He gets out of the car and reluctantly walks toward the crowded house. His body hurt for no reason. He felt pain from head to toe. The only thing that will ease the pain is **REVENGE**. The desire for revenge circulates his body through his veins with his blood.

No one speaks to him as he makes his way to his bedroom. In fact, everyone is silent until he goes into his room. He showers and puts on clothes. He has no plans to sleep tonight. He lays across his bed. He can hear the neighbors and his mother talking. His mind races from what to who happened to his sister.

Eventually, the house is quiet when all the neighbors leave. Je`Lynn locks herself in her bathroom to muffle her cries. He can no longer take the sound of her voice. Like a caged animal, Blue Jay needs to be free.

On a hot summer night, Blue Jay puts on a black hoodie and black steel toe boots. He grabs two of his guns and walks out the back door. He walks through the neighborhood thinking someone had to know who touched his sister. In his mind, everyone is a suspect. His blood boils in his body, and the only thing that will turn down the heat is to hurt someone like someone hurt Redbird.

The neighborhood is quiet, still, and dark. A gentle breeze sweeps through the Apex. Blue Jay walks around for about an hour. His min is about to explode with thoughts. Just then, he hears a girl scream. From nowhere, a hysterical girl, Gabrielle, ran into his arms panicking. Through her winded breathing she asks Blue Jay to help her; she says, "A man snatched her friend and took her into the alley."

Blue Jay pulls out his gun and the girl leads him to the alley. There stood known rapist and pedophile, Taymad Williams, a 26-year-old black male

9

from the Apex, who is responsible for five rapes, one-handedly choking a sixteen-year-old girl while struggling to get her pants unfastened with his free hand.

Taymad just served seven years, seven months, and thirteen days in state prison for raping three girls. Since being released, Taymad regularly molested several of his younger relatives until a year ago when one told, and his family put him out of the house.

After being exposed and shun by his family, Taymad had to turn to the street to fulfill his sick need for young girls. In the last six months, Taymad had broken into several homes to rape teen girls, but was only able to complete the mission twice. Those crimes remain unsolved because the crime lab has a huge backlog of rape kits. Taymad knew it was only a matter of time before he went back to prison because his DNA was on file from the previous cases.

He was prowling for a victim when the girls practically walked right into his arms. When he saw the two girls headed toward him, he hid in the alley to grab Shawnna. He had been watching her for months waiting for the perfect opportunity to grab her.

Blue Jay quietly creeps up behind him, puts his gun to the back of his head covered with a baseball cap. Taymad removes his hands from Shawnna's neck. Blue Jay tells the girls to quietly run home and tell no one. Blue Jay promises that Taymad will never hurt anyone ever again. The girls thank him, and they did just what they were told. They ran home and never spoke of the incident.

Blue Jay interrogates Taymad about hurting girls, the death of his sister, and other men in the neighborhood that hurt girls. Taymad begs for his life; he swears he doesn't know anything about his sister's death. Taymad knows Blue Jay is ruthless and has hurt many people before for much less than rape.

Taymad knows he is in real danger. With the rage in Blue Jay's heart, Taymad's pleas are all in vain. Taymad is about to die. His death will pay for every rape he committed. Taymad must die because Redbird died. Boom! Boom! Boom! Boom! Boom! Taymad takes five bullets to the head to ensure he never lives again. The death of Taymad Williams is the birth of the **Apex Animal**.

Blue Jay takes off running down the alley and around the corner until he feels like he is free and clear of witnesses. He walks a little more, but now he walks with purpose. His mind feels a bit of relief. He walks around until sunlight breaks through the thick dark atmosphere.

When he reaches home, he destroys his clothes and boots. He goes to his room and searches the Internet for a list of sexual offenders in the Apex. There are more names than he expected, but this is a start. He thinks one of the sex offenders on the list must be the murderer. Blue Jay makes up his mind, he will kill the man who murdered his sister, and no one will stop him.

Jesse "Blue Jay" James avoids his mother as he leaves for work. He reports to work at eight a.m. without a wink of sleep. His co-workers are shocked to see him. His supervisor asks if he needs to go home, but he declines. Blue Jay plans to keep a low profile to avoid suspicion. Unlike crimes he committed in the past, the crime last night had purpose and he can't risk getting caught before he accomplishes his goal: revenge for his sister's death. He is even more closed off and quiet than normal. Blue Jay sees his sister's face everywhere he looks, but Blue Jay push through.

Jesse "Blue Jay" James takes his lunch break in the break room where his co-workers are watching the news. The murder of convicted rapist Taymad Williams in the Apex area is the lead story. Jesse James sits watching the news as he eats. His co-workers talk about how Taymad deserved to die because he was a rapist.

After work, Blue Jay goes home to shower and sleep until nightfall. When night falls over the Apex, Blue Jay dresses in all black with a black New York Yankee cap and carries a pair of black leather gloves in his pocket. Blue Jay hides weapons in his socks and waistband.

He makes his way to 15142 Apt 2 on Livingston Street; the home of target 1: Athaniel Mirks guilty of rape and molestation of five minor females between the ages of six and nine. Athaniel, who has been on house arrest for the last year, must report to his house before sunset every night, no exceptions. Athaniel doesn't know it, but the grand reaper is coming for him this very night.

Blue Jay takes a deep breath before climbing through a cracked window in the back of the house. Blue Jay is determined to get information from

11

Athaniel. The creepy, old house is completely dark and silent. Blue Jay slowly creeps through the house holding an Emerson Karambits combat knife in one hand and a Glock 18 in the other hand. He peeks into the first bedroom, but there's a woman asleep in there. He goes to the next bedroom; there's a child sleeping in that room. He checks the last bedroom; there is Athaniel Mirks.

Blue Jay walks up to the bed and puts the gun on his face. When Athaniel opens his eyes, Blue Jay whispers with a tone of aggression, "If you move or scream, I will kill you." Blue Jay whispers, "Did you rape and murder a little girl yesterday?" Athaniel swears it wasn't him and he doesn't know who did it. Blue Jay asks if he is sure because this is the time to confess. Athaniel swears he didn't do anything, and he doesn't know anything.

Blue Jay believes him, but he asks him one more question: why do you hurt little girls anyway. Athaniel shamefully professes, crying yet whispering, "I am sick! Man! I don't know what is wrong with me. My brain is sick. I can't help it. I'm sick!" Blue Jay stands over him calmly; he whispered: "You're sick huh? Well, I think I got the cure." With all his might, he covers Athaniel's mouth and swiftly jabs the knife through Athaniel's throat.

Blue Jay watches the life drain from him as he gasps and gargles for air through the clots of blood filling his throat. When Athaniel is devoid of life, Blue Jay leaves the room and creeps out of the house undetected. Blue Jay quietly makes his way back to the street and heads to mission 2: 17113 Ravette Street (just a few blocks from Athaniel Mirks' home) the home of twenty-nine-year-old Jayrod Stevens, known predator of teenage girls.

Jayrod doesn't rape girls. He seduces them with money, gifts, rides in his car, and attention. Jayrod, a small-time drug dealer, spends his days sexing truant middle school girls and his evenings and nights with high school girls.

As Blue Jay turns the corner, he notices Jayrod sitting in his running car in front of his house. Blue Jay sees Jayrod is distracted by his phone, so Blue Jay takes advantage of the opportunity. Blue Jay hops in the car totally startling Jayrod. Jayrod yells at Blue Jay and demands Blue Jay get out of the car. Blue Jay shows Jayrod his gun, and tells him to pull off. Jayrod drives around while he inquires what Blue Jay wants with him.

As they ride down the street, Blue Jay asks about his sister's murder, but Jayrod swears he knows nothing. Blue Jay laughs and says, "Okay drop me off on Elm and Albany." When they get to the intersection, Blue Jay instructs him to pull around to the alley. Jayrod reassures Blue Jay he knows nothing of his sister's murder. Blue Jay opens the door, laughs, and shoots him five times in the head. Blue Jay wipes down the door handle and walks away from the car. He patrols the street until just before sunrise.

He returns home, destroys his clothes, and showers. He lays across the bed wide awake staring at the ceiling fan until it was time to go to work. He continues to avoid his mother. He hated her more now than ever. He never knew why he hated his mother. He just always did, and she felt it even when he was a baby. From the moment Jesse James was born, he pierced his mother with eyes of disdain and detest. He has no sympathy for her. NO SYMPATHY at all for Je`Lynn James.

Before work, Blue Jay stops at the mini market to get lunch. As he approaches the counter to pay for his food, he and Shawnna look directly in each other's eyes. Shawnna's eyes water as she stare at Blue Jay. She mouths thank you; she quickly turns to pay for her stuff and runs out the store. Blue Jay feels a sense of righteousness as he watches Shawnna run from the store. Blue Jay pays for his food, and leaves the store to go to work.

While on his lunch break, Blue Jay watches the news. The deaths of sex offender Athaniel Mirks and petty criminal Jayrod Stevens are the leading story. The reporter speaks of the recent three murders like they were community service.

After lunch, he goes back to the factory thinking of his next target. He couldn't think of one person in the Apex that would test him. Everyone in the Apex knows him and his ruthlessness. He has a reputation for being brutal, so there is no way anyone in the Apex would harm his sister. He thinking: It's an OUTSIDER.

At the end of his work day, Blue Jay asks his supervisor for a two-week leave to deal with the funeral arrangements. His supervisor is more than agreeable. Blue Jay is surprised when his supervisor presents him with a bag of money donated by the entire staff to help pay for the funeral. Blue Jay leaves work with a new plan that he has two weeks to accomplish.

Blue Jay goes to the office supply store, to make flyers to solicit information regarding the murder. He downloads pictures from his phone.

13

types a heartfelt message with a description of the crime that took his sister's life. Blue Jay has been saving five hundred dollars every month for the last five years to send his sister to college. He decides to use that money for the reward. He prints 200 copies of the flyer he created.

Trentin West (called Tren by her friends), an employee at the office supply store, checks on Blue Jay to see if he needs help. They talk about the flyer and his sister. Trentin is overwhelmingly saddened by the story. She read about the story in the newspaper the day before, but it was something about meeting Blue Jay that made the story real.

Tren secretly talks to her co-workers and convinces them to chip in to pay for the flyers. Blue Jay is extremely grateful for their help; Blue Jay is especially grateful to Tren for her empathy, attention and concern. Tren is not from the Apex; she has never heard of him, so she didn't hold any prejudice against him. Tren truly feels sympathy for him. Tren befriends Jesse James, his first real friend. They exchange phone numbers. Tren promises to come to the funeral. Jesse James is so grateful.

Blue Jay uses the money donated by his co-workers to pay the funeral home. When he makes it home, his mother is with Mrs. Sawyer and Brucille Liggett planning the funeral. He doesn't even look at either women as he hands his mother the receipt showing the funeral expenses were paid in full.

Blue Jay isn't ready to deal with his negligent (in his opinion) mother. It didn't matter what Je`Lynn did, in Jesse James' eyes, she is always the blame. Blue Jay changes his clothes and moves to put his new plan in action: 1) hit the pavement and hand-out flyers all day, 2) patrol the streets in the evenings, and 3) continue interrogating known pedophiles at night.

He puts flyers in every store. He puts flyers in gallon-sized freezer bags and staples them on light poles at every intersection in and around the Apex. He stops every passerby to plea for any information. As he speaks, he comes across as mature, articulate, caring, motivated, sensitive, and deeply saddened. People are empathetic and intrigued and the reward besides no one ever wanted to see someone get away with murdering a child.

He passes out flyers until sunset before going home to change his clothes. To keep true to his plan, he conducts his nightly foot patrol of the Apex neighborhood. As he walks down Fairway Road, he sees Kyrie Kelp, a nineteen-year-old high school dropout dressed in a black hoodie and a black baseball cap, breaking into the home of Sister Pasree` Johnson who lives with her daughter and granddaughters since her husband passed away three years ago. Blue Jay knows Kyrie as a harmless, petty thief.

Blue Jay sneaks up behind Kyrie, and forcefully grabs him and pulls him down from the window. He turns around to see it is Blue Jay. Simultaneously, he is relieved it's not the police, and he is afraid because it's Blue Jay. People fear Blue Jay more than they do the police.

Blue Jay convinces Kyrie to leave the house full of sleeping women. They walk and talk for a while. They talk about his quest to find Aria's killer. Blue Jay tells Kyrie that violating vulnerable females isn't right. Blue Jay tells Kyrie, "Those girls need protection from us not predation. As men we are the very ones God sent to lead and protect the girls." Kyrie promises to be more mindful in the future and to keep an ear out in the streets for information on Aria's death.

After talking to Kyrie, Blue Jay makes his way home. He yearns to sleep, but the anger and adrenaline keep him wide awake. His mind races with memories and questions as he lays across his bed feeling mentally fatigued. He can hear his sister's voice in his mind. He can see his sister's face in his mind. He watches the sunrise through his bedroom window. In a hazy daze, he has a vision of a red bird flying toward the sunlight. Tears pour from his eyes.

He can't take the thought of his sister in a casket. The funeral is only thirty hours away. He wonders how he is going to hold it together; he thinks about the funeral as he showers and brushes his teeth. He has no idea how to prepare himself for the funeral. When he hears his mother moving around, he goes out to ask if she needs anything. They sit at the table not looking at each other and having small talk. There are so many things they want to say, but don't. Instead of mourning with his mother, Blue Jay leaves to get things he needs for funeral.

Blue Jay goes to see Don Sumrell, the most popular salesperson in Detroit, at Exclusive City Suits to purchase a suit and a pair of shoes. He stops to have breakfast. After eating, he talks to patrons, he hands out flyers. People in the restaurant are very empathetic toward him. The restaurant's collects money to from the patron donate toward the reward.

15

After leaving the restaurant, Blue Jay stops by the funeral home to talk to the director and make sure the arrangements for the services are set. Blue Jay looks solid and calm on the outside, but internally he is broken and fatigued. Despite how he feels, he carries forth with his plan for the day.

Blue Jay drives back to the Apex. He goes door to door handing out flyers and soliciting information about his sister's murder. Normally, people were afraid or uncomfortable around Blue Jay, but today people are caring and empathetic toward him. They intently listen to him, and promise to keep an ear out for information and report it back to him.

Blue Jay continues soliciting information until nightfall. When he returns home, his mother is cooking with Mrs. Sawyer and Brucille Liggett. Blue Jay goes straight to his room. He showers and lays across his bed in the dark. Tears roll from his eyes into his ears as he watches the spinning ceiling fan.

The motion of the fan puts him in a trance. He finally drifts into a dream of walking through the Apex on a hot summer day. The hot sun scorches his skin as he walks down an unfamiliar street. The block is full of big, beautiful brick colonial houses. The joyous sound of happy children fills the air. Some children play in the sprinkler. Some children ride their bikes. Some children play tag.

As he walks, a red bird comes flying toward him. He stops and stares at the bird. The bird hovers over Blue Jay's head. The bird's wings flap so fast that they look as if they are moving in slow motion. The red bird wants Jesse to follow it. The bird leads him into a house with an opened door. Suddenly, darkness covers the Apex, as he enters the home. He sees a young man with a black baseball cap and hoodie standing over his sister's beaten, bruised, dead body. Blue Jay tries to grab the man, but he can't reach him. The man runs out the backdoor and into the alley. Blue Jay chases him through the alley, but loses him.

Blue Jay tries to go back to get his sister, but she is gone. The red bird flies around the empty house. Blue Jay panics as he runs around the house looking for his sister. The red bird lands on Blue Jay's shoulder. He turns his head, but he wakes up before seeing the red bird.

Staring at the ceiling again, Blue Jay lays in the dark on his back. He is so exhausted and fatigued. He drifts back off to sleep and into another dream.

He looks up and there is the face of Old Man Addison leaning over him as he lays in the bed.

Blue Jay looks directly into the eyes of the dead face of Mr. Addison. Mr. Addison sits on Blue Jay's bed, and says, "Young man, you killed me, why did you kill me?" Mr. Addison reaches his hand out to touch Blue Jay's shoulder, saying, "What did I ever do to you?" Before Mr. Addison could touch Blue Jay, Blue Jay wakes up.

The death of Mr. Addison was an accident. Blue Jay never meant to hurt anyone. One day, he decided to play a joke on Mr. Addison. Blue Jay threw a brick through Mr. Addison's window. The crashing noise scared Mr. Addison and the shocked caused a heart attack.

James Harold Addison died of a heart attack as a reaction of Blue Jay's actions. Blue Jay never thought he would kill Mr. Addison by throwing that brick through the window, but he did, and the guilt is something that has bothered Blue Jay since the day it happened. Blue Jay has made peace with the fact that the guilt will haunt him for the rest of his life.

Blue Jay wakes up with a mixture of feelings: guilt, anxiety, sadness, pain, and pressure. Maybe all the bad stuff he has done in his life has come back and cursed his sister? Maybe her death at someone else's hands was really his fault? Blue Jay deal with his emotions in his mother's house. He needs a clear space. He gets up and packs his clothes in duffle bags and suitcases.

He showers and brushes his teeth. He puts on his suit, brushes his hair, and tells his mother goodbye. He is so ready to leave that even the thought of riding in the family car with his mother and Mrs. Sawyer doesn't intrigue him. He packs his stuff in the backseat of his car and drives to the funeral home.

When he pulls up to the funeral home, he has a complete breakdown. He sits in his car alone and cries like a sad child. After crying, Blue Jay gathers himself before entering the funeral. The funeral is packed with the Apex community. The entire community has shown up. The staff from the office supply store comes as they promised.

Tren West greets Blue Jay as he walks toward the casket. He grabs her hand and asks if she will come to the casket with him. Tren, with empathy for Blue Jay for losing his sister, finds herself attracted to Blue Jay.

17

Blue Jay adores Tren and everything about her. Tren is the first person outside of Redbird to treat him like a good person.

For the first time in all his life, Jesse "Blue Jay" James really likes a girl. Tren, a smart graduate from a suburban high school, with a full ride to Spelman College for her academic achievements and her athletic achievements in track and basketball. She maintained a 4.0 since first grade. She was the star of her high school's championship girls' track team. Tren was also the starting point guard for the championship girls' varsity basketball team.

Along with being gifted, talented and beautiful, she goes to church faithfully with her mother and grandmother. Her father works six days a week as a supervisor at a factory in the Detroit area. Her mother is a registered nurse who works in the emergency room at the hospital five miles outside the Apex.

Tren grew up in a two-parent home in a suburb of Detroit. Tren is the opposite of Blue Jay, so dating Blue Jay is not something anyone would expect of her. Tren was raised to be kind to others, and do right even when no one is looking. While Blue Jay spent his whole life causing havoc and chaos, Tren managed to stay out of trouble. Tren is preparing for college in the fall; Blue Jay is a vigilante murderer.

One may ask what would a good girl want with such a bad guy, but Blue Jay makes her feel safe. Blue Jay listens to her and cares about her thoughts, dreams, and accomplishments. Tren calms the savage beast in Blue Jay. The idea of Tren being his girlfriend makes Blue Jay want to change his life and attitude.

Tren is deeply saddened by J.J.'s (as she called him) circumstances; she holds his hand all the way to the casket. Empathy is another factor that pulls Tren to Jesse James.

When Tren and Blue Jay reach the casket, she looks at Blue Jay with sympathetic eyes as she rubs his back. He touches his sisters cold face covered in makeup to cover the bruises. Aria looks like a sleeping angel dressed white dress and neatly twisted ponytails encased in a white casket with gold trim.

He takes small stuffed red and blue birds from his pocket and places them in the casket. He and Tren walk away and take a seat in the front row.

Blue Jay refuses to let go of Tren's hand throughout the entire service. Blue Jay never reaches out to his mother to comfort her, which makes her even more sad. Je`Lynn is devastated that her son hates her so much that he won't console her at the funeral of her baby girl.

Je`Lynn screams with sorrow and her screams fill the entire funeral home. Mrs. Sawyer and Brucille hold, fan, console, rock, carry, and support Je`Lynn the entire service. Before the casket is closed, Mrs. Sawyer and Brucille walk Je`Lynn to the casket for a final goodbye. Je`Lynn falls down screaming before the casket.

Je`Lynn's body trembles. When the pallbearers carry the casket down the aisle, Je`Lynn cries uncontrollably as she walks supported by Mrs. Sawyer and Brucille following the casket to and through the exit of the funeral home.

After the service, Blue Jay and Tren stand by his car. Tren makes Blue Jay promise to call her whenever he needs to talk. Tren's concerned about him grieving properly. Somehow, she can tell he doesn't have anyone to lean on or talk to about his loss. Tren can sense Blue Jay is troubled, but she has no inkling of the true dangerous side of Jesse "Blue Jay" James. Blue Jay is thrilled that Tren asked him to call her. Before Tren walks away with her co-workers, she and Blue Jay hug as she expresses her sympathies one more time.

After the funeral, Blue Jay goes to the Palmer Place apartment building on the edge of the Apex. Blue Jay pleas with the owner for an apartment. Blue Jay tells the owner of the building that he can't live in the house where his sister resided from her birth until her death any longer.

The owner, maintenance worker and manager, Sterling Silvers, rents him an apartment purely because he empathizes with him. Silvers, a longtime Apex resident, knows what it is like to have family murdered in the streets of the Apex. Silvers hands Blue Jay a key and leads him to the apartment. Blue Jay carries his three bags and two suitcases into his new empty apartment that is now his home.

That evening the Apex is hot and quiet in the Apex. Blue Jay goes to the diner near the apartment building to get something to eat. As he leaves the diner, he hears a woman in distress. He follows the screams to find a woman being beaten between two houses. He quietly walks over to see a man punching and smacking a woman in the face.

Blue Jay calmly tells the man that a real man fights men; real men don't hit women. The man pushes the woman to the ground by her face then walks toward Blue Jay with a smirk on his face. The man playfully asks, "Oh, so you're out here playing hero tonight?"

Blue Jay replies, "Nope, but I'm not letting you hit her again," as he steps closer toward the man.

The man walks toward Blue Jay as he asks, "So, you think you can dance?"

Blue Jay unbothered by the man's presence, said, "I got that get down."

The man raises his fist and laughs; he said, "Little boys these days have no respect for their elders." Before the man realizes what's happening, Blue Jay quickly rocks the man's face with a combination: left jab then right hook. The beaten woman sits on the ground watching the fisticuffs. That was one thing about Blue Jay. He was a right-handed person, so he always stung his opponents with his powerful, fast left hand.

Blue Jay is naturally muscular and strong. Born with the strength of an ox and the temperament of a short-fused deadly bomb, Blue Jay was born with the talent of a powerful, skilled boxer. Blue Jay continues to sting the dazed man with fists that move like lightning and hit harder than a runaway train. Blue Jay gives the man ten punches unlike any punches he had ever felt before.

The man falls swollen, bruised and knocked-out like a blown light bulb. Blue Jay steps over him, and says, "Is that enough respect for you, Old Timer?" Blue Jay goes over to the shocked woman to help her get up. He asks if she can get home. The woman says yes and thanks him. The woman looks at the man lying on the ground in a deep sleep. She stares for a moment than takes off running. Blue Jay leaves the man on the ground.

Blue Jay walks to the park. He sits on a swing and calls Tren. They get to know more about each other, and they enjoy talking to each other. For Blue Jay, it is refreshing to hear an innocent voice with kindness and affection for him. Tren hates to end the conversation, but she needs to rest up for her summer league game in the morning. She invites Blue Jay to come to the game. He happily accepts, and the two say good night.

The next morning, Blue Jay happily attends the game. He watches the game in awe of how well Tren can play basketball. He had not expected such a beautiful, feminine girl to be such an amazing athlete. Tren leads her team in points, assists, steals, and blocks in the game. Tren's summer league team has the best record in the city. In the four years that Tren has participated in the summer league, her team never lost a game.

While Blue Jay is watching the game, Kyrie comes to sit next to him. When he notices Kyrie, they shake hands and greet each other. Blue Jay asks how did Kyrie know he was at the rec center. Kyrie tells him that he keeps an ear to the streets. Kyrie says, "That information that you want, I got it. Meet me at midnight at the park." They shake hands. Kyrie leaves the recreation center.

Tren and Blue Jay go to lunch after the game, and later they decide to meet up that night for dinner. After dinner, they walk around the Downtown Area. When they turn down a dark street, they see two young girls scantily dressed walking towards them. A car pulls up next to the girls. One man hops out the car and runs toward the girls. He grabs them and drags toward into the car. The girls scream and fight, so the man beats them as he pushes them toward the car.

Startled by the commotion, Tren and Blue Jay stop in their tracks. Tren screams, "You have to do something to save those girls." The girls continue to resist, but are getting closer and closer to the car.

Blue Jay takes off running toward the commotion. Blue Jay catches the guy just as he is about to push the girls into the car. Blue Jay punches the attacker. A second man hops out the car, and points a gun at Blue Jay. Blue Jay takes the gun and punches him. Blue Jay and the first attacker fight. The second guy forces the girls into the car. Blue Jay manages to get a hold of the second guy as well. The girls were crying trapped in the backseat, The interior rear-door handles have been removed, so the girls cannot get out.

The two men together cannot handle Blue Jay. Blue Jay's fierce punches and brute strength overwhelmed both men. The two potential kidnappers try to fight off Blue Jay, but neither of the potential kidnappers are fast or strong enough to stop Blue Jay. Blue Jay beats both kidnappers in their faces and head until they lose their balance.

Blue Jay now securely holds and points the gun. POP! Then stillness. The second guy falls to the ground holding his stomach. Blue Jay shoots the man a second time in the forehead. The first man moves toward Blue Jay and Blue Jay shoots him twice in the chest. The first man falls to the ground and Blue Jay also shoots him in the forehead.

Blue Jay open's the car door. Blue Jay tells the girls to take their sweater and wipe anywhere they touched to remove any fingerprints. The girls do as they were told. "REMEMBER: You never saw me, and I never saw you," he says. "NOW RUN!" He says and the girls take off running. Before walking away, Blue Jay says, "Real men don't have to rape girls, enjoy death punks!"

Blue Jay runs back to Tren who watched the whole thing. They take off running back to Blue Jay's car. As Blue Jay drives, he apologizes to Tren for things getting out of hand. Tren says, "You had to protect those girls. Those guys were probably sex traffickers or rapist. You did the right thing. They planned deaths tonight, they just didn't expect those deaths to be their own. This is all they're fault, not yours. Somebody has to stand up for black girls."

Blue Jay says, "I knew you were a special person." He asks, "Do you want to ride somewhere important with me?"

Tren says, "Sure!" The two drive back to the Apex, where they dispose of the gun after wiping his fingerprints off the guns. They drive to the park where Kyrie sits waiting on the swings.

As they walk over to meet Kyrie, Tren asks "Who is that guy?"

Blue Jay answers, "The guy who knows who killed my sister."

Tren mouth drops; she says, "WHAT? Are you sure you can trust what he says?"

Blue Jay replies, "At least, it's worth listening."

When they reached Kyrie, he stands up and pulls out a cell phone. He shows them a picture of John Kemp. He explains what happened the day Redbird was murdered, "The day your sister was murdered, John just happened to be visiting (he swiped the phone screen to display the next pictures) his cousins, Keith and Kennith Kemp.

"John is here running from the police in his hometown for well you guessed it. He raped a little girl who told on him. He ran up here with his tail between his legs to avoid going to jail. John was walking to the store when he saw your sister. He snatched her off the bike, and took her to the abandoned house. Keith and Kennith has been hiding him in a trap house outside the Apex. (Going into his messages, he shows them an address). This is the address."

Tren asks, "How do you know this?"

Kyrie says, "I know people who know people who know things!"

"Are you sure it was this guy, John," Tren asks.

"He's the rapist," Kyrie proclaims.

Blue Jay says, "Thanks for looking out! I'll get you the reward money tomorrow."

Kyrie replies, "Keep your money and let's go run up in this house and kill everything moving."

Blue Jay asks, "Are you sure you're up for this?"

Kyrie says, "Take your girl home and meet me at my house in an hour. I got a chopper and some fireworks."

Blue Jay says, "That'll be too loud. We need something quiet."

Kyrie says, "I got you," as he and Blue Jay shake hands and they leave the park.

Blue Jay drives Tren home. Blue Jay says, "This night did not turn out the way I had hoped. I am not sure why, but I'm just a terrible person and wherever I go; whatever I do; misery and disaster are there. From the moment I was born, I've been miserable. My mother always hated me; I could sense it. I was a burden to her. Every teacher hated me because they thought I was a terrorist. Tonight, wasn't the first time I killed someone, and when you get out this car; I'm going to kill again.

"You're such a good person. You have so much going for you. I understand if you never want to see me again. I would love to see you again, but I know someone like you and someone like me don't mix. I can't live knowing the person that killed my sister is breathing and living well, and that might scare you. If you allow me in your life, I promise these things: I will change after tonight. I'll always protect you. I'll never yell at you, raise a hand to you, or curse at you. I'll never hurt you or cheat on you. I'll always provide for you. I will support you and your dreams. I'll go back to school while I work full-time."

Tren is touched by what he said. They kiss. She says, "If someone killed my little sister, I would feel the same way. Just promise you won't get hurt or caught. Be safe and call me as soon as it's done." Blue Jay takes her hand in his and kisses the back of her hand. He tells her to have a goodnight and promises to call. Tren tells him to be careful before she gets out the car.

Blue Jay goes back to his apartment to change his clothes. He burns the clothes he was wearing before driving to Kyrie's house. Kyrie hopped in the car; he said, "Let's do this!" Kyrie opened his bookbag to display two sawed-off shotguns, two handguns with silencers and three Molotov cocktails.

They hatch a plan before driving to the trap house where Keith, Kennith, and John are hiding. The trap house is the second house from the corner, so they park around the corner. They cover their heads and faces with hoods and masks. They slowly walk down the alley and across the backyard blending into the darkness.

Kyrie picks the lock on the backdoor. Blue Jay walks into the house holding a handguns with a silencer. Kyrie goes to the side of the house. He throws the first Molotov cocktail hitting the side of the house. He quickly runs to the front of the house to hit the front door with the second Molotov cocktail. He sprints to the next side and hits that side with the last Molotov cocktail. He runs to the back to enter the backdoor.

Blue Jay is agile and quiet as he slowly tiptoes through the house looking for John Kemp, all while hoping that John is really the one who killed Redbird. Kyrie catches up to Blue Jay, Kyrie signals to Blue Jay that they need to hurry up because the burning house is quickly filling with smoke. They come across the three men sleeping in the living room. Keith, lying on the couch, opened his eyes, coughing from the smoke. Kyrie shoots him twice immediately with his handgun with a silencer.

The smoke wakes up John and Kennith. They both jump out of their sleep full of fear and choking. Kyrie turns and shoots Kennith in the head twice. John tries to get up and run, but Blue Jay shoots him in the leg. John falls face first onto the floor. Blue Jay walks over to him and kicks him. Blue Jay says (full of rage), "Look me in my eyes." John turns over. Blue Jay stands over him and points the gun to the center of his face. "Did you touch my sister?" Blue Jay asks.

John acts as if he doesn't know what Blue Jay is talking about. Kyrie stands next to Blue Jay. Kyrie says, "Tell the man about the little girl you raped." Kyrie shoots him in the other leg and both arms.

John (crying in pain) says, "Okay man okay! (raising his hands) Don't shoot me, again! Please!" Kyrie aims the gun at him. John (angrily crying): I raped a little girl!

Blue Jay asks, "Why my sister?"

John cries out: "I don't know your sister. I saw a pretty, little girl and I couldn't help myself."

Blue Jay asks, "How many little girls have you hurt?"

John hesitates. Kyrie shoots him in both hands. He screams in pain. John yells, "Come on man! Okay, man! Five!" Blue Jay rapidly shoots him 5 times in the chest.

Blue Jay and Kyrie run out of the burning house. Boom! The house explodes and then collapses. By the time emergency response workers arrive on the scene, the house and the men are only fragments of memories.

Blue Jay and Kyrie burn their masks, clothes, hoodies and guns in an abandoned house in the Apex. Blue Jay drops Kyrie off at his house. Before Kyrie gets out of the car, Blue Jay thanks Kyrie for all his help.

Blue Jay goes home and calls Tren. Tren is glad to hear his voice, she says, "I've been so worried about you. I'm glad you and Kyrie made it out okay."

Blue Jay says, "Besides my little sister, you are the only person to ever care about me. I appreciate you. I'm glad you answered my call. You must think I'm an animal!"

Tren responds, "No! I don't think you're an animal. You had the courage to do what most people would want to do." She adds, "I've been thinking. In a few weeks, I'm moving away for school. Maybe you should move too. You could get an apartment near campus. Getting away from the Apex and getting a fresh start might be good for you."

"If you're cool with that, I'm down. I could use a fresh start with a good girl. Maybe I can turn my life around and go to college," he says.

Tren says, "I'll help you!"

Blue Jay smiles (for the first time in life: he smiles from being happy) he says, "Sounds like a plan." He asks, "It's really late. I better let you get some sleep. Can I call you tomorrow?"

Tren responds, "I look forward to your call!"

"Sweet dreams," Blue Jay says.

Tren says, "Thank you, goodnight!"

Blue Jay says, "Good night!"

Over the next few weeks, Tren and Blue Jay prepare for the move. Tren already had a dorm on campus, but they are hoping to find Blue Jay an apartment as close to campus as possible.

A week before Tren and Blue Jay are scheduled to move, Blue Jay is pulled over by the police. The officers make him get out of his car. They cuff him and put him in the back of their squad car. They drive him to the precinct, sit him in an interrogation room and read him his rights. Two detectives walk into the room. They ask him about the triple homicide a few weeks ago. They inform Jesse James that someone saw his car around the scene of the crime. When they asked what he did that night, he swore he was on a date with his new girlfriend. Besides his alibi, Blue Jay doesn't speak a word.

They place him on a seventy-two-hour hold while they gather more evidence. He sits in his cell thinking, I must be cursed. One week away from happiness, and they lock me up.

That night the story breaks on every channel that Jesse James is being held for suspicion of committing triple murders in the Apex. The journalist covering the story, Jennifer Jensen, refers to Blue Jay as the Apex Animal. Jennifer suggests the killings may have been revenge for the death of Jesse James' little sister, Aria James. She also notes the criminal history of all three victims. She sums up the story by saying, "A chilling end for a group of despicable men with sinister pasts."

One of the girls, Bria Benton, Blue Jay rescued downtown is watching the news with her parents. The fifteen-year-old starts crying and runs to her room. Her dad, Brian Benton, is a politician with deep family ties in the Detroit community. He follows her to her room. Mr. Benton knocks on the door; he says, "Sweetheart, what's wrong? Why are you crying?"

Bria says, "Dad, promise you won't get mad or tell mom. It's bad!"

Mr. Benton says, "I'm concerned, baby, tell me what's going on and I will fix it or help you."

Bria says, "That guy on the news that was arrested…"

Mr. Benton cut her off, "Did he hurt you? Did he touch you?"

Bria says, "No, actually the opposite, he saved my life." She explains how frightened she and Kayman Smith, Bria's best friend, were when two men snatched them off the street. She tells her dad how that the man on the news came and fought the two guys and killed the would-be-rapist. Bria proclaimed excitedly, "Those men were going to rape and kill us, and he risked his own life to save us. Those men had guns and he fought them with his bare hands. When he got us out of their car, he told us to wipe our fingerprints off the car and run."

She ends her story by begging her dad to help the man and tell him thank you. She also, begs him not to tell her mother. Bria says, "I'm so ashamed of myself for sneaking out the house and going to a club with a fake ID. I don't want her to know I did something so bad." Mr. Benton agrees to keep her secret only if, she promises to go talk to Dr. Stall, a psychologist who specializes in helping young girls survive trauma.

Mr. Benton is shocked. He asks Bria, why she hadn't told him sooner. Bria says she didn't want the man to get in trouble, so she just tried to forget it. She admits she had been having nightmares. Mr. Benton thinks to himself how Bria had been noticeably different lately, but he never thought something this drastic had happened. Bria had been quiet, almost zoned out at times, she hadn't gone anywhere but to school for weeks, and she rarely spoke on the phone.

The next morning, Mr. Benton goes to the police commissioner. Mr. Benton convinces the commissioner to let Blue Jay go because there was not enough evidence to charge him; he says, "Besides the one witness statement stating his car was in the area, you don't have evidence to justify keeping him in custody. The police found nothing incriminating on his person, in his apartment or in his car."

Mr. Benton goes to the Wayne County Jail to see Blue Jay. Blue Jay is shocked when Mr. Benton walks into his cell. Mr. Benton shakes Blue Jay's hand; he says, "I'm not here today as a politician or businessman, I'm here as a father, Brian Benton. Those girls you saved Downtown are my fifteen-year-old daughter and her best friend.

"Last night she saw you on the news and told me what you did for her. I understood and I'm not accusing you, but I'm just saying I understand if you did kill those men for harming your sister. I for sure, am grateful that you killed for my daughter who thanks you."

Tears roll down Mr. Benton's face. He says, "If you weren't there that night, I would be in this cell with you. If I can arrange for you to get out of jail today, you must leave Michigan immediately and never return. If you leave town permanently, I guarantee you no one will ever come looking for you in relation to any Apex murders or the things that happened Downtown."

Blue Jay says, "I have plans to move to Atlanta, Georgia next week with my girlfriend."

Mr. Benton hands him his personal cell phone, and says, "Call your girlfriend right now and tell her you have to leave tonight because you start a job in two days. I have a good friend that owns several businesses and apartment buildings, he owes me a big favor. If you leave tonight, I will have an apartment and a job for you by the time you cross the state line. Just don't ever return here."

Blue Jay says, "I have no reason to return, my sister is dead and she's all I had here."

Mr. Benton gets up to walk out of the cell. He says, "Young man, stay out of trouble. Be safe! God bless you!"

Blue Jay says, "I am starting a new life with a good woman. I have no reason to get in trouble."

Mr. Benton leaves the cell and tells an officer to take him back to his apartment give him ten minutes to pack and drop the young man off at the bus station, now.

Two officers escort Blue Jay to his apartment. They gave him a cellphone to call Tren to say goodbye for now as gather all his belongings. Blue Jay explains that he has a get out of jail free card if he leaves today, and he will have a job and apartment when he gets there.

Tren is happy he is free, and they could move forward with their plans. Tren parents aren't thrilled that she has become attached to Jesse so quickly, but they trust her and decide not to interfere.

The two officers escort Jesse James to the Greyhound Bus Station in Downtown Detroit. They told him he would receive a text with an address by the time he gets to Atlanta. Go there and meet Jonathan Caruso. He'll have an apartment and job for you.

After the long bus ride, Blue Jay makes it to Atlanta, Georgia. Blue Jay's first stop: a church across the street from Caruso's building. Blue Jay walks into the church with all his belongings. He kneels at the altar and prays for peace, forgiveness, salvation, a healthy future with Tren, a chance to go to college and to have a prosper career to provide for Tren.

After Blue Jay says Amen, the pastor of the church walks over to him; he says, "Son, you're praying really hard like you've been through something."

Jesse says, "My six-year-old sister was raped and murdered back in Detroit, I moved here today to get a fresh start. I have a good girl in my life, and I don't want to bring the bad from my past to ruin her bright future. I've done some pretty bad things. I feel like I've been cursed my whole life. My life has been covered with a dark cloud, but Tren is the sunshine I've always wanted. I need God to help me because I don't know what to do on my own. I know that on my own I am no good, so I'm hoping he will help me."

The pastor replies, "Well you have taken the first step. You are open and seeking, and that's exactly what he wants you to do. Now, you need to study the word. Everything you need to know is in the good book. I'll sit with you personally and help you study. You are welcomed to attend any of our services. Do you have somewhere to stay?"

Jesse says, "Yes! I am getting an apartment across the street."

The pastor asks, "What's your name, Son?"

"I'm Jesse James," Blue Jay says.

The pastor says, "I'm Pastor Helms, and I welcome you to Atlanta."

Blue Jay leaves the church and walks across the street to the apartment building to meet Caruso. Caruso gives him the address to a factory, where he will make twenty dollars an hour.

The next week, Tren moves into the dorms. Tren and Jesse were making the best of life. Tren helps Jesse get into Atlanta Technical College. Jesse takes classes in Automotive Collision Repair and Automotive Technology. He hopes to open his own shop. Jesse faithfully attends church and studies with Pastor Helms.

A year flies by, the young couple is doing well. Tren has upheld her promise to her parents. Tren excels in both academics and athletics. Blue Jay is committed to not disrupting or distracting Tren's focus or interfering with her education. Blue Jay supports and encourages Tren; he wishes her parents would see that. He figures they will see he is good for Tren when he opens his own auto repair shop.

Tren goes home for the summer leaving Blue Jay in Atlanta. He takes summer classes and works full time. Tren calls Jesse every night, but one night she calls with strange news. A rapist is terrorizing the streets of the Apex, and the sketch on the news looks just like Kyrie. She explains that the rapes occur on warm nights with clear skies about once or twice a week in homes with small girls, elderly guardians and no men.

Blue Jay thinks about Kyrie's behavior last summer. He caught him about to break into a house with young girls, an elderly grandmother, and no men. Kyrie mysteriously got information that led to the killer, but could never say where he got the information. Kyrie knew his sister, and no one would have questioned him for talking to her. Kyrie never let John, Keith or Kennith speak that night. Kyrie played Jesse and Jesse fell right into his trap.

Jesse goes to his new pastor. He confesses that he needs to do something that was not of God, but he had to do it to protect innocent lives and to avenge innocent girls who had been hurt. The pastor asks if the police could handle it. Jesse tells him it was too personal to leave to chance. The pastor sees he couldn't talk Jesse out of following through, so he prays a prayer of protection and forgiveness for Jesse.

Jesse and Tren hatch a plan to sneak Jesse back into Detroit to kill Kyrie. Jesse left his cell phone in Atlanta, so no one could track him in Detroit. He rents a car from a trusted friend and drives to the Michigan-Ohio border where Tren waits for him. Before Jesse gets in the car, he tells Tren, "This is the absolute last time I will risk what we have. You mean everything to me, and I don't want to ruin you with my crazy life. If I make it through this, I want to marry you and live happily ever after."

Jesse climbs in the trunk and Tren drives him into the city and drops him off in the Apex. The plan is to meet him at that exact location and drive him back to the parked car at the Michigan-Ohio Border.

Under the disguise of night, Jesse roams the streets of the Apex on a night with a clear sky looking for Kyrie. Jesse thinks of all the girls living with their grandmothers. He checks the Stanton home, but there is no activity. He checks the Wesson home, but there is no movement. He checks the Gardener home; no one is around. He checks Mrs. Johnson's house, and nothing. Jesse, feeling discouraged, thinks he will not find Kyrie tonight. He decides to check one last house, the Luther home.

Success! Kyrie is there climbing in the back window. Kyrie didn't expect the grandmother to be awake and moving around the house. He knocks her in the head with the handle of his gun and ties her hands up. With the grandmother unconscious and tied up he is free to go into the little girl's room.

Jesse climbs in the same window; quietly and slowly walking through the home looking for Kyrie. Blue Jay sees the grandmother. He wakes her up, unties her hands, and tells her to be quiet. He says, "I'm here to save your granddaughter. Where is Kyrie?" The grandmother points. Jesse slowly creeps in the direction of the little girl's room. Kyrie so focused on raping the seven-year-old that he didn't notice Jesse creeping up behind him.

When Blue Jay reaches the room, Kyrie is climbing into bed with the petrified little girl. Before Kyrie could touch the little girl, Blue Jay knocks him in the back of the head with a bat. Blue Jay takes all the weapons from Kyrie's unconscious body and places them in the pocket of his hoodie.

He takes Kyrie by the hood of his hoodie and pulls him with one hand and holding the bat with the other hand while wiping his footprints from the floor by dragging Kyrie through his footprints. The terrified little girl follows as Blue Jay drags Kyrie out her room and down the hall. The little girl runs to her grandmother. Blue Jay promises that Kyrie will never hurt them or anyone else again.

Blue Jay pulls Kyrie into the alley behind the Luther home. Blue Jay throws Kyrie on the ground. Blue Jay kicks him until he wakes up. When Kyrie realizes Blue Jay is attacking him, he yells, "Blue Jay, it's me Kyrie. Man, what are you doing?"

Blue Jay says, "It was you, Kyrie. You raped and killed my sister."

Kyrie says, "I wouldn't touch your sister."

Blue Jay says, "Stop trying to play me. I figured you out." Blue Jay swings the bat several times hitting Kyrie in the face and head. Kyrie's face and head pour blood as he lays on the ground dazed and confused.

Jesse wipes his prints off the bat, and throws it on the ground. Mrs. Luther and her granddaughter watch the whole incident from their back door. Blue Jay takes Kyrie's hoodie, he pulls the string from Kyrie's hoodie and ties his wrists to the Luther's fence. He tells Mrs. Luther to call the police.

Jesse takes Kyrie's weapons and wipes his prints off; he hands them to Mrs. Luther. He tells Mrs. Luther if Kyrie moves shoot him. Jesse wipes down the window he used to climb into the house and the door knob of the back door. Jesse James tells Mrs. Luther and her granddaughter to never tell anyone he was there. Jesse sets Kyrie's pants on fire and runs off.

Jesse runs to the meeting point where Tren awaits him. Jesse climbs into the trunk. Tren hurriedly drives Jesse to the parked car. Tren drives back to her parents' house and climbs into bed. No one ever knew she left the house. Jesse drives back to Atlanta and returns his friend's car. Jesse goes to work, school, and church as if nothing happened.

The police make it to the Luther home just in time to save Kyrie's life. He will live but his lower body is completely covered with a third-degree burn. Kyrie burns were just a portion of his comeuppance. A few weeks after Kyrie was caught, Kyrie's DNA is linked to Aria James' rape and murder; six rapes before her death, and ten rapes after her death.

When news break of Kyrie's arrest, Jesse's phone rings. It's an unknown caller. Mr. Benton's voice said, "I guess, we owe you the thank you for catching and stopping the real Apex Animal."

The End

Brad says, "If someone touched my sister, I would do the same thing Blue Jay did."

Mrs. Campbell says, "That's understandable, the desire to hurt who hurt you. That is a very human emotion. Guys, did anything in the story sound familiar to you? Can you say that happened to me or I have felt the way he felt before?"

Niko says, "I feel angry. I always feel angry like Blue Jay. I don't know why, but I do."

Mrs. Campbell smiles; and says, "Thanks for sharing, Niko. Anyone else?"

Lucas says, "Having everyone hate you, the neighbors, your family, all your teachers." Mrs. Campbell thanks him for sharing.

Levi says, "My big brother was killed, so I know how he felt losing his sister."

Mrs. Campbell with empathy for Levi, says, "That couldn't have been easy to share, Thank you, Levi. Anyone else willing to share?"

Mega says, "Hurting someone when I didn't mean to. He didn't mean to kill that old man; he was just playing."

Mrs. Campbell says, "Guilt is a hard emotion to process. Thank you for sharing."

Tucker says, "Wanting to hurt someone so badly that you can't think straight. It's like rage takes over you."

Brad says, "He blamed his mother, but she really didn't do anything wrong. I know how that feels."

Jace says, "I know what it's like to be hurt by someone for no reason, and you're not strong enough to fight back. No one does anything to them because they lie and run. I'm glad Blue Jay got Kyrie for his sister because everyone deserves to have someone stick up for them."

Mrs. Campbell thanks him for sharing, and asks Xander to share. Xander says, "Not getting along with your mother. It's hard to be together. It's hard to talk. Every time we are together, she just ends up hollering." Mrs. Campbell thanks him for sharing.

Eli says, "Not really having friends and not knowing how to talk to people. I just stay to myself."

Caleb says, "Lying and betrayal, two of the worst things someone can do to you. Kyrie lied to him and betrayed him, Blue Jay had to get him back."

Mrs. Campbell says, "The human experience and emotion can be universal. Things good or bad happen to many people, but each person will have their own reaction. There are ten of you sitting in the same place, but all relating to Jesse James' story differently. You all heard the same story, but each person took away something different. Can everyone see how a shared experience can result in unique reactions? Our past experiences help shape our reactions; they trigger emotions.

"You may never know what someone has been through and how your actions can cause trauma and damage. Just as a violation of you or your space can trigger or deepen your past trauma, you violating someone can cause him or her trauma. Before we act quickly, we must think about everyone involved and the possible consequences that can result.

"The guilt and pain tormented Blue Jay. He was spiraling out of control. He didn't know how to deal with his emotions. He was intent on getting revenge, but something changed him. In the end, Blue Jay lets Kyrie live. He didn't want to go back to that dark place. What changed Jesse, and stopped him from going down that familiar road?"

Tucker says, "He found a girl. She was a good person and she really liked him."

Eli says, "He went to church."

Mrs. Campbell says, "So he learned how to better deal with his emotions. The concepts of love and God helped him. We all need something big, great and good to believe in, so when we face hard times there's something to give us hope. Does anyone have something in their life that gives them hope?"

After a brief moment of silence, Mega answers, "Basketball!"

Mrs. Campbell says, "Is anything worth risking your love of basketball?" Mega shakes his head no. Caleb and Tucker say football. Brad says he loves video games.

Eli says, "Music!"

Mrs. Campbell says, "Does your love of music give you peace when you face difficult times?" Eli shakes his head yes. Mrs. Campbell asks the remaining boys if there was anything either of them were interested in pursuing as a hobby. Niko, Lucas, Levi, Jace, nor Xander can think of anything. Mrs. Campbell suggests to them to find something that gives you hope. She adds, "We all need something. Trust me, having something to believe in will help you throughout your life." They promise to give it some thought.

While Mrs. Campbell talks with the boys, Mrs. Miller and the mothers talk about the challenges of raising sons without positive male models in their lives.

Rita and Stephanie are both in tears thinking about the future. Mrs. Miller explains that it's helpful to have somewhat of a mentor, a mother who has been where you are and made it through a similar circumstance. She says, "Mentors are evidence, but they can also be examples. They teach us new and give us a new perspective. The first three meetings of every session, we invite mothers who have completed the program as support and examples of success.

Mrs. Miller asks Rita and Stephanie to share what led them to the group. Ashamed and embarrassed by their sons' behavior both were reluctant to speak, but they are so desperate for help that they consent to tell their stories.

Stephanie speaks first, "Bradley's dad was murdered when he was just a baby, so it's just me. My mother and sister help as much as they can. He hates that I work a lot, but it's my responsibility to provide a home for us.

'Since day care, Bradley just has sporadic outbursts. He knowingly gets in trouble a lot, and he really has no excuse for his behavior. This year at school, we have had a few incidents, but the last one landed us here. Bradley beat one of his classmates with a book. Bradley swears it was self-defense and the boy was a bully. The judge said he needs an intervention because he was too young to be so angry."

Mrs. Miller thanks Stephanie for sharing. All the mothers acknowledge that they have had similar experiences. Mrs. Miller asks who has moved passed this stage with your son. Several women raise their hand. Mrs. Miller asks if anyone is willing to share how they were able to be successful. Bren, who has had three sons successfully overcome their emotional issues, volunteers to share her story.

Bren says, "There's no one way for every child, so I had to find what worked for each of my sons. After my husband died, they started to act out. They were in the streets too much because I had to work more. First, each son got involved in something to keep him busy until I got home from work. For my oldest son, football was enough. His coaches were tough on him, but they were teaching him to think and be a man.

"My second son and my third son needed therapy, and it worked. Through the process we discovered my second son had a disorder. Doctors worked with the medication until they found the combination he needed. It took a lot of effort on everyone's part. The boys had to want to do and be better. Once they wanted it, it happened." Mrs. Miller thanks her for sharing.

Mrs. Miller asks Rita to share. Rita begins to explain how Niko's behavior has affected the family and his classmates. Rita says, "Niko came out the womb fussy.

He was a mean and explosive toddler who had tantrums and meltdowns at the drop of a hat. He would cry, hit, and kick for hours, and no one could soothe him or stop him. As he got older, he would openly defy all adults. Tell him no; he'd do it anyway. He never followed rules or directions. He is rarely settled and happy. Holidays, gifts, trips, or fun don't make him happy. Mr. Niko thinks he is righteous, but he jumped in a fight and one of the boys ended up needing stitches in his forehead."

Bren says, "That sounds like my second son. Don't be discouraged! Once you find the right team to support his needs, you will see a change. Don't give up!"

Rita says, "Thank you, that's encouraging."

Bren says, "This is a good first step. You've found a good place to be." The other moms agree, they encourage Rita. With the meeting coming to an end, Mrs. Miller wraps up the mother's circle while Mrs. Campbell wraps up the boy's circle. Mrs. Campbell and Mrs. Miller thank everyone for participating as the participants exit the door.

Second Saturday

Mrs. Campbell and Mrs. Miller stand at the door to greet everyone as they walk through the door. The mothers encourage their sons as they part ways for the presentations. The mothers go to their room and the sons go to their room. When the presentation begin, the circle leaders review key points from the previous meeting.

Mrs. Campbell asks the boys if anyone had any questions or anything they needed to discuss. Tucker asks Mrs. Campbell, "When is it okay to get people back for what they did? It just seems fair that people get what they give."

Mrs. Campbell says, "No one ever said vengeance is our job or duty. It's only human to want revenge, but we have a judicial system meant to serve justice. It's not perfect, but it's what we have."

Tucker says, "What if that's not good enough?"

Mrs. Campbell says, "That's when your love of football helps you deal with those feelings. If someone hurts a family member and you in turn hurt that person, it won't undo the harm or take away the pain your family member experienced. For most of us, life never goes back to the way it was, but with time you will learn to live through the pain. Tucker, is there something specific that would make you want to get revenge on someone?"

Tucker says, "There's a gang in my neighborhood that mess with everyone. Everyone is so afraid of them. They kill people, rob people, and hurt people. They laugh and party after they hurt people like nothing happened. They murdered my cousin and they're getting away with it. I hate them all."

Mrs. Campbell says, "Tucker, the feelings you have are very understandable and normal. Anyone would feel the same way in your situation, but it wouldn't help your family if you were to cause harm to someone and you go to jail for a very long time. Your family wouldn't feel better; they would be mourning two losses instead of one. Your cousin is gone, you're in jail for years, and the remaining gang members go on terrorizing the neighborhood."

Tucker says, "It's not fair. I got in trouble for fighting, and they get away with murder. Mrs. Campbell, the system is broken."

Mrs. Campbell says, "You're right Tucker, the system isn't perfect. It is not fair, but vengeance is not the answer."

Levi asks, "What is the answer?"

Mrs. Campbell says, "There isn't one answer, but there are things we can do to help us deal with the emotions that result from the trauma we experience."

Levi says, "So, someone hurts us, and we have to learn to deal with it?"

Mrs. Campbell says, "Being a mature adult means you learn how to control your emotions, overcome any difficulties, and manage stress and adversity."

Levi says, "That sucks, Mrs. Campbell." The other boys agree.

Mrs. Campbell says, "Life is that way, Levi!"

Mrs. Campbell says, "Dealing with gang violence is tough. It takes a toll on every citizen. The violence is devastating, and can cause the nicest citizen to want the violence stop by any means, but we appropriately handle our emotions because things can quickly spiral out of control.

"Innocent people get hurt when someone is looking to hurt someone and is so blinded by their own agenda, they can't see past what they want for themselves. I am not saying it is easy to do the right thing. It's not just hard for you all. Many people struggle with overcoming traumatic experiences.

"Even the police suffer with watching innocent people succumb to or survive violence. Violence is taxing to the whole community." Mrs. Campbell tells the boys a story while the mothers discuss ways to deal and cope with stress. The moms discuss topics like: implementing rules, creating boundaries, making schedules, setting deadlines to complete specific tasks, consistency, fairness, rewards, and consequences.

Red, White, Blue Crew Vs. The Girls in Blue 1

The Tilley Family Murders

Sunday started as a calm quiet night for the Tilley family on Chandler Park Drive. After enjoying dinner at Mama Tilley's home, Marshall Tilley and his wife, Veronica Tilley sit down to watch a movie with their kids: Marshall Jr. (10), Camille (7), and Kayla (4).

Mama Tilley goes to the kitchen to microwave popcorn when an incredibly loud boom sounds through her house. The shock scared Mama Tilley into a panic. Marshall runs toward the kitchen immediately upon hearing the noise made by six armed, masked men dressed in black jeans, black Timberland boots, and hoodies. Three assailants are wearing red hoodies and three have on blue hoodies over white t-shirts.

The first man through the door shot Marshall on sight without hesitation. When Veronica hears the shot, she takes Kayla in her arms and covers Kayla with her body as she got down on the floor. The second man through the door, grabs Mama Tilley making her kneel on the floor. He aims his forty-four-caliber weapon to her head.

The gunman says to Mama Tilley, "Where's the money at old lady?"

Mama Tilley replies, "We don't have any money." Two men guard the family while the other four rummage through the home taking anything of value: electronics, jewelry, petty cash, clothes, and the keys to all the Tilley family vehicles.

After about five minutes, the man standing over Veronica and the children whistles, "Choo-woo," which was the signal to wrap it up. The other men running out of the house. The man standing over Veronica and the children opens fire striking Veronica, Marshall Jr., and Camille in their heads and bodies multiple times. The man guarding Mama Tilley strikes Mama Tilley in the head.

Mama Tilley manages to make it to the phone to call the police. The first to make it to the scene are Officers Smith and Warren followed by Detective Cori Chalone and her partner, Detective Alana Marrow. The house is silent as the officers approach the home. The officers go to the back of the house to see the backdoor ajar. The detectives follow the officers through the door with extreme caution. Upon entering the kitchen, they immediately come upon Mama Tilley profusely bleeding from her forehead crying over her son's body.

"Ma'am, are the men who broke in your home still here?" Detective Chalone whispers.

"No, they are gone. All gone! Everyone is gone," Mama Tilley answers, crying and in pain.

"Call for backup and emergency medical assistance for her. I will clear the house," Chalone says to Marrow. Detective Marrow applies pressure Mama Tilley's wound with a towel she grabs from the cabinet as she called for assistance.

Detective Chalone quietly and carefully proceeds through the house. Marrow checks Marshall's pulse. Mama Tilley says, "He's gone. Everyone is gone."

Detective Chalone sees people lying on the floor in the front room. First, she checks the two kids, but instantly can see they are gone. Next, she checks Veronica's pulse, but she quickly finds out there is no need to provide aide. As she walks away from Veronica, she feels a tiny hand grab her ankle.

Frightened, Detective Chalone jumps and clinches her gun. Quickly, she realizes the hand around her ankle belongs to a child. It is four-year-old Kayla Tilley. Detective Chalone holsters her gun, and scoops up Kayla who is soaked with her mother's blood. Detective Chalone quickly heads outside to the emergency medical vehicle that just arrived on the scene.

42

As they walk toward the emergency medical vehicle, Detective Chalone asks the scared little girl, "What's your name?"

"Kayla," the little girl answers.

"Kayla, that's a pretty name for a pretty girl. Are you hurt, Kayla?" Detective Chalone asks.

"No," Kayla says, "This is my mommy's blood all over me," Kayla adds sadly.

Det. Chalone says, "I'm Cori and I am going to get you and your grandmother help."

"Are you going to get that bad man? That mean, bad man shot my mommy, my brother, and my sister," Kayla asks.

"Did you know the bad man?" Detective Chalone asks.

"No, but I saw his face!" Kayla answers.

Detective Chalone asks, "Have you ever seen him before?"

Kayla answers, "No, never ever!"

One of the paramedics grabs Kayla from Detective Chalone's arms and puts her in the back of the ambulance. The other paramedic goes for Mama Tilley. He brings Mama Tilley out of the house on a gurney. Kayla begins to cry out for Detective Chalone, "Ms. Cori, Ms. Cori, don't leave me," Kayla screams, panicked with fear.

Detective Chalone tells Detective Marrow, "I'll ride to the hospital with them. Meet us there!" Detective Marrow nods and goes to their patrol car. Detective Chalone got in the back of the emergency vehicle, and they take off.

On the ride to the hospital, Kayla describes what she saw. "The man shot my mommy first, two times. Pow! Pow! Camille screamed, so he shot Camille twice. My brother stood up and the man lifted his masked. He asked my brother if he wanted to be a hero. When my brother stepped forward, the man shot him twice. Before he shot my mommy, she told me to be very still and very quiet. Even though I was scared, I didn't move or say a word just like my mommy said," Kayla says as Detective Chalone cleans her face.

Detective Chalone asks, "What did he look like?"

Kayla answers, "He was tall and dark like my daddy with a moustache around his mouth and sloppy hair."

"Did anyone say anything else," Detective Chalone asks.

"The only other thing I heard was a sound like choo-woo. Like a weird whistle," Kayla answers. "Ms. Cori, I am scared. What's going to happen if that mean man comes back?" Kayla asks. Detective Chalone can't answer, so she grabs Kayla to hug her.

After getting checked out, Kayla and Mama Tilley go to the precinct to talk to a sketch artist. After giving statements and describing the assailant who shot Veronica and the children, Detective Chalone and Marrow take Mama Tilley and Kayla to a hotel outside the city limits.

Before they leave, Mama Tilley tells them, "I worked for thirty-five years to build a family, and in five minutes they came and took all I had. My son, my grandkids, my daughter-in-law, my home, my peace of mind are all gone. You don't work hard to have it all taken from you for no good reason.

Those bastards left me with nothing, and they had no right to take everything," Mama Tilley says with frustrated, devastated tears streaming down her face.

Kayla climbs in her lap and says, "You still have me, Grandma. We still have each other." Mama Tilley bursts into an emotional cry grabbing Kayla and pulling her close.

"That's right we have each other," Mama Tilley replies as she rocks Kayla.

Detectives Marrow and Chalone watch the interaction in silence with heavy hearts. Kayla grabs her little pink Hello Kitty two-way texting device, "Ms. Cori, may I send you a message when I get scared?" Detective Chalone takes her Hello Kitty two-way SMS device, and saves her number in it under her name Cori, she says, "You can text me anytime."

Kayla says, "My big sister taught me how to use it, and I can spell a bunch of words all by myself."

Detective Chalone says, "I'm so proud of you."

Kayla gives Detective Chalone a big hug, and says "I'm going to miss you!"

Detective Chalone smiles and says, "I'll miss you, too!"

Detectives Chalone and Marrow leave the sobbing grandmother and her granddaughter with two uniformed officers outside their hotel room door.

For the next few days, Kayla texts Detective Chalone: Good Morning, Cori every morning and Goodnight, Cori every night. Detective Chalone programmed a special ringtone for Kayla's number, so she can reply immediately with Good morning, Sunshine in the morning and Sweet dreams, Sweetheart at night.

For some reason, Detective Chalone and Kayla form an instant bond. Detective Chalone became extremely fond of Kayla the moment she took her into her arms the night of the murder. She felt a huge amount of empathy for Kayla because she witnessed the massacre of her family.

While Detective Chalone and Detective Marrow investigate the Tilley Family Murders, they stumble upon six very similar robberies that happened within the prior two weeks. Those crimes are being investigated by the Robbery Division in the precinct where Deputy-Chief Cane-Chalone is head of the command.

Detective Hunter Hill and Detective Meka Trueheart are part of the Robbery Division, and are good friends of Detective Chalone and Detective Marrow. The four strong, dedicated females look out for each other in their heavily male-dominated profession. The four female detectives meet to discuss the previous case and to show Detectives Hill and Trueheart the sketches comprised by Kayla and Mrs. Tilley's descriptions of the assailant who removed his mask during the Tilley Murders.

Detective Hill identifies the man as: Carl Watts AKA Blackman, a gunman in a street gang committing crime all over the city. Detective. Trueheart pulls out pictures of known associates of Carl Watts. Anthony Hoskins, AKA TrainWreck, who has a criminal history of petty theft and possession. Rico "Relo" Lawrence, who has a history of possession with intent. Gary Miller AKA Lil G, who has priors for burglary, assault, and possession at the ripe old age of seventeen.

Arthur Miller AKA Lucky, the brother of Gary has four prior arrests: criminal sexual assault, assault, possession with intent, and armed robbery. The ring leader, Torren "2 Guns" Monroe, has no prior arrests or convictions mainly because everyone has been too afraid to say anything about him.

Torren "2 Guns" Monroe is the leader of the criminal enterprise that the streets referred to as the Red, White and Blue crew. Torren hadn't officially named the crew, but the men run together in clusters and everything from their cars to their clothes are red, white or blue. In total, there are about twenty-five main members of the crew, twenty-five second tier members, and fifty young men eager to join the crew.

The four ladies decide surveille the crew's known hideouts. First, an abandoned apartment building that the gang refers to as the Manistique Manor. The gang renovated the building without any permits and illegally cut on all the utilities. The four detectives sit in an unmarked car parked down the street. They take pictures of everyone going in and out of the manor.

They witness heavy foot traffic of men. Drug sells are usually quick and don't require entry. Men are going in and staying for about thirty minutes to an hour. The detectives believe this location is used for human trafficking. Detective Trueheart and Detective Hill explain that the gang took over a desolate block of abandoned homes. The gang fixed up the houses to sell a different drug out of each house. The gang refers to the block as Coconut Grove.

The four female detectives drive two the block known as Coconut Grove in two different cars and sit on opposite ends of the block. They document every car and every person that enters the block. Detective Marrow notices Chauncey Brown riding around the corner on a mountain bike.

Chauncey is a petty thief that is known to the police as someone who will snitch to get out of trouble. "Bingo," Det. Marrow says, "That's our way in, Chauncey the snitch," she adds. Marrow and Chalone high-five each other.

Chalone radios Trueheart and Hill, "Ladies, let's call it a night. We got what we need. Meet us at your precinct in the morning."

Who's Who of the Good Old Boys (Girls) in Blue
Cori Chalone

Cori Chalone is a twenty-five-year-old, lifelong Detroiter. The youngest daughter of Detroit Police Department Lieutenant Mason Chalone (recently retired after being shot and partially disabled while on the job) and Deputy-Chief Carolyn Cane-Chalone, both with over twenty-five years on the force. Cori graduated at the top of her class with a BS in criminal justice before going to the academy.

Cori has a muscular build after years of running track, dance classes and combat training. Cori is a dedicated detective with a sincere love of the City of Detroit. Cori lives in the city with her boyfriend, Jalen Billingsley, a five-year, Detroit SWAT team member. She has dated Jalen for two years.

Cori gained favor in the department quickly because she was sharp, smart, dedicated and an excellent shot. Lt. Chalone started taking his girls to the range every week when Cori was nine years old. Cori has been involved in two fatal shootings, saving lives and garnering high praise.

Jalen Billingsley

Jalen, the Alpha Team Leader of the Elite Unit, is a dedicated officer. He lives and breathes the SWAT life. Jalen has ten years on the job; spending the last five as a star of the Detroit SWAT. Jalen loves Cori, and is happy with their relationship.

Jalen works out furiously and is in supreme physical condition. Jalen is well-liked among his team and throughout the department. His friends and family think he and Cori make a perfect couple. Cori is ridiculously and hopelessly in love with him. Cori describes Jalen as GOD's favor in human form; a man with a Goliath sized heart; and mighty like the son of an angel."

Deputy-Chief Carolyn Cane-Chalone

Deputy-Chief Carolyn Cane-Chalone is a smart, articulate woman who does everything by the book. The community has learned to trust her and feels confident in her ability to uphold the law. Deputy-Chief Cane-Chalone spent her years as a patrol officer building a rapport with the people in the community.

She is always fair, so the community sees her as someone they can trust. Deputy-Chief Carolyn Cane-Chalone raised her kids, loved her husband, and excelled at her job without missing a beat. She tries to give her daughter space to grow on the job, but she has sky-high expectations of her daughter.

Lt. Mason Chalone (Ret.)

Lieutenant Mason Chalone is a great father, husband, and honest cop. Lt. Chalone made a name for himself very early in his career when he and his partner responded to an attempted armored truck heist. He and his partner engaged in a shootout with the two suspects. They stopped the men without any civilians being harmed. Both suspects eventually surrendered after suffering nonlife-threatening wounds.

Lt. Chalone career came to end when he unknowingly stumbled on a robbery while stopping at a bank to use the ATM. Lt. Chalone's exchanged fire with two gunmen resulting in all three men being seriously wounded. Lt. Chalone was shot in the arm, leg, and neck. His doctor didn't want him to return to full duty. He refused to take a position at a desk, so he decided to retire and be a supportive husband and father.

Detective Alana Marrow

Alana Marrow is a twenty-eight-year-old lifelong Detroiter. Alana joined the academy as soon as she was of age. Alana is a quiet girl, but she is tough. She survived the mean streets of Detroit on her own. Her mother and father were both addicts and often spent time in prison. Her grandmother died just shy of her eighteenth birthday. Joining the force was a dream and means to survive for Alana.

Detective Hunter Hill

Hunter Hill is a no-nonsense, but extremely girly girl. Hunter didn't leave the house without a full face of make-up and remarkably perfect hair. Her mother is white and her father is Native-American and African American. Her beauty helped her become one of the best undercover cops. She earned respect as an undercover for hundreds of stings.

Hunter is very physically fit. She boxes and weight trains to stay in shape. Hunter Hill was in a long-term relationship with Sergeant Williams in the Narcotics division. Hunter and Khalid Williams have been married for three years and together for years. Hunter is twenty-nine-years-old with eight years on the job. Hunter loves being a detective, but she had her eye on promotion and advancement.

Sgt. Khalid Williams

Sergeant Williams is a good cop in the Narcotics Unit. Sergeant Williams is a smooth, yet quiet man. He has fifteen years on the force. He has the face and smile of a male model. Sergeant Williams oozes confidence, strength, and sophistication. When Hunter joined the force, the men were knocking each other over to get a chance. Hunter focused on her career ignoring them all until she came across Khalid Williams. Khalid was mostly infatuated at the beginning of the relationship, but eventually Khalid realized he had met his match. The moment she gave birth to their first child, Khaleem, Khalid learned what love meant. Two years later, they had a little girl named Khareem. Khareem is the one that stole his heart.

Detective Meka Trueheart

Meka Trueheart lives and breathes the job. Meka has a ridiculous knowledge of weaponry and destruction. Meka wears a ponytail, jeans and Timberland boots. Meka is more likely to play sports than go to a nail salon with Hunter. Hunter is always badgering Meka to dress more feminine, but Meka prefers comfort.

Meka has always dreamed of protecting and serving the community. Meka is a hard-nosed cop known for her toughness. Meka is thirty years old with ten years of service on the force. Meka's biggest thrill in life is solving cases and making arrests. Meka's priorities aren't the big promotions like Hunter. Meka has one thing in mind: keeping the streets safe.

Red, White & Blue Crew
Torren Monroe

Torren dropped out of high school in the first semester of ninth grade. Torren had his first interaction with police when he was in the fifth grade. Torren had contact with the police on a monthly basis as a teenager for aggressive behavior, but was never arrested. Torren lived in the streets, day and night. He educated himself in destruction, terror, and fear. Torren's antics throughout the neighborhood made him a feared man. Torren earned his named 2-Guns because he kept two custom-made guns in his waistband every day, all day.

GangStarr

GangStarr is a psycho street thug who terrorizes women and children. GangStarr is Torren's number one handler. GangStarr earned his name fist fighting and brawling in the city's streets. GangStarr has a huge slice across his face because his grandmother cut him when he tried to kill her by asphyxiation when he was twelve years old. His reputation has made him a ghetto superstar.

GangStarr has the intelligence of a gnat, but the physique of a Greek god. GangStarr eyes were empty and blank from his birth. He barely blinks, and keeps a toothpick in his mouth. GangStarr rarely has a thought that doesn't revolve around being violent.

GangStarr runs the Manistique Manor, and he rules with an iron fist. Unfortunately for the women, GangStarr is extremely brutal for his own pleasure. Some of the girls are held against their will, but the majority of the girls owe a debt to the crew for drugs, and the rest are young and naive girls who were lured by Torren, Carl, or Anthony.

Carl "Blackman" Watts

Carl Watts is a cold, soulless killer. He killed his first victim eight months before the Tilley murders. Once he got a taste of blood, he couldn't stop. The plan wasn't to kill the Tilley family, Carl killed them because he liked to kill. He got his nickname not from the color of his skin, but from the suspected color of his heart.

Carl and a few of the crew members heard Marshall Tilley had a small-time drug distribution business that he ran out of his mother's home. It wasn't until the job was done that they realized they targeted the wrong man. The man they wanted was Marcus Tilley, Marshall's cousin.

Anthony "TrainWreck" Hoskins

Anthony Hoskins is also known as TrainWreck because wherever he went there was trouble. Anthony was kicked out of school every year by October. Anthony was kicked out of preschool for stabbing a girl in the face with a

50

pencil. He was kicked out of kindergarten for setting his teacher's dress on fire. He was kicked out of first grade for fighting the gym teacher.

He was kicked out of second grade for setting lockers on fire after looting them for valuables. He was kicked out of third grade for slicing his teacher's arm with a box cutter that he stole from the corner store. He was kicked out of fourth grade for stealing the principal's car. In the fifth grade, he poured gasoline at each exit of the building and threw a lit match at each door.

He was kicked out of sixth grade for bringing a knife to school to stab a classmate in attempt to steal his hand-held video game system. By seventh grade, the city paid his tuition to an all-boy private reform school, but he ran away, and no one ever went looking for him (not even his mother).

Anthony lived in the streets, which is how he met Torren. Torren gave Anthony a place to stay and a bag of money to entice lifelong loyalty from Anthony. From that moment, Anthony would do anything for Torren, and Torren took full advantage of Anthony's devotion. Torren used Anthony to handle his dirty work. Torren was the head coach who created the plans, and Anthony was the star point guard that directed the players on the court.

Rico "Relo" Lawrence

Rico Lawrence is a very cunning, charming, clean-cut, twenty-five-year-old drug dealer. Rico is an articulate communicator. Rico doesn't prescribe to the violent life of Torren and his flunkies. Rico isn't a street thug. Rico is a businessman. Rico is money-making-minded. Rico has monetary motivation and drive. Rico associates with Torren for one reason: mass distribution.

Rico never touches the stuff, he has major connections south of the US border. Rico's connections move inventory across the border and Rico sells the product to people like Torren. People trust Rico because he has a reputation of making money multiply while staying under the radar of the authorities. Most importantly, Relo has more connections than anyone else in Detroit.

Arthur "Lucky" Miller

Arthur has been shot three times and fully recovered each time. The whole hood called him Lucky. Lucky is a reserved thug. He does things in a discreet manner. Arthur doesn't always agree with Torren, Anthony, and GangStarr.

51

Arthur is the conscious of the group. Arthur is consistently telling the crew to be cool and calm.

Running drugs for Torren and many other distributors has made Arthur very rich. Arthur is like the plant supervisor of the drug business. Arthur knows who, what, when, where, and why everything going on in Torren's business. Arthur is the one who named the block Coconut Grove because he said it was a hard nut to crack. Coconut Grove is his meal ticket, and he doesn't take his duties lightly.

Gary "Lil G" Miller

Seventeen-year-old Gary "Lil' G" Miller never went to high school. Gary gets his secondary education on Coconut Grove. Gary is on the block with his brother from sun up to sun down to sun up again. Gary watches his brother's back and makes sure nothing goes wrong on the block. Gary is what you may call head of security, and Gary takes his job seriously. Gary and Arthur run Coconut Grove like a well ran assembly line.

Holland Street Homicides

Just forty-eight hours after the Tilley Family murders, five black Chevrolet Tahoes turn on to Holland Street and park in the middle of the block. Two black Chevrolet Suburbans park in the middle of each intersection preventing cars from entering or exiting from either end of the block. Simultaneously, the drivers' side windows of the Suburbans roll down exposing AR-15s. The drivers of the Suburbans have one job: make sure no target made it off the block.

Immediately following the exposure of the assault rifles, masked men dressed in red and blue hoodies storm like U.S. Army soldiers toward the four houses in the center of the block. The men each holding an AR-15 run in groups of four kicking down the front doors simultaneously. The sieged men are caught off guard. A few men jump from the second floor to escape the chaos, but they were shot as they approached the corners by the AR-15s that surveilled the street.

Blackman entered the first home shouting, "Get down!" The men had no time to react in a defensive manner, so they complied. However, Blackman and his henchmen shot them anyway.

Blackman and the two crew members head to the basement where they know the drugs and money are stashed. Two other foot soldiers go to the second floor to ensure no witnesses are left. The other three houses are raided in the same fashion. The whole gang prescribe to Blackman's motto, kill them all and take everything valuable.

In a total of five minutes and fifteen seconds, they stole about twenty kilos of street drugs, about three hundred fifty thousand dollars in cash from the four houses, and left thirty-two dead bodies from the houses to the street. Even after the shooting stopped, no one dared look out of a window or open a door.

The four raided houses are storage houses for ShowTime and SugaSain's massive drug operation, but neither were on scene. The houses are equipped with high-quality surveillance cameras and recording equipment, which alone told the police the story. The police are shocked by the volume of victims.

Police go door to door, but no one admit to seeing or hearing anything. The police know they must find the perpetrators before ShowTime and SugaSain because this is sure to start a war. The last thing the mayor wants during an election year is a drug gang war.

Hill, Trueheart, Chalone, and Marrow are monitoring the manor when they hear of the mass murder on Holland Street, and the assailants wore red and blue hoodies. The detectives figure the crew would take the loot to their stash houses, so they rush to Coconut Grove.

As soon as the ladies park, one of the Suburbans pull up followed by the five Tahoes and the other Suburban. The ladies record GangStarr, Blackman, TrainWreck, Lucky, Lil' G, MookMan, Pearlie, Got'em, Quest, Maynard, Ray, Touchy, Murda, TinyTim, Dragon, Goon, Budda, PacMan, Lyon, Will, Pitman, Kid, Creme, Black, Face, Dame, OG, Elwin, CHI-Town, Cocoa, Dino, LowLife, and Sham each carry a black duffle bag exit the vehicles involved.

Soon, 2 Guns and Relo arrive on the scene. They have a brief conversation and Relo quickly leaves. 2 Guns goes into the basement. PacMan, Lyon, LowLife, Sham, Kid, Cocoa, and Quest each took off in one of the SUVs. Hill, Trueheart, Chalone, and Marrow followed them to an abandon warehouse recording the entire ride. They call in the suspicious vehicles as possibly the vehicles that were used in the Holland Street homicides.

The detectives watch as the gang members drove the vehicles into a warehouse and leave on foot. Suddenly, flames scorch the interior of the warehouse. Trueheart radio for fire and rescue. The four female detectives decide to split up. Two plan to follow the gang members and other two plan to get to the evidence.

Hill and Trueheart approach the burning building, while Chalone and Marrow follow the men. There's a blue Expedition awaiting the fleeing gang members two blocks over. Chalone and Marrow get pictures of the men fleeing the burning building and entering the Expedition driven by CHI-Town.

Hill and Trueheart bravely rush into the burning building. They get hoodies and masks out the back of two of the trucks. With hoodies and masks in their hands, Hill and Trueheart turned to rush out of the building.

As Hill and Trueheart are leaving, they notice two of the trucks have keys in the ignition. They take a closer look to find the trucks are filled with the weapons used in the Holland Street murders. They throw the hoodies and masks into the trucks and drive out of the burning building. The fire department quickly arrive followed by Deputy-Chief Chalone.

The flames are quickly extinguished, and the crime scene unit retrieves the remaining vehicles with only exterior damage. Deputy-Chief Chalone is not happy with Trueheart and Hill for risking their safety to get the evidence, but she half-heartedly congratulates them for potentially solving a mass murder.

Deputy-Chief Chalone wants the recovery of the evidence to he held from the press, so she orders the removal of the vehicles to be expedited. Deputy-Chief Chalone told Trueheart and Hill to be in her office in sixty minutes ready to debrief. She stares at her daughter with eyes thanking GOD she is alive, but she dare not speak to her. Not only is her daughter assigned to another precinct, but Deputy also-Chief Chalone never wants anyone to think she shows favoritism to Detective Cori Chalone.

Hill and Trueheart return to their precinct to explain how they with Marrow and Chalone came to find the SUVs to Deputy-Chief Chalone.

Deputy-Chief Chalone wants every detail of the case. She also wants the details of the Tilley Family murders and the prior six robberies. While Hill and Trueheart debrief with Deputy-Chief Chalone, Detective Chalone and Detective Marrow go back to surveille Coconut Grove.

Immediately, Marrow and Chalone spot Chauncey Brown on his bike. They record him riding up to purchase drugs from MookMan before riding off the block. They follow him and when he is a safe distance away from the Grove, they pull up next to him, Marrow grabs the rack on the back of his bike and orders him to stop.

Chauncey jumps off his bike and runs through the alley. Detective Marrow hops out of the car and takes off on foot, while Chalone drives around the corner to the enter the other side of the alley.

Chauncey cuts through a backyard, so Marrow cuts through a backyard two doors down. Marrow gets close enough to him to elbow him, knocking him into the car as Chalone pulls up next to him.

Chalone and Marrow cuff him and put him in the back of their car. They take him to the Downtown Precinct, so Trueheart and Hill interview him. Chalone texts Trueheart: "We have a little birdie to sing." Trueheart convinces Deputy-Chief Chalone that she needs to take a call. She leaves Hill to finish the debrief.

After Trueheart leaves Deputy-Chief Chalone's office heading for the elevator, she sees Sgt. Williams sitting at Hill's desk. Trueheart tries to rush to the elevator to avoid Sgt. Williams because she knows he is angry that she and Hill ran into a burning building. Sgt. Williams corners her just before the elevator's doors open; he says, "Running in a burning building like this is Die Hard! What were you two thinking?"

Trueheart hesitates with frustration that he caught her; she says, "You know your wife, the hero, I couldn't stop her!"

"I'm going to kill her," he whispered in anger. Just as he finished the sentence, Detective Hill walks out of Deputy-Chief Chalone's office.

When Hunter catches a glimpse of her angry husband's face, she tries to sneak back into Chalone's office, but Sgt. Williams shouts, "Hunter," before she can make it through the door.

Detective Hill smiles as she walks to the elevator to cheerfully greet her husband, "Honey, what are you doing here?"

He responds, "Don't play with me, Hunter, what were you thinking?"

"It wasn't as bad as it sounds, I swear," she responds.

"There isn't a pleasant way or easy way to understand a building on fire. What, just the edges were burning," he responds sarcastically.

"Exactly!" Trueheart says as she pushes Hill on the elevator.

Sgt. Williams angrily says, "This conversation isn't over, Hunter!"

"See you at home, Honey!" Hill replies jokingly. Hill blows Sgt. Williams a kiss as the elevator's doors closed.

Trueheart explains to Hill that Chalone and Marrow have Chauncey. They take Chauncey to an interview room. Chalone and Marrow go back to their precinct while they wait for Hill and Trueheart to complete the first step of their plan. Chalone and Marrow have big plans for Chauncey. Detective Chalone receives a call from her mother who is calling as a concerned mother not as an angry deputy chief. Detective Chalone assures her mother and ranking officer that all is and will be well. Deputy-Chief warns that she is watching.

Woo-Wong Family Restaurant Robbery

The next day, Chalone and Marrow decide to stop at Chalone's favorite take-out restaurant for lunch. Chalone eats at the restaurant two or three times every week, so the whole family knows her well. The restaurant seems normal as they approach, but they hear shouting before entering. They both pull their guns, and duck low. Marrow goes to the back. Chalone slowly approaches the front door. Chalone sees two men with big guns dressed in black jeans, black Timberland boots, and red hoodies over white t-shirts.

One of the armed gunmen has the owner of the restaurant, Mr. Wong, by his neck with a forty-caliber gun held to his head standing at the cash register. The gunman demands Mr. Wong to remove the cash. Mrs. Wong and kids watch with the second man pointing a large handgun in their faces. The Wong family knows Cori because she has been their best customer since the restaurant opened ten years ago. Cori's eyes sees Chen Wong, Mr. Wong's sixteen-year-old son. Chen is a black-belt student of Aikido. Chen won so many competitions that his family has a room in their house just to house his trophies. When his eyes met Cori's eyes, he feels a hint of relief.

Chalone aims her gun at the man holding Mr. Wong at the register. Marrow enters the restaurant through the backdoor. She stays close to the floor and takes aim at the man holding the family hostage.

The robber holding a gun to Mr. Wong's head cocks the hammer of his gun and tightly hugs the trigger, "Hurry up old man," he shouted, "Or your family will see your brains splattered on the wall." Cori winks at Chen and he instantly kicks the gun out of the second robber's hands.

Before the robbers could react, Cori yells police put your weapon down. The first robber turns his gun in Cori's direction. Cori yells police put your weapon down. The first robber shoots at Cori and Marrow shoots him. The bullet went into the back of his skull and burst through his forehead. Marrow comes through the kitchen with her gun on the second gunman. When he pulls a knife from his pocket and lunges at Chen, Marrow shoots him in the back.

The Wong Family is covered in blood splatter. Mrs. Wong fell to the floor crying in relief. Her husband and youngest son rush to her side. Chen stands looking at the dead man at his feet. Chalone consoles him, while Marrow notifies dispatch of the incident.

The Wong family thank Marrow and Chalone for saving them. Mr. Wong promises Marrow and Chalone free food for life. Chen Wong is the most affected by the whole event. Chen feels violated and helpless. It's as if the Red, White, and Blue Crew intentionally targeted his manhood. In the moment of watching them humiliate his father and degrade his mother, Chen changed from innocent to rageful. He won't speak as police question his family. Chen sits with a blank look on his blood-splattered face.

Who Lay Dead on the Floor of
THE WOO-WONG FAMILY Restaurant

Known as the best Chinese cuisine in Detroit, the Woo-Wong Family Restaurant is the scene of a double fatal officer involved shooting. Hill, Trueheart, with Deputy-Chief Chalone promptly arrive on the scene to support Detective Chalone and Detective Marrow.

Robber one: Paul Withers also known as PacMan. PacMan was a low-level member of the Red, White, and Blue crew. He was a murderer, he was one of the men with Carl "Blackman" Watts on the night of the Tilley Family murders. Now Paul knows firsthand how the dead members of the Tilley family felt on that fatal night. He was shot while pointing a knife at Chen.

Paul was rowdy and uncontrollable at an early age. He occasionally attended school only to cause trouble. Paul ran the streets with Sham, Lyon, LowLife, Kid, Cocoa, and Quest since they were in second grade.

Lifelong criminals, they are now almost thirty-year-old men who never held a job or contributed productively to society. From theft to assault to possession with intent, the men had been arrested so many times that the county prosecutors and judges know them by name.

Paul fathered ten kids with ten different women, but he wasn't ever a father. He never paid either woman a penny of support. He wasn't involved in any of the children's lives. He kids wouldn't know him if they ran across him in the streets.

Torren told the crew a long time ago to stop the petty robberies because they were risking exposing the much more profitable trafficking trade businesses the crew ran, but many of them had addiction problems and no self-control with their money. Robbery was a quick and easy way to get money on the side.

Torren was livid when he found out about the Woo-Wong Family Restaurant robbery. PacMan and Quest thought they could get in and out quickly with a few hundred bucks with little risk.

Robber two: Quest born Quincy West almost seemed to never have a chance. Quest's mother was a twelve-year-old learning disabled and socially impaired girl when she gave birth. Impregnated by her stepfather, her mother abandoned her when she got the news that she and her daughter were expecting sons by the same man.

It wasn't like his mother was willing to be an adulteress with her mother's husband, he violated her by force regularly whenever his wife left them alone from the day they came home from their honeymoon.

Quest and his mother were taken into the system because no one in her family had the financial ability to care for two children. Quest and his mother went from foster home to foster home until Mrs. Johnson adopted them when he was four and his mom was sixteen. When Mrs. Johnson died two years later, Quest became uncontrollable. With the mental challenges of his mother, the court saw it best to remove Quest from his mother's care. Now Quest is reunited with Mrs. Johnson, the one soul who could soothe Quincy's soul.

Marrow's gun is taken. Chalone and Marrow must report to their precinct to be interviewed. The Wong Family give statements to the Internal Affairs Unit as well. Mr. and Mrs. Wong insist that Detective Chalone and Detective Marrow saved their lives.

After giving statements, Marrow and Chalone are given the rest of the day off. However, Marrow and Chalone meet up with Hill and Trueheart to discuss the Chauncey interview and the Holland Street homicides.

Trueheart tells Marrow and Chalone, "The lab hasn't tested every gun, so we're still waiting on ballistic reports." Chalone asked what's the hold-up; Trueheart tells her the lab said it would be a while before they get the results because the quantity of casings and guns was so large.

Chalone replies, "These guys are terrorizing the city; we have got to do something. Quickly!"

Hill adds, "Chauncey is in the box for a few days. The desire for freedom will convince him to wear a wire for us when he buys drugs from the Coconut Grove houses."

Marrow replies, "We need him to get in the houses and that apartment building ASAP."

Trueheart added, "Ladies, our plan will be in play soon; Chauncey will be a lot more agreeable after forty-eight hours in a cold, hard cell."

Hill responds, "Detectives go home, relax, gather your thoughts, and compose yourself." Marrow and Chalone check in with each other before going home.

Hill and Trueheart continue the investigation; they track down Marcus Tilley, the Nephew of Mrs. Tilley. Marcus is only willing to talk to Hill and

Trueheart because they make it clear: they only thing they want to discuss the murder of his family.

Marcus profusely exclaims, "Marshall was a good, hard-working man who would never harm anyone or do anything illegal. Marshall was a computer geek and school boy. He had no ties to street gangs. No one had a reason to kill him. The streets are saying they were after me and my money. Killing those kids wasn't right!"

Hill agrees, "Definitely not right, Mr. Tilley. Do you know anyone capable of such violence that may want to harm you?"

Marcus Tilley answers, "Any and everybody in these streets. One may never truly know."

Trueheart replies, "Many may know and never tell."

Marcus says, "That's a possibility as well."

When Cori opens the door to her home, she is met by Jalen Billingsley. She is shocked and happy. They embrace, and she exhales as she relaxes in his arms. Cori is strong, but there is something about Jalen that allows her to feel vulnerable. "Are you OK," he asks.

"Yes, I'm OK," Cori says.

Jalen says, "It's the after that's hard. Seeing a person die is never easy."

Cori replies, "Alana did what she had to do. The risk is a part of this job. She knew if she didn't get them, they would get us. But, a part of me thought they deserved it for what they did to that poor woman and her family."

Jalen prepares dinner for Cori. Jalen has been keeping tabs on the crew, and he's worried about Cori having to investigate such cold, unregulated killers. While they eat, Jalen tells Cori everything he knows about the Red, White, and Blue crew. Cori listens and takes notes in her cell phone.

The Crew Laments

Word spread fast through the streets about PacMan and Quest. The crew is livid. Torren is very upset that PacMan and Quest disregarded his order to stop the petty robberies. Although he is mad at PacMan and Quest, he blames the lady cops who killed them. The whole crew gathers to lament in the inner courtyard of the Manistique Manor. Emotions are running high as Torren gives somewhat of a eulogy for the deceased.

Torren leads the crew in pouring out some of their drinks simultaneously. After expressing their sorrow, the crew smokes together. After the memorial, Torren reminds the crew to lay low before he leaves to proceed with making big money deals. Before leaving, The crew begin to discuss the robbery, and they all reach a mutual agreement: the cops must pay. They blame the women for shooting. Although everyone knew PacMan and Quest would've killed everyone in the restaurant before going back to jail. GangStarr proclaims the cops weren't in danger and the shootings unjustified.

GangStarr rallies the troops to rage against the establishment, he says with authority, "They need to feel the pain we feel. They need to understand that we are not to be played with."

As the night progresses, the more inebriated the crew becomes and with the inebriation grows an increase in violent agitation. The crew becomes wild and volatile. They decided to make the whole neighborhood pay for their sorrow.

Lyon and LowLife make Molotov cocktails. The whole crew piles in a parade of car with criminal intentions. The first stop is the restaurant, "Let it burn for our bros," LowLife yells before he lights the Molotov cocktail and throw it at the Woo-Wong Family Restaurant. The igniting flames incite the urge for revenge even more. LowLife says, "A gangster rapture will rain down on the city, and the police is not exempt."

One group went to the Fifth Precinct and a second group went to the Ninth Precinct. They throw the final two Molotov cocktails at exactly 3:13 and 3:15 into the lots full of patrol cars before speeding off and gathered in the inner courtyard of the Manistique Manor. 3:13 and 3:15 are significant because those are the reported times of death for PacMan and Quest.

After setting the fires, the crew quietly disperse to lay low. About 4:30 a.m. a patrolling cruiser rides pass a shimmery blue, eighty-four Impala driven by MookMan with passengers Kid and Cocoa. The shimmery blue, eighty-four Impala was reported to be on the scene at the time of the Woo-Wong Family Restaurant fire.

61

The police makes a U-turn to get behind the car. Immediately, the lights and sirens are engaged. Instead of pulling over, the very intoxicated MookMan flees. A high-speed chase ensues through a residential area. MookMan turns down Chalmers trying to get to Interstate-94.

MookMan lead Officer Alante` Crews and his partner Sabrina Rabiscoe at speeds topping one hundred miles per hour. As MookMan turns sharply but swiftly to enter the freeway, he lost control of the vehicle, crashing into the embankment then flipping over three hundred sixty degrees all the way down the ramp.

Officers Crews and Rabiscoe get out of their cruiser to approach MookMan's car. Walking slowly with their guns raised, Crews and Rabiscoe repeatedly announce, "Detroit Police! Stick your hands out of the window!" Instead of complying with their request, Kid opens fire on Crews and Rabiscoe. Crews and Rabiscoe recede to their car to take cover and call for backup.

MookMan, Kid, and Cocoa get out of the car with minor injuries. They instantly fire on the cops hiding behind their police patrol vehicle.

After thirty shots were fired, Crews and Rabiscoe take a defensive stance and fire back. MookMan, Cocoa and Kid take off running in different directions. Before they get to far, another cruiser pulls up. The two officers: Derek Moore and Clive Clemens take off after MookMan. Crews runs after Kid, and Rabiscoe chases Cocoa. Cocoa's injured leg prevented him from running far. Rabiscoe cuffs him without incident. Rabiscoe places Cocoa in the back of the patrol vehicle, and she notifies dispatch that one suspect was in custody.

MookMan makes up the embankment, and into the alley behind the Coney Island and a nightclub. Officers Moore and Clemens are right behind him, yelling, "Detroit Police! Stop! Throw down your weapon! Put your hands up." MookMan is tired and wants to create some space, so MookMan turns to shoot at the approaching officers. Moore and Clemens return fire, killing MookMan with two shots to his chest. Moore calls in the shooting as an officer involved shooting.

Kid hear the shots as he runs past through the intersection one block away from the accident. A few cars stop at the intersection to watch the chase.

Kid's heart is pounding three times as fast and hard as normal. He is too intoxicated and fatigued to run any further. He turns and raises his gun, taking aim at Crews. Crews stops and takes a defensive stance, shouting, "Put your weapon down! Put your hands up!" Kid gently squeezes the trigger, but Crews is much faster.

Crews shoots the gun out of Kids hand. The force of the bullet knocks Kid to the ground unharmed. Crews yells, "Roll over on your stomach. Spread your legs and stretch out your arms." Kid rolls onto his stomach. Crews approaches cautiously and slowly. He places cuffs on Kid's wrists. Another squad car pulled up to take Kid away. More police cruisers arrived on scene with their lights flashing. The flickering, flashing lights in the early morning dark sky makes the crime scene look like the night before Christmas.

With the capture of Kid and Cocoa, the Blue Crew is down five men. By early the next morning, word spread through the streets of the loss of three Blue Crew members. The crew mourns MookMan. Another soldier laid to rest by the police and two locked up. Torren is livid with GangStarr for allowing the crew to be so reckless.

Torren ceases the Coconut Grove operation and Manistique Manor operation as retribution for violating his authority. The closure of the Manor and the Grove operations meant no income for the crew members. Torren sends a message to his soldiers: listen to me or I will stop your money. They are disappointed with his decision. With their extreme propensity to abuse many different drugs and alcohol, they need money and fast.

GangStarr was not the type to be okay without having money and he was for sure not about to go without revenge. GangStarr believed in blood for blood.

He is a maniac without a soul or conscience. GangStarr calls some of the low-level young members because he knows they were reckless and unconcerned with death or jail. GangStarr is loyal to Torren, but he doesn't agree with him on this one. GangStarr calls for tribulation.

GangStarr vows that the police are going to carry the full burden of GangStarr's demented lunacy. GangStarr hatches a secret plan that would bring despondency on the city and the police department. GangStarr tells Blackman, TrainWreck, Lucky, Lil' G, Pearlie, Got'em, Maynard, Ray,

Touchy, Murda, TinyTim, Dragon, Goon, Budda, Lyon, Will, Pitman, Creme, Black, Face, Dame, O.G., Elwin, CHI-Town, Dino, LowLife, and Sham to recruit as many viable foot soldiers as possible. They plan to meet in the park after dark, and Torren cannot know about the meeting.

A Succession of Unsolved Store Robberies

The gang gathers in a pack of more than one hundred, eager to either obtain fair monetary appropriation or capitulate to death or jail. In some way, they are as disposable as a Hefty bag in their own eyes. They didn't give a second thought to living or dying.

They listen to GangStarr speak of their potential demise and their desolate spirits radiate enthusiasm. The insanity of GangStarr strikes a chord with the crowd. For the first time ever, Blackman, TrainWreck, Lucky, Lil' G openly disagree with and disobey Torren. The plan is suitable in their acumen, but they all know Torren could not know of their doing.

All good plans need one thing to be executed with perfection: funding. The Red, White, and Blue crew is going black: all black everything from head to toe.

GangStarr's speech convinces the desperate crew members to execute the groundwork of his plan despite the knowledge that Torren didn't want any more trouble. GangStarr's plan is to ravage and raid the small business community.

Mass Liquor Store Robberies

Stage one of GangStarr's plan: in groups of five, raid the twenty most popular liquor stores across Detroit at the same time. GangStarr gives each member a Bluetooth ear piece. GangStarr appoints each group a leader, a lookout and a timekeeper. GangStarr gives each crew leader a script with strict instructions to stick to the script. Dressed in all black with ski masks covering their faces and holding assault rifles, the untrained Blackout crew practices the plan without a flaw. GangStarr knows the police can't respond to all the robberies, so he feels confident, but he stresses the need to manage the time wisely.

At dusk, twenty inconspicuous cars occupied with five masked passengers in each car slowly roll up to the most trafficked liquor stores in

Detroit. One man stays in the car, one man goes to the rear, and the armed majority enters the store. Immediately, one shot is fired from an AR-15. The leader holds the biggest gun and does all the talking.

As the leader instructs the innocent patrons to get down on the floor, another armed man robs the patrons. The other two-armed men go directly to the cash registers and safes behind the counter. The women and children scream and cried as the men rummaged through their pockets and purses.

The Blackout Crew is in and out in minutes. Each crew goes somewhere to lay low before initiating phase two of the plan. The liquor store robberies are just the beginning of GangStarr's depravity. The Blackout Crew is planning a Titanic-sized hit that very night. At midnight, the Blackout Crew is armed, masked and ready to strike.

Hop, Roy, Magic, Moe, Don Juan, Ray Kay, Poppy C, Tone, Manny, and Kelo all ran lucrative illegal pharmaceutical businesses within the city limits. Unfortunately, they made the list of the ten spots the crew was hitting at 2 a.m. Being that the Red, White, and Blue Crew knows the men very well and are familiar with how the men operated their businesses, this part of the plan seems as easy as taking candy from a baby.

Jimmy "Hop" Hopkins runs a small crew out of the first floor of a two-family flat near the freeway. Hop and his crew doesn't deal with customers. They are strictly into distribution. Hop and his crew take payments from local crews in exchange for drugs from his international connection. They always have major cash on hand, so it was logical to make him a target.

Roy is a courier not a dealer. Roy gets packages and delivers them. Roy works alone and stays under the radar. When Roy is working, most people mistake him for a homeless man. At any given time, Roy has enough drugs at hand that he can make any street dream a concrete reality.

Mike "Magic" Scott specializes in controlled substances. Magic got his name at the park, playing basketball, but he tore the ligaments in his knee as a teenager. Magic had dreams of basketball fame, but he settled for street fame. Magic's operation includes doctors, senior citizens and mental health patients. Fraudulent patients fake sicknesses or injuries, get a prescription, and sell the medication to Magic. Magic has a supple supply worth a pretty penny.

Moe owns a few auto shops, which cover for his big-time drug business. Don Juan has several houses that peddle any and every drug an addict may ask for with exceptional quality and quantity. Moe and Don Juan are good friends, and they often do big deals together. Moe and Don Juan are known for frequently throw big parties that attract a mass. These parties rake in big cash for Moe and Don. The parties are just another way to clean their dirty money. The Blackout Crew knows Moe and Don Juan store large amounts of cash and drugs at a house occupied by Moe's aunt and uncle.

Ray Kay is short for Raymond Kaymer. Ray Kay runs an auto theft ring and chop shop. Ray Kay's employees sell drugs out of his shop and give him a cut. Ray Kay's chop shop at any given time houses about ten stacks, and the Blackout Crew wants that money badly.

Poppy C's government name is Carlos Carleton born and raised in one of the biggest drug-dealing families in Detroit. Poppy C's uncle and dad were millionaires a couple times over before death became them. His dad and uncle were murdered by rivals in the drug trade, and no one ever faced consequences for their deaths. Poppy C was left to run the family's empire with his cousins: Tone, Manny, and Kelo.

Poppy C is the leader. His savvy and distinct street business tactics puts in a different class from his cousins. Tone, Manny, and Kelo all push major weight and bank roll serious dollars, so they don't mind sitting in a lower level from their big cousin Poppy C.

When the clock strikes 2 a.m., the Blackout Crew assembles for one purpose: put all ten men down and take all their money. One hundred men dressed in all black with black ski masks and black gloves broke into ten groups of ten with fully loaded assault rifles. GangStarr assigns each group a target and given instructions to leave no witnesses. The main key to the plan is to strike each target at the same time, so no target will have time to warn another target.

Moe's uncle and aunt are awakened by a crash. A group of men rush into their home and grab them out of bed. They instruct Moe's uncle to open the safe, while they held a gun to his wife. After Moe's uncle opens the safe, the money stuffed into large leather duffle bags. Without notice, Moe's uncle and aunt are shot in the head.

Simultaneously, a black SUV pulled up next to Moe's Cadillac with Don Juan in the passenger's seat at a red light. As soon as the cars are stationary, the black SUV passenger's side rear and front windows roll down and assault rifles put thirty shots in Don Juan and Moe killing them before they could react.

Ray Kay and a few of his employees are counting the week's receipts when masked men holding AR-15s kick in the door and begin to spray bullets throughout the room. Ray Kay and his men drop like flies being sprayed by Raid. On the table, now, lay stacks of blood-soaked U.S. currency.

After life escapes Ray Kay and his men bodies, the masked men bag the money in two large leather duffle bags before they exit the chop shop's back door.

Roy is riding down the service drive on a bike with a large bag strapped across his back. A car stops at the corner, and immediately opens fire. Roy tries to turn around, but he is hit three times before falling to the ground. Another car rolls up and a man quickly jumps out the car to snatch the bag from Roy's dying body.

Hop, his driver and bodyguard are heading to the freeway with a truck full of product on the way to make a deal. As they turn to enter the freeway, a car cuts in front of them and one pulls up behind them. The cars box Hop's car in on the ramp. Masked men instantaneously jump out of the cars with AR-15s and began shooting. Before Hop and his comrades can comprehend what is happening, the truck is riddled with bullets. One of the masked men pops the trunk of Hop's truck to confiscate Hop's intended delivery.

Magic is asleep in his bed with his wife. Magic's children are asleep in their rooms. Suddenly, Magic's room is filled with tear gas followed by an invasion of masked men through his bedroom window. Dazed and confused, Magic jumps up and is frightened by the large guns pointing at him. The men don't speak as they snatch Magic and his wife from their bed and lead them out of their bedroom window.

Magic and his wife are put in the trunk of a car, and driven to Magic's main spot. After Magic gives the masked raiders the code to the security system of his stash house. As soon as the door is open, magic and his wife are shot execution style and left at the threshold of the entrance of the stash house. The masked men raid Magic's stash in less than one hundred seconds.

The remaining four teams hit Poppy C's, Kelo's, Manny's, and Tone's trap houses like well-trained SWAT teams. Masked, armed men dressed in all black enter through doors and windows simultaneously. Shooting upon entry, the masked men show no mercy on the unsuspecting victims. Blood sprays all over the ceiling, floors, and walls. The houses filled with smoke and glass as the masked men pilfer the Carleton family fortune.

As the five masked men move through the home on Cordelle Street, Kelo and Manny pull up in a car. They notice there is something going wrong.

They pull out their guns and cautiously enter the house. As soon as they spot one of the intruders, they open fire. The masked intruders return fire. Kelo and Manny's gun power could not match the power of the intruders' AR-15s. Kelo and Manny fall as the seventh and eighth victim of the hit list. After killing Kelo and Manny, the masked intruders leave the house with drugs and cash worth two hundred fifty thousand dollars.

Tone is working in his spot on Kercheval and Mack with a few handlers packaging product and counting money when armed masked men burst through windows and doors. Tone and his handlers begin shooting at the masked men. The masked men return fire. The masked men had much more fire power.

Tone tries to take cover, but the bullets from the AR-15s tear through the tables and walls. After a minute of gunfire, Tone and his handlers are dead. The masked men gather the bounty and quickly exit the house.

Poppy C drives his Camaro into his girlfriend's driveway with the intention to head home to his wife in about an hour. A hail of bullets rain upon him before he could get out the car. Poppy C is killed instantly without ever knowing all his fortune had been taken for his stash houses and his cousins were murdered. With the tenth murder, the mission is complete. The Detroit drug world suffered the biggest night of bloodshed and robbery that the city has ever seen.

The Blackout crew brings the accumulate stolen riches to a female ally house. GangStarr, Blackman, TrainWreck, and Lucky count the cash. GangStarr tells Lucky and Lil' G to flip the drugs and bring back the money.

68

After selling the drugs, the crew has more than enough money to purchase weapons and ammunition to wage war on the police and enough for each man to pocket ten thousand dollars. GangStarr tells the crew it is imperative to keep a low profile and a tight lip. GangStarr could not risk Torren getting word of their murderous, ravenous rampage.

By five o'clock, word spread throughout the city of the ten murders and robberies. No suspects are mentioned. The Detroit Police is all over the city investigating the crime scenes. One question bothers the whole city: who has the manpower and the gallantry to pull off such a heist. Hill, Trueheart, Marrow, and Chalone have a hunch that the Red, White, and Blue crew is responsible; they just have to prove it.

Chapter 7

Gas Stations Become Necrosis

The city is set ablaze with a spirit of take, steal, kill, and destroy. In Detroit, you take or be taken and the Blue Crew posing as the Blackout Crew is out for the taking. Anyone making bank in the streets is on the list to be took. With the infamous night of murder and robbery being the talk of the town, the city is plagued with a spirit of larceny.

In one night, the Blackout Crew became street legends. With their personal economy in a downward swing, the Blackout will kill for a few thousand dollars in cash. Suddenly, there wis multiple murders committed during carjackings at gas stations across the city. The treacherous Blackout Crew destroys the citizen's peace. Murder-minded low-level Blackout Crew members victimize innocent people filling their tanks with gas.

Torren has had time to cool off, so the Blue Crew assembles as usual at the manor and on Coconut Grove. Torren keeps tabs on the murder investigation of the ten drug involved homicides, but he still has no idea his Blue Crew is the Blackout Crew. Nor, does he know about the war about to be waged against the police.

GangStarr isn't backing off the idea that the cops must pay for his slain brethren. The Blue Crew continues to secretly assemble as the Blackout Crew to discuss their plans. They are paced to strike at the right moment. In the Blue Crew's down time, they make the gas stations of Detroit more deadly than a warzone. Victims range in age from infants to the elderly. Pumping gas into your own vehicle couldn't be more innocent and righteous. Nevertheless, the Blackout Crew persecute patrons of the gas stations.

Lives Lost Pumping Gas

Victim: Barbara Whittaker, fifty-six-year-old mother, shot in the head dead pumping gas into her Ford Taurus with her three crying grandkids watching the entire incident. A masked man walked up and shot her without warning before pulling her grandkids out the car and taking off in her car.

Victim: Earl Fleming, eighty-four-year-old retired veteran of the US Navy was beaten ferociously about his head for his station wagon. Earl Fleming was punched in his head so many times that it tripled in size. Earl laid in a coma for three days before succumbing to his injuries. Earl's attack outraged the city because the consensus is beating a frail, old man was too much.

Victim: Teon Wilks, forty-four-years-old, went through the drive thru of KFC to get food for his wife and kids before entering a BP and never leaving out. Teon was shot five times in the chest while pumping gas into his Mercury.

Victim: Camille Turner, twenty-three-years-old, shot in her head before she could fully exit the car. As she opened the door of her Honda Accord, an assailant dressed in all black walked up and shot her in the head. Camille's body went limp and fell out of the door. The masked assailant rolled over with her own car as he sped away.

Victims: Maya Dingle and her husband, Jarrod Dingle, were shot execution style at a Sunoco while their toddler daughter and infant son were in the back seat of their minivan by four masked assailants. The heartless thieves took the babies with them and dropped the babies off two miles away on a corner still strapped in their car seats.

Victim: Julius Monroe, forty-two-years-old, shot in the head, neck, and chest a total of fifteen times. Julius was robbed of his expensive jacket, SUV, and Cartier sunglasses while standing outside a gas station talking to his friends.

Each of the above ordeals were caught on high-quality gas station surveillance cameras and repeatedly played in entirety on the news for days and weeks following the crimes.

Piracy of the Elderly in Detroit

Walking back to their senior citizen housing complex from the casino, a group of elderly people are attacked for their winnings by the Blackout Crew. Some Blackout Crew members beat the elderly women until they gave up their purses and the men until they gave up their wallets.

When the incident is the leading story on the six o'clock morning news and on the cover of both the Detroit News and the Free Press, the whole city is in an uproar. Many citizen and advocacy groups are outraged. This incident is just a beginning to a host of assaults on the elderly.

Every day the lead story on the news is an attack on the elderly ranging from battery and robbery to murder. There were two incidents that made the citizens say enough is enough. Betsy Robinson eighty-nine-years-old was beaten and robbed at gunpoint in her own home.

Her daughter, Randa Robinson-Ropes, drove from Ohio to see why she wasn't answering the phone. When Randa found her mother, she grab her chest and began to hyper-ventilate. Randa manages to call 9-1-1 before falling to her knees. The EMS responders put Betsy and Randa in the EMS vehicle on a gurney for transport to ST. John's Hospital. Randa and Betsy spent three days in the hospital recovering.

Irene Draymond was riding in the car with her disabled husband, Isaac Draymond when they were ran them off the road by four masked men. They murdered Isaac, beat and robbed Irene, and left her on the side of the road.

The citizens are demanding the police do something to stop the attacks on the elderly. Patrol officers are paid overtime to work double shifts to keep the streets flooded with a police presence. The tension was high between the police, the people, and the Crew. The police are under pressure to stop the Blue Crew and the new anonymous Blackout Crew.

Chen Strikes Back

Chen is furious about the humiliation his family suffered. His humiliation transforms to frustration then to the desire for revenge. Chen learns that the Blue Crew hangs at the Manistique Manor. He sneaks his father's gun and makes up his mind that tonight is the night to get revenge. Chen dressed in all black with a black ski mask, stumbles onto a group of six men hanging out at the rear of the manor smoking and playing around.

Touchy, Murda, TinyTim, Dragon, Goon, and Budda are waiting on the major members the crew. Goon walks behind the dumpsters to relieve himself. Chen creeps behind him and strangles him to death with his own hoodie. Goon's body falls to the ground with his eyes open. Chen believes if you die with your eyes open, you deserved to watch your own death.

Chen take the gun from Goon's body, quietly walks around the dumpster, and hides behind the building looking for a way to get the other five men. TinyTim comes to the back looking for Goon, as TinyTim turns the corner he run into Chen. Face-to-face for less than 3 seconds, Chen knocks TinyTim in the bridge of his nose. Chen picks up his head to snap his neck.

Chen takes the gun from TinyTim's waistband. Chen notices the silencer; Chen feels like God is on his side. Chen shelters by a brick wall, takes aim. One by one he quickly shoots the remaining four men. Now six dead bodies of the Blue Crew lay dead on their own territory.

When Blackman, Lucky and Lil' G find the bodies of the dead men, they panic. The Crew cannot have a police investigation at the manor. Police on scene would kill the business again. They load their friends into one of their SUV's and dump the bodies in a nearby hospital's parking lot.

The GangStarr meets with Blackman, Lucky, and Lil' G the discuss possible motives. Blackman thinks someone found out the Blue Crew has been posing as the Blackout Crew and decided to retaliate against them. To hide their knowledge and involvement, GangStarr told everyone to conceal the facts of their comrades' murders. Blackman stresses that Torren could not get wind of what happened because that could expose the Blackout Crew's scheme to get money.

Tension Within

Evidence has finally been analyzed and the reports on the Tilley family murders and the Holland Street murders are ready. Police issue warrants of arrest for Lyon, LowLife, Blackman, TrainWreck, Lucky, Lil' G, Pearlie, Got'em, Maynard, Ray, GangStarr, Will, Pitman, Creme, Black, Face, Dame, O.G., Elwin, CHI-Town, Dino, and Sham. Either their DNA was found on one of the hoodies or their fingerprints were on a gun recovered from one of the SUVs discovered in the burning warehouse.

The police raid every known address of the wanted members of the Blue Crew. A few (GangStarr, TrainWreck, LowLife, Dino and Sham) were able to hide after word spread of the raids. All the other wanted crew members are caught and arraigned.

At Blackman's arraignment, he discovers the existence of Kayla Tilley, the only eyewitness to his execution of Mama Tilley's daughter-in-law and Mama Tilley's two grandkids. Mrs. Tilley testifies to how her son was shot for no reason, the terror she felt when the men stormed her home, and the emptiness that now fills her life in the aftermath of the murder of four of her family members.

Detective Chalone and Marrow also testify to what the scene was like when they arrived. Chalone details how she found the little girl under her mother's bloody, dead body. The entire courtroom is appalled at Blackman's cold heart. The judge orders Blackman held without a bond, but the other Blue Crew members were given one million dollar or ten percent cash bonds.

When GangStarr hears of Mama Tilley testimony, he assembles the soldiers two make two pleas: 1) all monies collected by the Blackout Crew was to go towards the bond of the arrested soldiers, and 2) Mama Tilley, Kayla Tilley, and the two female detectives must die before the next court appearance. GangStarr collects donations from the soldiers to give to Torren. Torren comes up with the remaining bond to get incarcerated soldiers out of jail.

Torren is suspicious of how GangStarr had so much money after the brief shutdown, but he doesn't speak on it. Torren was on high-alert and in full investigation mode to find out how GangStarr had almost a million dollars of cash.

The police keep Mama Tilley and Kayla Tilley in a safe house while GangStarr has the crew hunt for them day and night. Detectives Marrow, Chalone, Hill and Trueheart are still gathering evidence to secure the cases against the Blue Crew.

The Cover-Up Murder

As the unmarked car carrying Mama Tilley and Kayla Tilley to their next court appearance led by an unmarked car and followed by another unmarked car drives to the courthouse, the entourage is ambushed by a hail of AR-15 bullets. Out of nowhere, bullets fly through the windows and the body of the cars striking every adult in the cars. Kayla is unharmed nestled in Mama Tilley's arms. When the car carrying Kayla comes to a stop, a masked man takes Kayla from Mama Tilley's dead hands.

At the exact same time, Detectives Marrow and Detective Chalone's homes are hit by a drive-by. Detective Marrow is riding down her block when she notices commotion in her rearview mirror. She watched bullets fly from the car and into her empty house. She turns the corner calling in for backup. She hit a U-turn and hid at the corner until the car comes to the intersection.

Detective Marrow bumps the speeding car's rear bumper as the car turns the corner causing them to spin out of control and crash into a tree. No one in the car is wearing a seatbelt, so the men in the rear seat are ejected through the windshield. Both rear passengers hit the tree. The driver tries to run but Marrow hits him with her car. The shooter in the passenger side seat shoots at her as she hit the driver. She dips low and slides out of the car. Shielded by a parked car, Marrow takes aim at the shooter, and shoots him in the head.

Detective Marrow cuffs the driver. She checks the two ejected passengers; one was dead, and one was dying. Backup and emergency vehicles arrived on the scene to find Dino and Sham dead, Lyon is dying from a traumatic brain injury from hitting his head against the tree, and LowLife is in custody. LowLife is done for trying to carry a hit out on a cop. Like Carl Watts A.K.A. Blackman, he will never walk the streets as a free man again.

The Murder of One of their Own

As the botched hit on Marrow is carried out, Chalone's house is hit with a hurricane of assault rifle bullets from a car parked outside Chalone's house.

Chalone is in the kitchen, but Jalen is leaving out the front door. Jalen is shot ten times before falling to the floor. The car is occupied by four Blue Crew members. Once Jalen is down, they get out of the car. They have one mission: kill Chalone. Chalone tips over the refrigerator and snatches the rifle and ammo taped to the back of the refrigerator.

Chalone runs out the back door. She hops the fence. She hops the next fence. She comes to the front two doors down. Protected by the house, Chalone aims and shoots Lucky and Lil' G who die instantly. Head shots and their bodies fell to the ground causing thuds. Chalone reloads her weapon and walks towards her house. Pearlie comes out of the backyard. She and he fires at each other. He misses; she doesn't.

Two shots to the throat, Pearlie's whole neck evaporates before her eyes. His head rolls off his body as it drops to the ground. Chalone reaches for her service weapon from her hip holster and walks up her driveway. When she reaches the backyard, Got'em is coming out of her back door. She hit him in the chest four times.

Chalone checks her empty, cold house room by room. She finds Jalen dead on the threshold of their front door. Chalone falls to the floor screaming. She grabs Jalen. She begs him to get up, but Jalen is gone. The chaos spooks her neighbors so badly that fifty calls are placed to 9-1-1. Sirens fill the neighborhood. Soon police are securing the home and forcing her out the door.

Mama Tilley is dead. Kayla is kidnapped. Eight Blue Crew members are taken off the street: seven dead and one in custody. Detectives Chalone and Marrow are taken to headquarters to be interviewed. They learned of each other's ordeals and the newest Tilley Family murder during their interrogation. Chalone is out of her mind and inconsolable. Normally, her mother would stay out of her work affairs, but this morning Deputy-Chief Chalone sit through the interview holding her daughter as she sobs and cries as she explains the events that led to Jalen's death.

Deputy-Chief Chalone is normally by the book, but coming for her daughter is her breaking point. She puts a BOLO out for Torren "2 Guns" Monroe, Marcus Tilley, and Rico "Relo" Lawrence. She wants the three men located immediately and brought to her for a personal conversation.

Police hit the streets looking for their known vehicles and hit every known address associated with the three men.

The first one found is Relo. Relo is brought to a parked SUV with tinted windows. Deputy-Chief sits in the back seat of the black SUV. She tells him to sit. First, she lets him know this is not about drugs, this is about her daughter and the missing little girl. Next, she lets him know it isn't him she's after. There's a knock on the window.

The door opens and Marcus Tilley enters the vehicle. Relo says man look I sell drugs. I do not steal, kill or take little girls. I, for sure, am not trying to kill any cops or old ladies. That's sick and sadistic. Deputy-Chief Chalone tells Marcus Tilley and Relo, the violence has to stop. The Blue Crew and the fake Blackout Crew needs to be stopped. She shows the men pictures of the Blue Crew posing as the fraudulent Blackout Crew committing robberies.

Marcus asks what do you want with me. Deputy Chief says, "I want to know everything you know about this Blue Crew. I want every detail of their operation."

Marcus says, "I don't snitch."

She tells him, "This is your once in your lifetime chance to get exactly what you want and have someone else do your dirty work. All three of us in this car want these men stopped today. Do we not gentlemen?" Both men agreed. Deputy-Chief says, "Tell me everything you know, and all of our problems will be solved with these men."

The men tell her everything they know. She tells the gentlemen that no one will know of their conversation. They two men leave her vehicle and drive to an alley to hatch a plan to get what they wanted. Relo wants the product and money. Marcus wants revenge. Marcus says, "They've got to pay for touching my family. I've been lying low, but my aunt this morning was too far."

Relo says, "I got you! Let's do this!"

Deputy-Chief Chalone receives a call that Torren is located. Patrol cops pull him over on the freeway. Patrol cops cuffs his passengers and put them in the backseats of squad cars. Her driver drive her to his car. She gets in his backseat. She asks why are you coming for my daughter. He is baffled.

She shows him pictures of his seven dead soldiers resulting from trying to kill two officers. She shows him pictures of Mama Tilley dead and the six cops that was with her. She shows him pictures of the Blackout Crew in various robberies and murders. She shows him pictures of ten dead drug dealers who were robbed by his soldiers pretending to be a new crew. Torren said, "I sell drugs. I don't rob, steal, or kill innocent women or children."

He swears he has no knowledge of any of those things and none of those orders came from him. He says, "I didn't call any of those shots, but I bet I know who did, GangStarr. GangStarr is crazy and his antics are like a terrorist's. Because of his reckless behavior, I haven't given them anything new to sell." He explains why he shut his crew down for their reckless behavior.

He says, "The Tilley murders were the last draw for me. I sanctioned the whole crew. I see they've gone rogue. I have no problems with your daughter, Mama Tilley, or any of the men in these photos. After today, there will not be a Blue Crew and there definitely will not be a Blackout Crew."

Deputy-Chief Chalone thanks him for his time. She tells him that she and her Blue crew are gunning for every member of his Blue Crew with an intent to eradicate the problem with no lawyers or courtrooms. Torren says I see we have a common goal.

When she gets out of the car, his friends: Credo, Lotto, and Mystro get back in his car. Torren tells them how his soldiers have gone rogue and must be taught a lesson. Torren says, "It is night-night for all of them tonight. Not one of them will make it to see the morning light." Torren asks his friend to find out every name of every person who was in the Blackout Crew.

Marcus and Relo Confederation: Coconut Grove Cracked

Marcus and Relo agree to rob Coconut Grove after darkness falls over the city. The plan is to assemble trustworthy teams big enough to hit every house on the block at the same time. Marcus and his crew will hit the left side of the street. Relo and his crew will hit the right side of the street.

They both agree to have very heavily armed men stationed at each corner and covering the alleys behind the houses. They also agree that no witnesses will be left, and each crew will take whatever they find and there will be no hard feelings if one crew gets more than the other.

Each man went to his crew and tell them the plan. The men assemble an extreme arsenal of weapons, including grenades, assault rifles, machine guns, a mortar, and night-vision goggles. This is retribution for the mayhem, murder, and destruction of the Tilley Family, the innocent citizens of Detroit, and all the business owners who were victimized. Relo and Marcus tell their soldiers to kill every member of the Blue Crew.

The Search for Kayla Tilley

As Relo and Marcus plans their attack, the police must deal with the murder of beloved SWAT team member Jalen Billingsley and the kidnapping of Kayla Tilley. Police raid every home, every known or previous address of every known member or associate of the Blue Crew.

Marrow and Chalone meet up with Hill and Trueheart. They search spots known for drug transactions and violence. They search abandoned buildings as they wait for a warrant to search the Manor. When the warrant comes, the detectives accompany the SWAT team on the raid of the Manor. They found girls chained to beds and locked in closets, but no sign of Kayla.

As night fell over the city, Marrow, Hill, Trueheart, and Chalone watch the Manor. The women discuss how they could use Chauncey the snitch to get to the ring leader, GangStarr, when Chalone's phone rings. When Chalone says hello, a little voice whispers, "Cori, will you save me?"

Chalone quickly sits up, puts the phone on speaker and says, "Kayla, Honey, where are you?" Kayla tells her she is stuck in the trunk of a car. Trueheart pulls out her phone to record the conversation with Kayla. Chalone asks if the car is moving. Kayla says, "No, and it's really, really dark in here. I am scared!"

Marrow calls to get a trace on Chalone's line. Chalone tells Kayla to stay on the phone; do not hang up.

Kayla tells Chalone that the bad men killed her grandma and the police officers. Kayla says, "They took me and locked me in here." Marrow gets an address. Chalone tells Kayla not to hang up, but if you hear anyone coming be quiet, very quiet. Hill starts the car, and the women take off.

Trueheart says, "I know that address. It's an abandoned building near the train tracks." As the four detectives rushed to find Kayla, Marcus and Relo lead their teams to Coconut Grove to execute their plan.

The Blue Crew is light on men after the raid on the manor. Pitman, Will, Dame, O.G., Elwin, and CHI-Town are awaiting orders from GangStarr as they guard the houses of on Coconut Grove with about twenty want-to-be crew members who are trying to earn their way into the gang.

While on guard, the Blue Crew members are mourning the loss of their fallen comrades: MookMan, Touchy, Murda, TinyTim, PacMan, Budda, Lucky, Lil G, Dragon, Goon, Quest, Got'em, Pearlie, Sham, Dino, and Lyon. The twenty-six men smoke and drink as they blast music and watch for potential customers.

They need money, so they are eager to poison people with their products. As the soothe their sorrow, they are oblivious to the fact that death was becoming them. Heavily armed men led by Marcus and Relo are secretly arriving on the scene under the guise of night in all black vehicles and dressed in all black and covered with body armor.

They Bleed BLUE; They Bleed to Death

Marcus and his team move through the alley like a well-trained group of Navy Seals approaching an unsuspecting enemy. Relo and his team spread out, approaching the houses from the rear. There are men stationed in all black SUVs at each corner and at the central point of the block on both sides. No one suspects anything because the Blue Crew members drive the exact same SUVs. Relo instructs his team to kill any Blue Crew member on sight.

Marcus and his men set a timer so they would enter the houses at the exact same time. When the timer signals, someone kicks open the door on each of the houses. After the doors are kicked open, Relo and his men firebomb the roof of each house on their side. With fire blazing, the Blue Crew members panic and arm themselves.

Relo and his men enter the homes with authority in sets of four. The first two men through the door are the shooters and the second set of men are the scavengers. Marcus and his men enter the houses like a SWAT team.

They strategically move through the houses in unison killing anyone they come across.

Once a house is clear, they disperse, and each person thoroughly checks a room.

Gunshots blaze through Coconut Grove. The Blue Crew is out manned, outnumbered, and out gunned. Bodies are dropping as the Blue Crew tries unsuccessfully to escape death. A few men jump out of windows, but are shot to death by assault rifles pointing out of the windows of the black SUVs parked on the street.

The Death of Pitman

Pitman sits in a chair at the table making calls trying to get the twenty on the next move. When Pitman hears the backdoor being kicked in, he assumes it's the police. Pitman grabs his gun from his waistband and ducks low as he tries to go out the front door. As soon as he hit the door, he sees the AR-15 pointing at him from the black SUV parked in the middle of the block. Pitman gets off a few shots, but his handgun is no match for the AR-15. Pitman is shot out of his shoes.

The Death of Will

Will and a few foot soldiers are leaving to go buy food. As they approach the backdoor, they are spray with bullets like roaches and ants are sprayed with bug spray. Will or the men can't get to their weapons. Their bodies are like cushions taking in needles and pins. They are all dead by the time their bodies hit the floor.

The Death of Dame

Dame wants to go out like an old-time gangster, in a blaze of glory. When Marcus comes through the door, Dame flips the couch over and begins to fire at Marcus. Dame strikes Marcus, but Dame's handgun isn't powerful enough to penetrate Marcus' body armor. Dame ducks and dodges bullets as he exchanges fire with Marcus. Marcus lets loose on Dame. The bullets easily tear through the couch and Dame's body.

The Death of O.G.

O.G. short for Otis Guildford. O.G. is alone in the corner house. When one of Marcus' men kicks in the door, O.G. hides in the closet like a child afraid of monsters in the dark of night. The intruders initially think the house is empty, so they begin looking for valuables and drugs. While in the closet, O.G. sits on the floor and covers himself with the shirts, towels and sheets in the closet. He tries to look like a pile of clothes. However, his toe is sticking out when someone opens the closet. The intruder immediately and repeated pulls the trigger and hits O.G. with fifteen bullets.

The Death of Elwin

Eldridge Winslow called Elwin jumps out a second story window of a burning house. Shawn Moxley, sitting in the SUV parked at the corner sees Elwin glide out the window and soar through the air. Shawn laughs and says, "Look at this angry bird!" He aims his assault rifle and shoots Elwin five times. Elwin died before he touched the ground.

The Death of CHI-Town

CHI-Town born as Chi McBride outlasted all his comrades. CHI-Town makes it to a car. He backs out the driveway, and that's as far as he gets. A gunman approaches the vehicle on the driver's side of the car and shoots CHI-Town before he can put the car in drive.

The Fall of GangStarr

The four female detectives pull up to the abandoned building. They strategize how they are going to enter the building and find the little girl. The detectives scope the entrances and the men guarding the building. The four detectives get dress in protective gear and agree that all are going home tonight by any means necessary. Hill calls her husband; Chalone calls her mother who in-turn calls her husband. These calls are personal. These calls aren't to report a crime; these calls are to wage a war.

The four detectives decide to separate. Each detective enters the building undetected by the guards positioned like trained snipers on the roof and in various windows. Chalone cautiously enters the building through the rear.

Hill cautiously enters the building through the front door while Trueheart and Marrow each climb into a window on opposite sides.

The detectives quietly and carefully move through the building on high alert with their guns in hands. When Marrow peeks into a dark room to check for any signs of life, Ray puts a gun to her head. Ray begins to mock her, telling her how she is going to die. He tells Marrow to put her gun down slowly. She complies with the request, but as she stands up, she pushes his gun away with her hands and knees him in the stomach. He grabs his stomach causing him to loosen his grip on the gun. She knees him in his ribs and takes his gun out of his hands. Marrow shoots him twice in the head with his own gun. Marrow picks up her gun, and secures his gun in her waistband. Marrow clears the remaining rooms in the area; each room is empty.

A foot soldier spots Trueheart. He shoots at her, so she takes off running. She runs down some stairs and into a makeshift chop shop. The gunman follows her shooting with an automatic weapon. Trueheart sees an SUV elevated on jacks, so she runs and slides under it. She makes it all the way to the other side of the SUV.

The gunman peeks under the SUV. Trueheart kicks a lever on one of the jacks causing the SUV to crash down onto the man's head. Just as the man's head is crushed, Maynard comes into the chop shop shooting at Trueheart. Bullets fly everywhere scraping the walls and bouncing off the ceiling and floor.

Trueheart, shielded by the SUV, takes her time, perfects her stance, aims, and shoots Maynard in the head. Trueheart walks over to Maynard, kicks his gun out of his hand and shoots him again. She checks the unknown man whose head was underneath the SUV. Only a neck and body survived the crash, the man's head was mashed into splatters of skin and brain matter.

Trueheart picks up Maynard's gun and takes off up the stairs. Trueheart and Marrow frightened each other as Trueheart runs through the door leading from the stairs. Relieved to see each other, they quietly embrace. Marrow indicates, she killed one. Trueheart signals she killed two. Marrow points to herself, then Trueheart before pointing forward, which indicates they will move forward together. Trueheart follows Marrow out of the door. As they walk down the hall a group of masked men shoot at them from down the hall.

The two women take cover in doorways as they return fire. As Marrow and Trueheart shoot it out with the thugs, Sgt. Williams, Deputy-Chief Chalone and Retired Lt. Mason Chalone pull up in separate vehicles. They are heavily armed, dressed in body armor and prepared for war. Immediately the snipers shoot at the new arrivals. Sgt. Williams drives his SUV up to the building as a cover to allow Lt. and Deputy-Chief Chalone to enter the building unharmed.

Sgt. Williams follows the Chalones into the building and up the stairs in search of the snipers. When they reach the top floor, they clear the first room as a unit. They move from room to room quietly until they crossed paths with a group of three, armed foot soldiers in a room. Rapid gunfire is exchanged between the two groups.

Sgt. Williams has had enough of them. He throws a flash bang into the room which stun the foot soldiers. They stop shooting long enough for Sgt. Williams and Lt. Chalone to enter the room and get the advantage over the young, inexperienced shooters while Deputy-Chief Chalone stands guard at the door. The foot soldiers surrender under the barrels of Williams and Chalone's gun. Just as they are about to place cuffs on the three men, a fourth man burst out of the closet shooting. Deputy-Chief Chalone with no hesitation shot the man in the chest.

Sgt. Williams and Lt. Chalone continue taking the three men in custody. The three men walk down the hallway with their wrists secured in zip ties leading the officers as they clear each room. As they walk toward the fourth room, the three detained men take gunfire from an automatic weapon. Their bodies hit the floor like trees cutdown in the forest.

Deputy-Chief Chalone dives into an empty room. Sgt. William and Lt. Chalone take cover across the hall. They communicate with their eyes and hand gestures. Lt. Chalone peeks out the door; he tells Sgt. Williams and Deputy-Chief Chalone that three men are approaching. Sgt. Williams crawls to the other side of the room. Lt. Chalone signals to Deputy-Chief Chalone to shoot high on the count of three.

Sgt. Williams finds a connected room with a door that leads to the hallway. As the three men approach, Lt. Chalone uses his fingers to count to three. When the third finger goes up. He and his wife quickly stick their guns out the doorway and shoot two of the three men.

Sgt. Williams simultaneously shot the third man in the back of the head. Relief is all over their faces.

Taking a moment to regroup after the elimination of the threat, they secure the weapons, check the bodies for a pulse and clear every room on the top floor. When they realized they were alone on the top floor, they proceeded down the stairs to the fourth floor with caution.

They clear the fourth-floor room by room. They quickly walk down the stairs to the third floor. They cleared the third-floor room by room. They quickly move down the stairs to the second floor. They could hear the battle of bullets on the first floor. They forego checking the next floor to go help. When they exited the stairwell, they enter a gun fight with the group of foot soldiers who are shooting at Trueheart and Marrow.

As the five of them shoot it out with a group of gang members on the first floor, Det. Hill cautiously searches in the darkness of the front of the building. The front of the long, old car manufacturing plant is weather-torn and worn down. Holding her gun in one hand and a flashlight in the other, Det. Hill slowly moves through the darkness vaguely hearing the gun battle.

Many scavengers have torn into this part of the building taking every piece of metal they could find. Birds and small animals have made a home in this part of the building. The sounds of night have Hill on edge. She sees light through the crack of the door. She cautiously approaches the door. She leans her back against the wall before she opens the door.

Stillness lingers on the other side of the door. The light emerges into the darkness. She hears no movement, so she cautiously proceeds through the door. Before she can fully get through the door, TrainWreck punches her in the face knocking her to the floor. She losses her grip of her gun and flashlight. He grabs her hair and drags her to his side of the door. He kicks her in the stomach and ribs. He tells her, "I knew you were coming." He adds, "Smile for the camera," before he kicks her again.

Det. Hill balled up in the cradle position slowly reaches for the knife strapped to her ankle. She conceals the knife behind her wrist as TrainWreck stands her up. Just as he grabs her by the throat, TrainWreck is violently thrust forward onto the knife and knocked off his feet. Det. Hill gasps for air as a masked figure dressed in all black attacks TrainWreck with martial art techniques.

Det. Hill gets on all fours to search for her gun as the masked figure continues to kick and punch Trainwreck who has the knife stuck in his chest. TrainWreck pulls a gun from the back of his pants. Before he can shoot the masked vigilante, Det. Hill shoots TrainWreck dead in the center of his forehead. The masked vigilante takes off running searching for Det. Chalone.

Det. Hill, in pain with two broken ribs, gently and cautiously walks toward the sound of gun shots. She comes up behind the men shooting at her husband, partner, and the others. Det. Hill, despite the pain, aims her weapon and with all the strength she had left she quickly shoots three of the men in the back of the head before taking cover.

With three more men down, the daunting task seems a little lighting. Surging on the foot soldiers like Desert Storm Troopers, the police kill the Blackout Crew foot soldiers leaving GangStarr as the last Blackout Crew member standing.

Det. Chalone finally finds GangStarr. GangStarr sits in the rear of the building on the trunk of the car where he has the little girl. He knows Det. Chalone would come if the little girl called. Det. Chalone slowly walks into the old automation alley of the building where workers would assemble engines many years ago. GangStarr tells her to put her gun down or he will let go of the handle of the grenade he is holding. He says, "I don't think you want the little girl to go boom."

Det. Chalone slowly puts her gun down on the ground. She raises her hands, she says, "Ok! I put the gun down. Let me have the little girl."

GangStarr says, "You didn't think it would be that easy?" GangStarr flips the switch, and the conveyor belts starts to move. The car starts moving. GangStarr says, "You have to get the little girl out the car before it reaches the end of the line." He points to the big compressor at the end of the line. He says, "It will smash the car with her in it."

GangStarr takes off running. Det. Chalone rushes toward the car in a panic. Kayla Tilley bangs on the trunk of the car screaming help, which makes Det.

Chalone panic even more. She runs and jumps on the conveyor belt. She rushes toward the car. When she reaches the moving car, she pulls doors and the trunk only to find they are all locked. She frantically searches for something to pop the trunk open. As the car moves further down the line, a hanging hook comes into her sight. She slams the hook into the lock, opening the trunk.

Det. Chalone lifts the trunk and Kayla crawls out. Det. Chalone says, "Come on, Baby, we have to jump." Det. Chalone takes the girl into her arms, and she jumps off the conveyor belt. Det. Chalone lands and rolls on the ground protecting the little girl. Det. Chalone gets to her feet and rushes to get out of the building. Before she can reach the door, GangStarr hits her across her back with a pipe. She fell to the ground. She tells Kayla to run and keep running until she sees her friend.

She screams, "Go! As fast as you can and don't stop until you see my friend." Kayla takes off running. Det. Chalone knows she must fight for her life. As Det.

Chalone struggles to get on her feet, GangStarr picks her up and throws her into the wall. She falls on the pipe that he used to hit her. When GangStarr moves closer to her, she quickly jabs the pipe into his stomach.

She makes it to her feet and strikes him across the face with the pipe. GangStarr and Det. Chalone slug, beat, batter, and kick each other. Det. Chalone uses all her strength to strike him as hard and as many times as she could. She uses the pipe to strike him in the nose. Blood pours from his broken nose. The blow stuns him giving her a chance to strike him in the head. She darts to the door before he grabs her, the masked figure dressed in all black kicks him with both feet. GangStarr slides as if he were a plane landing on an air strip. The masked figure kicks him again. Det. Chalone watches as she backs out the door.

Det. Chalone turns to look in the face of Torren "2-Guns" Monroe. Fright becomes her face. She just doesn't have the energy to fight anymore. Torren says, "Relax, Detective, I am not here for you." Torren walks in as the masked figure and GangStarr struggle on the ground. GangStarr is on top of the masked figure. Torren walks up behind GangStarr. Torren aggressively takes GangStarr by the forehead exposing his throat. Torren takes a huge, sharp knife from his pants to slash GangStarr's throat. The masked figure rushes from the blood pouring from GangStarr's throat.

Torren tells the masked figure to help detective get out safely. The masked figure takes off the mask as he approaches her; she said, "Chen! You shouldn't be here, but I'm so glad it's you." She hugs Chen. Marrow, Trueheart, Hill, Sgt. Williams, and the Chalones searched the building for Cori.

They first come across Kayla who is running to save her own life. She runs right into Marrow's arms. She jumps and buries her tear flooded face in Marrow's chest. Marrow asks, "Did you see Cori?"

Kayla says, "She's fighting the bad man. She told me to run and find you."

Lt. Chalone asks, "Where is she?"

Kayla points and says, "They're all the way back there."

They all take off running. Marrow cradles Kayla in her arms as she runs in a panic. They are met by a fatigued and limping Det. Chalone and Chen. Det. Chalone takes Kayla in her arms as she tells the group, "It's over!"

As the group walks to their cars, the building explodes. Boom! Pop! They turn to see Torren fleeing the scene. Det. Chalone says, "He helped us!" They get into their cars and pull away to a safe distance to watch the building burn. Chen says, "The Blackout Crew is blacked out."

Det. Cori Chalone looks at Chen; she says, "We all can sleep a little better tonight."

Cori Reconstructed

Two years later, Detective Cori Chalone is now Sgt. Chalone. Sgt. Chalone drops the now six-year-old Kayla off at school. Both recovering from their losses, they've handled life as a team now for the last two years. Cori legally adopted Kayla. Cori still wears the ring Jalen gave her, but she sold their house. Cori purchased a new house for her and Kayla to make their home. When they pull up to the school, Kayla says, "Bye Mommy!"

Cori says, "Have a good day, Sweetheart. I'll pick you up!"

Kayla says, "Please be on time, it's Taco Tuesday."

Cori smiles and says, "For sure!"

The End

When Mrs. Campbell is done with the story, the boys want to know if it is a true story. Mrs. Campbell tells them it's a true story. The boys excitedly discuss the story.

Mrs. Campbell asks the boys, "Is there anything you can relate to in the story?" The boys list things they have witnessed or experienced: gun violence, robbery, betrayal, drugs, and murder.

Jace who had been quiet says, "I was adopted. Just like Kayla, my parents were murdered in our house. They made my brothers and me watch." The room is silent while Jace speaks. Everyone in the room immediately feels empathy for Jace.

Mrs. Campbell says, "Jace, I'm so sorry to hear of your loss. Would you mind sharing how life changed since that happened?"

Jace says, "We no longer had a home. We had to pack a bag and go stay with our aunt. It was horrible. The house was dirty. We barely had food. My aunt was never home. Mrs. Long our social worker took us away from her and we went to foster care. We were all in several different homes for two years. After two years away from each other, Mrs. Long found a place that would take us all. Mrs. Long said we were lucky because many kids are not lucky enough to be adopted by the same family."

The boys are speechless and humbled by Jace's story. Mrs. Campbell says to the circle, "Jace and his brothers' lives were totally interrupted by choices someone made. Is that fair?" All the boys said no.

Jace says, "Every night, I dreamt of hurting the man who hurt my parents for two years. I felt helpless watching him pull the trigger. The big sound of the gun was so scary. My little brothers woke up screaming in the middle of the night for months after it happened. We have a good family, but sometimes I can't deal with losing my family. I don't want my mom to get tired of us and put us out because I act up in school."

The boys are quiet again listening to Jace. Jace says, "Last thing I want is to cause my brothers to lose another mother. I don't know why I keep getting in trouble."

Xander asks, "What happened to the man who shot your parents?"

Jace says, "He went to jail for killing someone else?"

Levi asks, "Why did he do it?"

Jace says, "He was robbing our house. We were coming home from grocery shopping. My dad tried to protect my mom, and the bullets went through him and into my mom. He shot so many times that every body part of my father had a bullet in it."

Mrs. Campbell says, "Jace that cannot be an easy story to tell, but we thank you for trusting us with your story." She adds, "I can hear the love you have for your brothers in your voice, and I bet, protecting your younger brothers mean more to you than getting revenge. Jace, you answered the question. Your younger brothers matter more than anything. It'll take time and it's hard work, but we can help you learn to handle your emotions."

The boys encourage Jace. They tell him that they believe in him, and he can stay out of trouble. Mrs. Campbell says, "Jace, I know you can do it, and I am committed to help. Can anyone else relate to something that happened in the story?"

Eli says, "My grandmother and aunt were shot at a gas station in Detroit by some men trying to rob some other people. My aunt was driving. She pulled up to the pump just as five men with huge guns ran up to the two gas stations on the corners at an intersection. There was a man pumping gas into his Charger, a mother with her children in the back seat, two brothers in a mustang, a car full of teenagers, and a truck driver restocking the coolers."

Eli continues the story, "Not one of the men asked anyone for anything. They started shooting and didn't stop until five people were dead and several other people were hurt. People didn't even see it coming. My aunt was shot five times and died in her car. My grandmother died a few days later in the hospital. One of the brothers died, the truck driver died, and one of the children died on site. It was on the news for days after it happened. My grandmother was the person that loved me more than anyone else.

I couldn't believe she was gone for a car she had nothing to do with." The group empathizes with Eli and his grief.

While the boys discuss Eli's story, the mothers talk about surviving tragedies. Eli's mother, Abigail, tells the group about the murder of her mother and sister. Jace mother, Mecia, tell the group how she came to adopt Jace and his brothers.

Abigail says, "It has been hard for everyone, but Eli is taking the death of my mother the hardest. Eli has been inconsolable. Before it happened, he was a typical boy. After it happened, he became angry and malicious. So quick to fight. I never really know what to do with him and all his anger."

Mecia says, "That is exactly how I feel. My heart goes out to Jace, and I want to love the anger out of him. I haven't been able to reach him. His brothers are adjusting well, but Jace's emotional issues impact them negatively. I really don't want to lose Jace mentally or spiritually."

Mrs. Miller says, "Grief is a serious emotion. There's a natural process of grief. Think about encouraging them both to talk to someone about their grief. It's very important that the grieving person goes through each stage. We can refer you to someone."

Mecia says, "I would like that."

Abigail says, "I would too!"

The other moms encourage Abigail and Mecia to take Mrs. Miller up on her offer. Bren says, "Their grief support group for children is great. You will love it; I promise."

Shanelle who has two children who successfully went through the group says, "It really helped my children when their father died. I also learned a lot of strategies to help them. First thing I learned was to allow them time to spend with his family. They learned more about their father by listening to his family tell stories.

"It was like a custody agreement for two years; someone picked them up from school on Friday and dropped them off on Monday morning. When they got home to me, they were full of excitement telling me what they learned and what they did. I was just happy to see my kids smiling again."

Inga, who has a child in the grief group and a child in both the grief group and the boys' circle in the other room, says, "My son, Tucker, who is in the other room, and my other son, Gabriel, both go to the grief group.

When my nephew was murdered, my boys took it hard. That was their big cousin and they looked up to him. It was more than I could deal with alone.

"The group really has helped Gabriel, but Tucker keeps fighting that's why we ended up here. For one of their homework assignments, Gabriel had to gather all the pictures he could find of Gavin. He created a beautiful memory book. We look at it and talk about the good times and the good memories. Tucker has football, his coaches and teammates. Those relationships help, but his temper is so quick."

Mrs. Miller says, "Some kids take a little longer to make it through the process. This may seem like punishment, but this group may be just what Tucker, Jace, and Eli need."

Jane, mother of two former boys' group members, says, "My kids went through the grief group and boys' group. I learned two things to help: 1) create some ritual or ceremony to do on the anniversary of the tragedy, and 2) make sure each child has some special possession of the decedent.

"Every year on my eldest son birthday, we visit his headstone. We clean it up. We plant flowers around it. We buy a marble cake and have dinner at his favorite restaurant. Both of my sons took anything they wanted from his room, and they cherish everything of his that they have.

"My son, Brock, uses his computer, and he swears he gets better grades because his brother's spirit is in the computer. It took a while, but they both found their way. I'm sure the groups will help Tucker, Jace, and Eli find their way."

Mrs. Miller and Mrs. Campbell end day two with a quick game of Four Corners on the Obama Family. Each of the corners are labeled with a letter from A through D. All the participants stand in the middle of the room. When the facilitator asks the multiple-choice question, the participants run to the corner that corresponds with the right answer. The two people with the most correct answers, win a prize. The movement and laughter help all the participants lighten the load from the heavy conversation. The participants leave with smiles on their faces.

Third Saturday

Meeting three starts with role playing. The boys role play in groups of two one being the aggressor and the other the victim. Mrs. Campbell gives each group a different scenario.

Mrs. Miller breaks the moms into groups of two and gives each group a list of conversation starters. The moms practice using the conversation starters as a bonding exercise. After the groups are done with the exercise, each group review what they learned.

The boys agree that being a victim does not feel good. Mega says, "If you don't get someone, someone will get you." Some of the boys agree.

Mega explains, "When people see you beat up someone, they are less likely to try to fight you."

Levi says, "Adults do it to protect themselves, so we do it to protect ourselves.

Mrs. Campbell says, "Are we supposed to base our actions on what everyone else is doing?"

Levi says, "You have to survive."

Mrs. Campbell says, "You can survive by doing what's best for you even if it means losing some friends. If you spend your life doing what everyone else is doing, you'll never grow into the person God wants you to be."

Mega says, "How else do you let people know not to bother you if you don't make somebody an example?"

Mrs. Campbell says, "If you are yourself all the time, people will see. You don't have to do anything outside of being yourself, and live your truth. Focus on what's important to you."

Mega says, "This is how I got in trouble. A bunch of people was jumping on one person. It was funny so I hit him too, but I didn't mean to hurt him. He fell back and hit his head. We thought he was dead, so we all ran. He was in a coma for about a week. I felt bad because he never did anything to me. I was just playing."

Levi says, "I was tired of people messing with me, so I made an example out of one person. Now, I have no problems with bullies."

Mrs. Campbell asks Mega, "What if that boy was you? What if that boy was your son? Mega, you play games for fun not people. He could have really gotten hurt. He could have died because you wanted to have fun."

Mega says, "It's not good, Mrs. Campbell."

Mrs. Campbell says, "Following the crowd is never good." Mrs. Campbell tells the boys a story while the mothers discuss the importance of taking time to bond with each child individually.

The Price Paid

The Temptation

Xyla (pronounced Zy/la), Navaeyah, Zahra, Montreal, Ameko, Rena, and Kimma Lee sit around Rena's room listening to the radio. Jay Z's American Dreaming comes on; Montreal says, "Come on, Xyla let's freestyle pass the mic, this is my favorite Jay Z song. Xyla you sing the intro and chorus then pass the mic to whoever. They pick up where you left off and it keeps going to the end of the song." Xyla grabs a brush from Rena's dresser and pretends it's a mic.

(Xyla sings the intro):
Riding through the city
With my girl Kim Lee
Dripping with black girl magic
Hating is so tragic.
Roll up on Meko.
Killing cancer like chemo
Slow roll, stunting just like the boys do.
Brand new, Audi silver trim dark blue
Oh no, stepped on my new red bottoms.
Dollars! Got'em!
Let's go, it's on
(Xyla pass the mic to Kimma Lee. Kimma Lee takes the brush. Kimma Lee raps first):
Wrist blinged out, hair pressed out, jeans fitting got his eyes bugging out.
Stack-stack-stacking top popping out.
Dreams of our downfall, but they can't

94

My friends turnt in my Benz, looking good 'bout to roll out.
Dressed up top down, we run this town.
Everything cream, and Louis Vuitton Brown
For real, I'm only a teenage girl.
Black girl dreaming with my home girl.
(Kimma Lee passes the brush to Montreal. Montreal takes up where Kimma left off):
So sexy, thick dark and lovely black Stallion
Bag made of genuine leather it's Italian.
Face beat, hair is flawless, a Detroit darling.
A wonderful time, brand new show and me it's starring.
Black girl dreaming of living rich like Will and Jada
I snatch every crumb and stack my paper.
As pretty as Halle, thick as Janet
Bey says girls, we run the world, we own the planet.
(Montreal passes the brush back to Xyla to sing the chorus. Xyla sings):
For sho', we're killing the game it's on hold.
(Montreal says):
Black girl dreaming
(Xyla sings):
Bright glow, twenty-four karat shiny gold
(Montreal says):
Just black girl dreaming.
(Xyla sings):
Oh no, got them scared game tight it won't fold.
(Montreal says):
Black girl dreaming
(Xyla sings):
All eyes our way
Meko, you're on
(Xyla hands Ameko the brush. Ameko raps):
Oh wee! Those nice right there
And, these over here
The price quite fair
Oh! we're hot it's recreational shopping for new, fresh clothes.

Know how to pop it dip it low roll slow.
Make him feel heaven rocking on my tippy toes.
Ameko on fire, I'm a beast iced head to toe.
Open my eyes when the sun rises to realize
I'm only black girl dreaming
(Ameko passes the brush to Rena. Rena raps):
Only ride in hot cars
Detroit Rock City all-stars
Hang in the hottest bars
Popping bottles like black Hollywood stars
Push to start, beat the block
Gave me a ring, got him on lock
The love of my life, he will make me his wife
It's all a dream I'm still in high school
Stay woke, Homegirl, the streets stay scheming
On your own baby girl, feels good, black girl dreaming
(Rena passes the brush back to Xyla to sing the chorus. Xyla sings):
For sho', we're killing the game it's on hold
(Rena says):
Black girl dreaming
(Xyla sings):
Bright glow, twenty-four karat shiny gold
(Rena says):
Just black girl dreaming
(Xyla sings):
Oh no, got them scared game tight it won't fold
(Rena says):
Black girl dreaming
(Xyla sings):
All eyes our way
Zahra, you're on
(Xyla hands Zara the brush. Zahra raps):
Life of a black princess, Gucci bag full of signed checks
My head to the sky and the boy is impressed
He says my bottom too fat but my top too little

Love me so, my head to heart down the middle
So, he makes me like him after a couple of dates
He asks honey you're straight, he takes care provide my desire
My love on top don't stop so hot like fire
(Zahra passes the brush to Navaeyah. Navaeyah raps):
Surpass the thots, he treats me well
Covered in rocks, rings wedding bell
How blessed am I, spiritual health
He buys me wheels, he gives me wealth
Keep my appearance fly you can see for yourself
Asked the Lord for signs, he said black girl keep dreaming
And these chicks are plotting, I can read they mind
But she can't take what's mine, he's one of a kind
It's true he so faithful, give me all his time
I'm just black girl dreaming
(Navaeyah drops the brush on Rena's bed. The girls celebrate).

Montreal says, "We killed that!"

Xyla says, "Black girl dreaming, that life sure sounds nice."

Zahra says, "It does sound nice; unbelievable to beat the struggle."

Kimma Lee says, "I'm so tired of the struggle. We never have enough of anything."

Montreal says, "We can make our black girl dream a reality."

Rena says, "What are you talking about?"

Montreal says, "Sabrina and Ashley got fake IDs to work as dancers at a private club. They do parties. They go on dates. They get paid in cash.

We can do it too. We can save up our money to pay for studio time and make our own mixtape. We get in and we get out as soon as we make enough money."

Xyla says, "That sounds like a high price to pay to make some money."

Ameko says, "I don't know. That doesn't sound safe. Dates? Parties? They may do more than dance."

Montreal says, "All they do is dance and look pretty. We're all cute. We all can dance. We can do this."

Navaeyah asks, "How are we going to explain being out so late to our moms? My mother is not going to go for that."

Montreal says, "My mother will be too drunk to care. Everyone can say they are at my house."

Kimma Lee says, "Fast cash sounds nice, but I don't know about being so close to strange men."

Montreal says, "I can get us fake ID's. Just try it once. If we don't like it, we'll never do it again."

Rena says, "How do you know the owner will let us dance at that club?"

Montreal says, "He already said we can, and he knows how old we are. All we have to do is get fake IDs."

Xyla says, "I don't know about that."

Montreal all says, "Xyla, dancing beats living on the streets and going house to house. You and I are both basically homeless. We can make some money and find a place to stay together. Aren't you tired of looking for somewhere to go every night? I am!"

Montreal convinces the girls to go with her to get the fake ID's the next day after school. Kimma Lee says, "No one is going to believe we are twenty-one."

Montreal says, "It's just a technicality. Everyone knows how old we are. Men don't care."

Rena says, "We're going to jail if we get caught."

Montreal says, "We won't get caught. Just think about it as a means to an end: our album. Let's go tonight and try it out." The girls reluctantly agree to go. Montreal takes them to Ashley's house to find outfits appropriate for the stage.

After they select outfits to wear, Ashley and Sabrina take the girls to the club, Principle of Pleasure. Principle of Pleasure is a secret, private gentlemen's club only open to exclusive criminal members who can afford the high annual dues. There's a golf course, exquisite menu, exotic scenery, endless supply of any alcohol, readily available street drugs, and heavily armed security. Principle of Pleasure is hidden just off the Detroit River surrounded by abandoned buildings and illegal chop shops. The owner of the club, Turk, has numerous young girls and women to entertain his members.

No females are allowed in the audience, but the entire staff excluding the all-male security personnel is females from the bartenders to the janitors. The dancers and waitresses are friendly with each other. While some of the girls do more than dance and serve drinks, a strong majority are strict and only perform the duties of their job title.

Sabrina and Ashley told Montreal they only dance, but that wasn't the truth. Sabrina and Ashley were making so much money as dancers that crossing the line was very easy for them both.

Sabrina and Ashley dropped out of school to focus on making money. They were spending money as fast as they made it. Cars, Gucci purses, expensive clothes, hair, nails, outfits for dancing, and their personal hobbies and habits.

Sabrina or Ashley didn't have parents or anyone looking after their well-being. They were in charge of their own thinking and decisions. Sabrina and Ashley were living so fast they weren't thinking of the consequences of their actions or choices.

Montreal, so enamored with Sabrina and Ashley's fast success, is willing to follow in their reckless footsteps. Montreal knows in her heart and mind Sabrina and Ashley do more than dancing, but she wants what they have by any means necessary. Montreal lies to her friends in hopes that the love of money will blind their good sense. Montreal didn't even feel guilty about lying to the only people on earth that truly loved her. When it comes to the prospect of money, love and loyalty go out the window.

While at the club, Montreal convinces everyone to dance except Xyla. Xyla chickens out and runs back into the dressing room. While in the dressing room, Kiana strikes up a conversation with Xyla. Kiana Marks is one of the strict dancers who will not do anything other than dance.

Kiana explains that dancing is not for everyone no matter how desperate times may get some people can't stomach the reality of dancing for men. Kiana tells Xyla it's okay to be different and not follow the crowd. She tells Xyla, "You have to do what's best for you not what's best for your friends. Anyone who can't support your decisions may not be your friend."

Kiana's remarks make Xyla think. Xyla wants to go to college. She wants to make money, but not at the expense of her pride and dignity. She won't support their decision if they wouldn't support her decision. This is the crossroad where their lifelong friendship will end.

Xyla is hounded by one thought: where was she going to go. If Xyla decides to dance, she losses her pride. If Xyla doesn't dance, she losses her friends. Xyla thinks for a moment. She decides dancing is not an option for her. Xyla puts on her clothes and waits for her friends in the dressing room. When Xyla's friends return from the stage, they don't speak to Xyla.

At the end of the night, the girls discuss all the money they made. The girls are super excited as they count their money. As the girls change into their clothes, Montreal tells them that Sabrina and Ashley invited them to an after party to dance. Montreal swears the men throwing the party are rich, which could result in the girls doubling their money. The girls carry a whole conversation without ever acknowledging Xyla.

The girls agree to go and leave Xyla sitting in the dressing room with no place to go. They don't even check on Xyla before leaving. Kiana asks Xyla if she needs a ride home. Xyla tells her that she has no home or place to go. She explains her mom died and staying with her stepfather was not a healthy option for her. Kiana knew exactly what she meant.

The Break

Kiana offered Xyla an opportunity to stay at her home. Xyla was blown away. Kiana explains, "I was in your shoes in high school, but I was pregnant. My mother said I had to go. My boyfriend's mother said I couldn't stay with her. My boyfriend worked after school, so he had money to rent weekly hotel rooms.

After I had my daughter, Kiara, I started dancing here. He hates it, but he understands we need the money.

"My boyfriend works to pay the bills, we both go to college, and I dance at night to pay for our classes. He, Alex, could've left me out on the streets. He did an honorable thing by leaving his mother to help the baby and me. He stuck by me, so I'll always have his back. It's a struggle, but we are managing. Soon and very soon we will be making it. We both are very close to graduating. I pray our finances will get better soon then I can quit dancing."

Kiana says, "Dancing may be a means to an end for me, but that doesn't mean it is one for you. Come stay with us, go to school until you get on your feet. What do you want for yourself?"

Xyla says, "I want to go to college. I want to be a nurse. I want to sing."

Kiana says, "Those are all honorable goals. You don't need to be in the streets and you don't need to be in a club. Come stay with us. It's a safe place."

Xyla went home with Kiana to live with her, Alex, and Kiara. For the first time in a long time, Xyla had a stable, safe place to stay. Kiana makes a deal with Xyla, get good grades and she and Alex will take care of her for as long as she needed. Although Alex and Kiara are very accepting of Xyla, she is shy and scared at first.

To get to know each other, Kiana asks everyone to eat dinner as a family every evening. The first Sunday morning Xyla spends with Kiana's family, Kiana wakes Xyla; she says, "Good morning, Sunshine. Rise up, Sleepy Head."

Xyla says, "Good morning!"

Kiana says, "Get up. Get dressed. Eat breakfast. I'm going to take you to a place where you can sing, well, at least you can think about singing there one day."

After they eat breakfast, Kiana, Alex, Kiara and Xyla attend the eleven a.m. services at First Missionary Baptist Church. This is the church Kiana and Alex have attended since they have been on their own. Xyla is astonished by the church. Xyla had never been to church. Xyla listens to every word spoken. When the parishioners stand at the altar to give their testimony, Xyla hangs on every word.

101

What stands out the most for Xyla is that each parishioner says, "God saved me!" After testimonies, the choir sins for twenty minutes. Xyla never heard music like that before. The sound is so soulful, and the music has a message and a purpose.

After church, Kiana asks Xyla if she thinks she would like to sing with the choir. Xyla smiles and says yes. Kiana says, "Choir practice is every Wednesday at six p.m. I will take you if you want to go."

Xyla is ecstatic, she says, "Yes! I'd love to go." Xyla starts to see a spiritual meaning in Kiana's offer. She thinks to herself: God saved me. Xyla asks Kiana to teach her how to pray properly. Kiana pulls out her bible to show Xyla Matthew 6:9-13, The Lord's Prayer. Xyla prays every morning and every night.

While Xyla lives her best life, her friends are tangled between chasing money and school. Chasing money has taken over Montreal. She quit attending school altogether. The others aren't interested in school; they only attend often enough to keep the attendance officer from reporting them as truant. Montreal didn't care because her mother didn't keep an address long enough to get a visit from the attendance officer.

Each of the girls has changed so much since the night Montreal mentioned dancing. Xyla is going in the opposite direction of her materialistic friends. Despite their differences, the girls still loved Xyla. They would speak when they saw each other. Their friendship didn't matter to Xyla anymore. Xyla didn't love how the money had changed them.

The absence of their friendship has little effect on Xyla. She has Kiana as her number one cheerleader. Kiana teaches Xyla to be confident in herself and her choices. When the girls would flash their money and material gains, Xyla wasn't swayed or tempted to follow the girls. She pitied them for the choices they made. While they are living in the right now, Xyla concentrates on the future.

Like Kiana, Xyla was willing to work now and get her payoff later. With a steady place to sleep and three good meals a day, Xyla is free to focus all her energy on school. Kiana encourages Xyla to participate in after school activities and extracurriculars to increase her chances of securing scholarships. Tenth grade goes better than ninth grade. Xyla is earning all A's. Her teachers are impressed by her turn-around.

Xyla fulfills her promise and succeeds in school. After high school, Xyla studies nursing at Wayne State University on a full ride. After Kiana and Alex graduated, they got married and Kiana quits dancing.

Kiana and Alex became Xyla's unofficial adopted family, supporting her the entire way to earning a Bachelor of Science in Nursing.

The Sunday before her graduation, Xyla stands before the congregation to give her testimony for the first time in seven years. Seven years of week after week of watching congregants get up to tell their truth, Xyla finally felt like she had a story to tell worthy of praise.

The Testimony

Xyla's eyes are full of tears as she starts to give her testimony. Xyla explains how God sent Kiana and Alex to save her and they changed her life. Xyla thanks Kiana and Alex for saving her. Xyla continues by explaining the death of her mother.

Her mother died from an overdose after years of using drugs leaving Xyla to live with her abusive husband. Xyla ran away from him because he tried to attack her. She was homeless, staying with friends. She explains with sorrow how hopeless she felt.

Xyla goes on to talk about how Kiana offered her an opportunity to live with her for nothing in return. She says, "Your biggest blessings may come through people you don't even know, and the biggest curses may come through the people you love." She tells the congregation that Kiana and Alex brought her clothes, gave her food, and helped her through school.

Xyla explains how her friends were pressuring her to make bad choices for money. Xyla says, "If it were not for Kiana, only the Lord knows where I would be. I am so grateful to Kiana and Alex for their support and encouragement."

Xyla adds, "I ran in a group of seven girls. We all met in grade school. We were together just about every day of our lives. And on that faithful night that I split from them, the Lord saved me from a gruesome fate.

My friends bragged about the money they got, the stuff they bought, and the men they were with.

"They tried to make me feel bad because I didn't have the material things they had. But Kiana gave me a loving home, a loving family, and she brought me to church. They didn't understand that we I had was way more valuable than their purses and clothes. At First Baptist Missionary Church, I was able to sing soulful music for the Lord. I learned to sing gospel for the Lord. Kiana taught me how to pray. She fed me and taught me how to cook.

"My friends had stuff. They had temporary happiness, but I had something greater than anything money could buy. I have something no one can ever take from me. I am so grateful for what Kiana brought into my life, and all I can give to repay her is love. I have an education, I have a family, I start my career next week, and I have a redeemer named Jesus who paid the ultimate price for me. Where would I be without Kiana? Probably dead, strung out, or going nowhere living in the streets because that's what happened to my friends.

"My friends were enjoying the glitz and glamour of the fast life until one night their fast lives fell apart and they were never able to put the pieces back together. The fast life destroyed their lives, and to this day they haven't been properly introduced to the good grace of God.

"The seven of us would talk about our dream of making it into the music industry. The congregation was enthralled in and intrigued by Xyla's story. They listened in silence. Every eye in the church is on her anticipating the ending. They were willing to pay for that dream with their souls. I refused to sell my soul to profit the world.

"I learned from them we all make sacrifices, and we all have a price to pay. What each one of us must decide is what is the goal and what is it worth to you. I also learned the devil can work through the ones you love to expose your weaknesses and elicit desires, and use them against you.

The Price They Paid for Fast Money

Sabrina and Ashley invited Navaeyah, Zahra, Montreal, Ameko, Rena, and Kimma Lee to work a private party after leaving the club.

Sabrina and Ashley promised the girls an opportunity to make big money. The girls expected nothing out of the ordinary: dance and get paid.

The party was in honor of Wilson's bachelor party. Wilson and fifteen of his friends rented a hotel room after leaving the club. Wilson's friend purchased an extreme amount of expensive alcohol. When they arrived at the hotel, the men were already intoxicated. Ramell instructed Sabrina and Ashley to get the others to loosen up.

Ramell, Ashley, and Sabrina poured glasses of expensive champagne for the girls. They laced the drinks with something to make the girls relax. Ramell told Sabrina and Ashley the powdery substance would make the girls relax, which was a half-truth.

The girls were dancing for the rowdy men when Sabrina passed out the drinks. The girls immediately felt strange and light-headed, but Sabrina and Ashley encouraged them to continue drinking. The girls drank more champagne and within an hour they were all unconscious.

Sabrina and Ashley rummaged through their purses and stole their money. After pillaging the girls' purses, Sabrina and Ashley left the vulnerable six girls with no one to protect them from the sixteen drunken men. With six vulnerable, underaged girls at their disposal, things escalated from bad to the worst in a matter of seconds.

The girls woke up the next morning with a headache, no clothes on, no money, and no memory of what happened. Despite not having a memory, they all knew what happened. Montreal convinced the girls not to go to the police because they were underage and would get the club owner in trouble.

What a price to pay and a secret to keep. The girls were devastated beyond repair. They felt violated, invaded and betrayed. Montreal was more upset that her money was taken than her body.

The shame and embarrassment coupled with fear and an inability to do anything drove the girls to the edge of insanity. Life for all six of them was different from that night forward. Each girl had to cope on her own with the secret they promised to keep.

Rena

Rena was never the same after that night. Rena became withdrawn and quiet. Rena eventually broke from the pressure of the secret, and told her mother. She and her mother moved away, Rena switched schools and never saw the girls again. In a new place, Rena still couldn't cope. Rena took two handfuls of pills and got in the bath tub. Her mother found her and called emergency services.

The ambulance rushed her to the hospital, so the doctor could pump her stomach. When Rena woke up in the hospital room, she was screaming and pointing. She excitedly told the doctors she saw someone in her room standing in the corner with a knife waiting to kill her. Rena was frantically stuck in a paranoid delusional hallucination causing the staff to panic. The doctors gave her medicine to calm her down.

The doctors couldn't bring her out of the delusional state, so they sent her for a psych evaluation. She was diagnosed with schizophrenia with paranoia. Rena spent the next few years of her life in and out of mental institutions. Rena became a recluse; she rarely left the house unless she had a medical appointment.

Rena didn't talk to anyone but her mother and medical staff. Rena spray painted all her windows black. She had no television, cell phone, friends, no outside contact with the world. Rena nailed her doors and windows shut fearing that there was always someone lurking around her house to kill her. Rena spent her life alone and destitute of joy. Each year Rena detached more and more from reality until one day she just didn't wake up.

Kimma Lee

Kimma Lee tried to move on and continue dancing, but she never trusted Montreal, Ashley or Sabrina again. Kimma Lee lost respect for herself and her friends. She eventually moved to a new club, but continued performing at parties. She just never ate or drank at a party again. Kimma Lee unknowingly contracted HPV the night she was drugged. She never expected to hear a doctor tell her she had advanced cervical cancer. With little body fat, Kimma Lee could feel the knots and lumps of cancer all over her mid and lower body within months of her diagnosis.

The cancer was too advanced to treat. The doctors sent her to hospice where they tried to keep her comfortable while the nature of cancer took its course. When Xyla heard Kimma Lee was gravely ill, Xyla went to say goodbye and express her love. Kimma Lee was so happy to see Xyla. Xyla was shocked how the cancer had changed Kimma Lee's body. Kimma Lee was bone thin. She looked as if death was taking her any moment.

Kimma Lee and Xyla made peace before her death. Xyla and Kimma Lee hugged in silence with tears streaming down both their faces. They accepted this was the end of their friendship in this lifetime.

The other girls excluding Rena reunited standing next to her casket a week after Xyla's visit. The girls were mournful. It was unspoken, but a guilt hoovered over the sad moment. They felt responsible for her death. The love and desire of money cost them two friends.

Xyla's conscious was clear. She had nothing to do with that night. Montreal felt no guilt, no shame because she no longer felt any emotion. Cold and blank, the now grown Montreal stands starring at the former frame of Kimma Lee. Montreal could barely recognize what was left of her body because the cancer had ravaged her inside out.

Ashley

The saying that what you do comes back to you is befitting of what became of Ashley. Ashley, a beautiful statuesque girl, attracted a lot of attention.

One night at the club, she attracted the attention of a rich, older businessman from the suburbs. Problem with a lot of attention is some of the attention comes from dangerous people. Randy Motkins was the silent but deadly type. He never approached Ashley or talked to her; he stalked her in silence.

He followed her for weeks. He would quietly sit outside her house watching for any sign of her. One night her mother told her to take the trash out to the curb. Randy couldn't wait any longer; he decided tonight was the right moment. Lucky for him and very unlucky for Ashley, Ashley was alone and unsuspecting of her stalker. Randy quietly rushed up behind Ashley, covered her mouth and picked her up. Randy shoved her in his trunk.

Ashley's family frantically searched for her. Their pleas for her safe return are featured on the news. They search the city for days to no avail. Volunteers found Ashley dead a week later in an unkept field near the city airport. Ashley's family was devastated much like the families of Kimma Lee and Rena, but Ashley's family didn't know or understand the hand Ashley played in Kimma Lee and Rena's destruction. Unfortunately for Ashley, karma came with a big bill she was not prepared to pay.

Sabrina

Sabrina had five kids, all boys, over the next seven years. Each child had a different father with the same story: absent, uninvolved, unconcerned, and unknown to the children. Sabrina's children raised themselves because Sabrina wasn't raised enough to lead children through life. Sabrina spent her life being used by man repeatedly until she was all used up.

After giving birth five times, Sabrina's body could no longer afford her an abundant life. She never worked a real job or had a real relationship. Her children disrespected her, misbehaved everywhere they went, and they all dropped out of school to pursue a life of petty crime. Sabrina paid for her part in the destruction of Kimma Lee and Rena with everlasting unhappiness and poverty.

Navaeyah

Navaeyah tried to be strong after that night. She continued following Montreal on a downward spiral, eventually spinning out of control. She tried to be cold like Montreal and separate herself from that night, but she wasn't cold enough to succeed. Montreal led her down a path that led her to her last night of life.

Montreal took Navaeyah to house dance party given where drugs and alcohol were in an abundance. Navaeyah agreed to go to a room with two men for a dance. Navaeyah didn't know either of the men, but she went with the intent to dance for money.

Of the two men, one intended to get a dance in exchange for money and the other intended to take what he wanted. The dance started out very routine, but the second man was not entertained enough. He grabbed Navaeyah by the back of her neck and pushed her into the lap of the first man.

He told her you got to get closer. Navaeyah asked him to let her go, but he smacked her to the floor. The first man tried to stop the second man, but the second man was out of control.

The three of them tussled from the bed to the dresser to the floor. In the scuffle, Navaeyah inadvertently scratched the first man's arm just before the second man punched her knocking her unconscious. The first man was unable to stop the second man, so he left the room leaving Navaeyah alone and unable to protect herself. The first man bleeding from the scratches on his arm warned his friends and they left the house.

At the end of the night, Montreal, drunk and barely able to walk, went looking for Navaeyah. Montreal searched the house until she found Navaeyah dead on the floor. Montreal screamed as she touched Navaeyah's lifeless body. Montreal used her cell phone to call the police and she hurriedly left the house.

The police came to the empty house to find Navaeyah's body on the floor in one of the upstairs bedrooms. The forensic team processed the house: bagging all cups, taking prints from door knobs, they cut Navaeyah's fingernails for DNA, and swabbed her face and legs for DNA. The police notified her mother who was hysterical.

Navaeyah's mother told the police to contact Montreal because that is who Navaeyah left the house with that evening. Navaeyah's mother always warned Navaeyah that Montreal would bring about her downfall because Montreal's spirit was not in the right place.

When the police found Montreal, she proclaimed Navaeyah went to dance for two men, but she was too intoxicated to remember which two men from the party went in the room with her. Montreal professed the truth about their career started: Ashley and Sabrina luring them to private parties, the previous rape, and dancing while underage at the club. She cried as she talked about losing two friends, Kimma Lee and Rena, from their lifestyle choices.

"I'm so tired," Montreal said. "If I knew I would tell because our lives and deaths deserve justice too. We may not be upstanding citizens, but not even a dog deserves what has happened to us. I was a homeless, hungry teenager with nothing and nowhere to go or do. I never thought dancing would lead to us being violated and three of our deaths.

"The people who raped us the first time walk the streets freely unconcerned about what they did to cause the death of Kimma Lee and the destruction of Rena's mind. The person who kidnapped and raped Ashley walks the streets freely with no concern about the devastation he caused her family. Now the person or persons who raped and killed Navaeyah walk the streets unconcerned that they killed a good girl who didn't harm anyone. So, Sir and Sir if I knew who did it, and how I regret not knowing, I would tell you."

The police listened to Montreal's heartfelt explanation. They believed she would tell if she knew, so they let her go. Navaeyah's mother was not as forgiving; she blamed Montreal for Navaeyah's death. Montreal didn't appeal to her because Navaeyah was only there because Montreal asked her to come. Montreal accepted responsibility for Navaeyah's death, Rena's insanity, and Kimma Lee's death.

When the DNA from Navaeyah's body was processed, two male profiles were found: George Denny and Reggie Fullerton. The police searched both names. Denny had no criminal record or encounters with the police. Fullerton had a long list of assaults. The police issued a warrant for both males.

Denny turned himself in and professed the truth: "We went into the room for a private dance. Everything was cool until Reggie went crazy and started beating the girl for no reason. I tried to grab her from him and as she held my arm, she scratched me. When I couldn't stop him. I got out of there."

Denny signed a witness statement and promised to testify against Fullerton, so the police did not arrest him. They told him to not tell anyone that he had any contact with police and to never mention anything he saw the night of the attack to anyone.

One officer suggested he leave town for a little while. Denny said he could go visit family in the south until things cooled down. Denny moved to Mississippi with his grandparents and never returned to Detroit. He got a job and lived life as a productive citizen.

When the police located Fullerton, he decided to shoot it out with the cops. Fullerton was shot thirty-two times standing next to his car surrounded by eight police officers. The death he caused Naveayah came right back for him. Case closed. No need for a judge, jury or witnesses. The guilty confessed when he shot at the police.

Zahra

Zahra met Nasir dancing at a private party. Nasir was taken by the young, naive beauty instantly. Nasir took Zahra home that night and never let her go home. Zahra became Nasir's main girl. Nasir was quiet and to himself, but he was also the biggest drug dealer under age twenty-one in Detroit. Zahra being young and naïve didn't understand the consequences of a relationship with Nasir.

Zahra made runs for him, picking up and dropping off drugs and money for him. Zahra left the other girls and the dancing life completely behind. She became first lady of Nasir's drug ring. When Nasir was out of town or making a run, Zahra called the shots.

One night, a group of ten men came to Nasir's stash house to rob him. Zahra and Nasir's runners were there preparing a shipment. When the men stormed the home, Zahra and the group had to shoot to save their own lives.

The shootout seemed to last forever in Zahra's mind, but it was about five minutes and thirty-seven seconds long. Nasir had trained Zahra to use a weapon when they first met just for situations like this. By the end of the shootout, Zahra was the only person living, having to take three lives to save her own. Zahra ran and hopped in an all-black SUV to get away before the police came, but she only made it about five blocks before she was surrounded by police.

Zahra surrendered to be the only living person to answer for fifteen dead men and twenty kilos of cocaine and heroin and an extreme amount of prescription pills.

Zahra was arrested and sentenced to fifteen to twenty years in the federal prison system. No opportunity to a fair trial with an all-white jury of Grosse Pointe residents. Zahra serve ten years with no support from Nasir. When she came home, Nasir had a wife and children. Together he and his wife owned and operated several businesses in the Metro-Detroit area.

Nasir never gave Zahra another thought after she was caught. Zahra came home to nothing. The federal government took everything she had the night she was arrested. Zahra had to stay at a half-way house for a year. She got a night job as a housekeeper with a company that cleaned hotels and office buildings and a day job as a cook. Zahra took culinary classes while in prison.

Zahra had to build her life from the ground as a former inmate of the federal prison system with a criminal history that included drug charges. Zahra could never get money to go to school. Zahra had to rebuild her life with only the skills and education she gained in prison.

Ameko

After Kimma Lee's funeral, Ameko disappeared without a trace. None of the girls ever heard from her or seen her again.

Montreal

After the death of Navaeyah, Montreal was overwhelmed with guilt and shame. Montreal numbed herself daily with drugs and alcohol. Each year her drugs of choice became stronger. Montreal went from being a dancer that used to get through the job to being a dancer that danced to get high. Eventually, she lost her physical appeal and no one hired her to dance anymore.

Montreal roamed the streets looking for means to get high. One day she met a group of users who introduced her to heroin. Montreal went from black girl dreaming of being a rapper to full time feen for drugs and alcohol.

Xyla

Xyla stood in front of the congregation and fell to her knees praising the Lord for his mercy and grace that saved her from the fate that consumed her friends.

Kiana, Alex, and Kiara came up to the altar to hug Xyla as she screams praises of hallelujah. The entire congregation was on their feet clapping and praising with Xyla.

Ten Years After High School Graduation

Xyla worked a double shift to cover for a good friend who had a family event with her children. Xyla and her friends at the hospital are very close, and they always make sure none of them missed important events with their children. They share the workload and do what is necessary to cover for each other. On this faith-filled night, Xyla covered the emergency room for a friend.

An ambulance brought a female suffering from a drug overdose into the emergency room. Xyla and the attending staff rushed into action to save the woman's life. The woman didn't look familiar, but her name surely sounded familiar. One of the other nurses said, "She has a unique name Montreal Karole."

Xyla looked at the unconscious lady with tubes in her nose and mouth. It didn't look like Montreal, but she knew it had to be. Not many females had the name Montreal. Xyla asked, "What's her D.O.B?"

The nurse said, "June twenty-second."

Xyla said, "I know her. We were friends when we were younger."

Xyla and the other nurses nursed Montreal back to health. Before Montreal is set to be released, Xyla cooks Montreal's favorite foods. Montreal feels special because Xyla still remembers what she likes to eat after all these years. Montreal was so happy to see real food. Montreal hadn't had a cooked meal in years. Xyla combed Montreal's hair and bathed her.

As Montreal eats, the two of them talked about Xyla's life. Xyla shows Montreal pictures of her husband, Martez, and three children: Marly and Martin six-year-old twins and two-year-old Myla. Xyla's face lights up with joy as she tells Montreal about her family.

Montreal smiles at Xyla, and says, "Back then I never would have thought you would be the one to live out loud the black girl's dream, and the rest of us paid a high price trying to take a short cut."

The End

When Mrs. Campbell finishes the story, Lucas says, "Montreal is like my sister. She's lost in the streets. We have the same dad, but different mothers. We used to be so close when we were little. When she turned fourteen and went to high school, she met new friends and changed.Our father doesn't know how to be a father. "He's like her friend, not her father. He's so busy running the streets that he doesn't watch her. She runs the streets doing whatever she wants. She is even doing drugs. She doesn't go to school. She has never worked a day in her life, but she has two kids at age sixteen.

"I know she and I are impulsive and learning in school can be difficult, but she's giving up. It's not that we can't comprehend. We both are smart and quick to catch on, but neither of us can sit long enough and focus to show what we know. We both like to be free, so rules and structure can feel too confining for us. My sister doesn't want to do better, so I can see her self-destructing like Montreal."

Mrs. Campbell says, "It's never easy to watch someone you love self-destruct. You must pray for your sister. Also, set an example for her. Even though you are the younger sibling, you can be the leader."

Mrs. Campbell asks the circle what theme or moral did they hear in the story. "Don't follow the crowd," Mega says.

Levi says, "It doesn't pay to take short cuts."

Tucker says, "Xyla found a loving family that helped her do the right thing."

Jace says, "Dreams are important, but should never come at the cost of your self-respect."

Brad says, "Something horrible happened to all the girls that followed Montreal. Xyla was the only one to survive because she didn't follow the crowd."

Niko says, "I heard what everyone else heard, but I also heard, Xyla was introduced to church where she was able to sing. She was able to do the thing she loved to do."

Eli says, "How quickly people turn on you when you don't do what they want you to do."

Mrs. Campbell says, "Very insightful! I'm so proud of each of you for actively participating, and I appreciate your honest, thoughtful answers."

Mrs. Campbell asks, "What can happen if you choose not to follow the crowd and how can you handle those consequences?"

Eli answers, "People will make fun of you, but you shouldn't let that bother you because you did the right thing."

Mrs. Campbell says, "Eli, that is a great answer. You have nothing to prove to anyone, and you will feel peace with yourself when you know you've made a good choice."

Brad says, "When you don't follow the crowd, you will probably stay out of trouble, and focus on what's important when you're at school. People who follow the crowd end up losers. I don't want to be a loser. Being a grown man and struggling to have money, unhappy, and in and out of jail. I don't want that life."

Tucker says, "I want to go to college to play football. Being in trouble all the time will not help my chances of getting a scholarship."

Mrs. Campbell asks, "How can we resist the temptation to follow the crowd?"

Caleb says, "We have got to think about the risks and consequences. Before I do something, I should ask myself: Is this worth me losing the chance to play football? If the answer is no, I shouldn't do it."

Mrs. Campbell says, "Think before you act. Go over the consequences in your head. I like that, Caleb, very noteworthy advice."

Levi says, "Don't go places where you know trouble happens. Stay away from people who are troublemakers."

Mrs. Campbell says, "Great solution, Levi. Avoid what we can. Don't"

Jace says, "It would be nice to go to a better school."

Mrs. Campbell says, "A fresh start can be great. A place where no one knows you or has no assumptions or prejudice based on your past."

Niko says, "Why do I even do the stuff I do when there's nothing good in it for me? I need to do better for myself."

Mrs. Campbell says, "That's right Niko. No one can love you like you love you. Once you love yourself, you will see your own worth, you'll take better care of yourself, and you will make better choices."

Mrs. Campbell, handing out mini framed boards, says, "I appreciate each one of you for participating in today's activities, but before we go, I want each of you to write or illustrate your vision for your future. If we can see it, we can achieve it. Having a clear vision of our desires, prayers, and passions for the future will help you keep a sharp focus on your future.

"You can draw several pictures, or you can draw one picture. You can write sentences. It's up to you. When you are done, I ask you to quietly for a few seconds look at your picture, and get that image in your mind. Whenever you need to get away from something or someone, go to that image in your brain."

As Mrs. Campbell speaks, she hands the boys a container of crayons, markers, and color pencils. Xander says, "It's like a vision board?"

Mrs. Campbell says, "Yes, Xander, it's like a vision board."

Lucas asks, "Can we keep them?"

Mrs. Campbell says, "Yes, you can keep them."

As the boys draw, the mothers take an emotion quiz. The mothers try to match each emotion to its definition. After the mothers finish the quiz, Mrs. Miller goes over the correct answers. The mothers are shocked at how hard it can be to name emotions.

Mrs. Miller asks the adults to consider how hard it may be for young people who may not have a mature vocabulary. She adds, "It is important to encourage young people to identify their feelings, so everyone involved can help the child appropriately work through the emotion or emotions the child is feeling."

Mrs. Miller gives the mothers sentence starters to help children identify the emotions they are feeling. While the mothers talk about the sentence starters, the boys quietly admire each other's artwork.

Mega draws himself dunking a basketball. Caleb and Tucker draw pictures of themselves playing football. Brad draws a logo for his future business that develops video games. Eli draws pictures of himself making music and the instruments he plays at school.

Niko draws pictures of shoes and clothes. Lucas draws pictures of expensive foreign automobiles. Levi draws pictures of horses. Jace draws a picture of his family including his biological parents and his adoptive parents. Xander's drawing was a representation of his global wish. Xander drew a picture of earth surrounded by happy kids. The boys look at their pictures and for a moment they all feel happiness.

The boys leave to meet their mothers in the lobby. The mothers greet their sons with gentleness to show their interest and concern of their sons. The mothers who attended the group in the past with their sons watch and smile at the change in the mother and son interaction in comparison to the first day. Mrs. Miller and Mrs. Campbell also noticed the positive vibe between the mothers and sons.

With all the participants gone, Mrs. Miller and Mrs. Campbell straighten up the rooms and prepare for the next meeting. They discuss the progress of the participants. They are both pleased with the groups thus far. Mrs. Campbell says, "I have a great group of boys. I am so impressed by how willing they all are to participate in the process."

Mrs. Miller congratulates Mrs. Campbell on the boys' progress. Mrs. Campbell says, "We do this every day hoping something changes for the people we serve. We never know if they really hear what we said or if they are motivated enough to stay committed. In all the years I've done this, I haven't wanted a breakthrough for anyone as much as I want it for Jace. He knows exactly what he needs to do. He wants it, and he has got to make it happen. I'm rooting for him."

Mrs. Miller says, "He deserves a breakthrough."

Fourth Saturday: Bridge Day

The remaining meetings are only for the ten boys and their mothers who have been ordered by the court to participate in the program. Meeting four is called Bridge Day. This day is dedicated to building a pathway of communication between son and mother. The last three meetings of the program are to improve the mother/son relationship.

Mrs. Campbell and Mrs. Miller are hoping to build a foundation of a lifelong bond between Mecia and Jace. When the boys walk in on day four, there's a gift box with a bow on each chair. The mothers walk into their room to see similar wrapped boxes in their room stacked on a table covered with a white linen tablecloth.

Mrs. Campbell and Mrs. Miller simultaneously start their meetings by giving their group directions for the activity. Mrs. Campbell explains to the boys to think of the ultimate gift to give their mother, but here's the tough part the gift cannot cost money. Mrs. Campbell explains to the boys, "The gift should be something for her head, heart, or spirit. Think of a way to physically represent that gift to put in the box for your mother."

She leads the boys to the Arts and Crafts room. She tells them you have ninety minutes to think and create. She adds, "When you are finished go through those doors. Mrs. Miller will meet you there."

The boys get straight to work. Mrs. Campbell watch the boys gather their supplies as they think through the process. Each boy is totally focused to accomplish the goal.

Mrs. Miller explains the directions to the mothers, "On the table, there is one box for each of you. When we get started, you will take a box and go to the Arts and Crafts Room. In the Arts and Crafts Room, you will create a representation of the one thing you want for your son more than anything else. It can't be something acquired with money. You will put your creation in the box and present it to your son. When your son opens his box, you will tell him what you created and why you want him to have it."

Mrs. Miller leads the mothers to the Arts and Crafts Room, and she tells them they have ninety minutes to work. She adds, "When you are finished go through those doors. I'll meet you there," she points to the double doors that leads to the atrium before the auditorium.

Just like their sons, the mothers think and work in silence. Mrs. Campbell watches the participants work while Mrs. Miller sets up for the presentation of the gifts. After about twenty minutes, people start walking through the double doors to meet Mrs. Miller in the atrium.

With the gifts they created, the participants nervously walk toward Mrs. Miller. There is a silent fear of rejection and disappointment in both the mothers and sons. Mrs. Miller has the chairs in the atrium set up in groups of two facing each other. The groups of chairs are far enough apart to give each group a sense of privacy. When she greets the participants, she tells them to sit in the chair with their name tag on the back of the chair.

Mrs. Miller says, "When mother and son are both seated, the son will present his box first."

The first mother and son pair to present are Niko and Rita.

Rita says, "Hey, Son!"

Niko says, "Hi! Mom," handing her the box.

Rita takes and opens the box. Rita sees a red heart torn into several pieces taped back together. Niko says, "If I could give you anything, I would take away all the hurt and sadness you ever felt especially the hurt and sadness I caused. Mom, I am sorry that I keep getting in trouble. I know it's a lot for you to deal with, and I'm going to do better." Rita cries as she listens to Niko speak.

Rita says, "Niko! Son! Thank you so much. I appreciate your intention to do better, and I forgive you for anything that occurred before this moment. Let's forget the past and just live in the moment. Can we do that, Son?"

Niko says, "Yes, Mom!"

Rita and Niko hug. She says, "I love you, Son!"

Niko smiles. He says, "I love you, Mom!"

As Rita embraces her son, she says, "Son, life is more than you think it is now. Life is hard and it takes a lot to survive, but Son, if you survive life can be wonderful. This world is so beautiful, and if I could, I would show you the whole world."

Rita hands Niko his gift. Niko opens the box to see his mother created a small replication of earth from blue and green construction paper. Rita says, "Son, I pray God blesses you with a long life and the ability to travel the world."

Niko says, "Thank you, Mom!"

Brad sits across from Stephanie; he hands her the gift he made for her. She opens the box to see a picture of her husband. Brad carried that small picture of his dad in his wallet for years. Also, in the box is a rose Brad made of red tissue and a green pipe cleaner.

Brad says, "If I could give you anything, I would give you your husband back. I can't imagine what all of this has done to you. I know the stuff I do makes you even more miserable. Mom, I am really going to do better. I can't give you your husband back, but I can do my part by stopping the behaviors that hurt you."

Stephanie hugs her son; she says, "I love you, Son, and I always will. You do not make me miserable, more like frustrated and disappointed, but not miserable. You're a growing young man. You're going to make mistakes that is how you learn to be a man. This won't be easy for either of us. If we stick together, we will get through it."

Stephanie presents Brad with her gift for him. Stephanie cries as Brad opens the box to see a picture of his dad and him when he was a baby surrounded by a hand-drawn house on the back of the box.

Stephanie colored the bottom of the box green. She drew their family happy and in-tact in the box.

Stephanie says, "Bradley, I did everything I was told to do: be a good girl, go to school, get a good job, get married, and be a good wife, so your kids will grow up happy. My intention and desire have always been to give you a good, happy family. I am so sorry that it didn't happen the way I thought it would.

"When I married your father, I never imagined he would be gone so soon. When I had you, I had no idea I would have to raise you alone. I want to take good care of you, and give you all the things you need. But in order to give you things, I need money. In order to have money, I must work.

"I know you feel like I am never around, like I'm not there for you. It's true, I've sacrificed us to make up for being a single parent. But Bradley, I do the best that I can. I didn't know what else to do. I figured, giving my three kids a good life would be the best thing for them. Clearly, I was wrong because there's something you need that I'm not giving you."

Bradley says, "Mommy, that is not true. It's not you."

Stephanie says, "I know that I'm a woman, and I can't teach you to be a man. Son, I'm trying, and I need you to do your part. Not for me, but for you. What kind of life do you want for yourself? You need to figure that out. If you want to go to jail, then stay on this course. If you believe there is something more for you, Son, you've got to do something differently. You can't keep fighting, and getting in trouble."

Brad says, "You're right. I know something must change. Mom, I'm going to change. I'm going to do better."

Stephanie says, "A part of being a man is honoring your word. When you tell a woman, you're going to do something, you must keep your word because if you don't, your word will be meaningless. A man should never say something or say he's going to do something if he doesn't intend to do it. Son, don't make promises just because you think that's what I want to hear. If you say, you're going to change, I am expecting to see something different Bradley."

Brad says, "Mom, I'm going to put more effort into school. I'm going to be the son you deserve to have. You work so hard to take care of us, and I don't appreciate it."

Stephanie says, "Son, if you're serious about changing, I would like us to go to therapy. Can you commit to really trying?"

Brad says, "I'll do whatever it takes to fix this."

Stephanie says, "Son, I am one hundred percent committed to the process. I want the best for my son, and I recognize I must do something differently as well."

Stephanie and Brad hug. Stephanie says, "I love you, Bradley!"

Brad says, "I love you, Mom!"

When Inga sits across from Tucker, Tucker gives her the box. Inga says, "Thank you, Tucker."

As Inga opens the box, Tucker says, "If I could give you anything, I would give you a better me. I don't know what is wrong with me. I hate to see you disappointed, but I keep making bad choices. If I knew how to fix me, I would. I'm sorry for all the trouble I get in." Tucker wrote his name and drew a picture of himself.

Inga smiles, "I love Tucker very much. I love you as you are. It's the behavior we need to change." Inga asks, "What do you need from me, Son, to help you?"

Tucker answers, "I don't know."

Inga says, "What if we found out together?"

Tucker says, "I would like that."

Inga hands Tucker his gift; she says, "Son, if I could give you anything, I would give you happiness because for so long you've seemed so unhappy. No matter what I do, you are never happy, and I don't know why. I don't know what to do anymore, and it's time we go see someone who can help us figure out what to do next. Can you take that step with me? I mean, really work with someone to figure it out."

Tucker says, "I can do it, Mom. I can, I promise."

Mega says to Megan, "If I could give you anything, I would give you a reason to smile every day at least three times per day. Mom, you cry so much and you're so upset all the time. More than anything, you need to relax and smile."

Megan smiles at her son; she says, "Awe! Mega, that's sweet." Mega drew smiles all over the inside of the box. Megan hugs Mega. Megan gives Mega his gift; she says, "If I could give you anything in the world, I would make your dreams reality. I would take you away from all the negative influences. I would put you in the best school with the best basketball team. I want you to get a good education and an opportunity to do what you love to do."

Mega says, "Thanks, Mom," as he hugs her.

Levi and Lea say hello to each other. Lea asks if he's okay. He says yes. Lea says, "I know you hate talking about your feelings, but this will be good for us, Son. It'll help us get to know each other better."

Levi says, "Momma, if I could give you anything in the world, I would give you your son back because I saw how much it hurt you to lose him. I hate to see you in any kind of pain."

Lea says, "Son, that's so sweet. Thank you, Levi!"

Levi gives her the box. Lea opens the box to see a picture of the sun. Levi explains, "Without him life just doesn't have the same light; life seems dull and dim without him. I thought giving you some sunlight would make our life better."

Lea hugs Levi: she says, "Son, that is so thoughtful. I love it, and I love you."

Lea hands Levi his gift. Lea says, "Son, art and drawing is not my thing, so don't expect much when you open the box. Levi, if I could give you anything, I would give you your innocence back. Before we lost your brother, you believed in things; you enjoyed things. Remember how much you used to love going to ride the horses when we visited granddad on the ranch. Your face would light up. Your smile made me smile.

"You're right, losing him did take the light from us, and I so want that back, Son. For my peace and sanity, I need to see you lit up and smiling again. I know those aren't much like the horses on granddad's ranch, but the joy you used to have when you were with the horses, I want you to have it back."

Levi says, "Thank you," as they hug.

Jace and Mecia look at each other. Mecia says, "Jace, you know I love you, don't you?"

Jace says, "I know you do, and I love you, too!"

Mecia says, "I am not trying to replace your mother. I never want you to forget her. I wanted children. I couldn't have my own. You needed an adult to love and care for you, and somehow the universe brought us together."

Jace says, "I'm so glad we have each other. If I could give you anything, I would give you the gratitude you deserve. I know my behavior doesn't say it, but I am so thankful you took us in when we had no one. The last thing I want to do is cause my brothers to lose another mother."

Jace gives Mecia the box. Mecia opens the box to see the words thank and you in big block letters. Mecia says, "Thank you, Jace for being my son."

Mecia gives Jace his gift. Jace opens the box. Mecia says, "As much as I love being a mother to you, I know that being with your mother would be best. I would give you more time with your parents." Mecia drew the face of an analog clock in the box. Mecia continues, "No child should have to see what you saw. I know that changed you, and I want to help you deal with your feelings. But in order to help you, I need to seek help to learn what to do. I think we should get family counseling. What do you think?"

Jace says, "I think it will help."

Mecia and Jace hug; he says, "I'm glad you're willing to help me even though I don't deserve it."

Mecia says, "Jace, you deserve a fair chance just like everyone else."

Lucas hands Melinda her gift; he says, "Mom, If I could give you anything, I would give you a cure for lupus. I see how much you struggle every day. I hate to see you hurting. I know my behavior makes the lupus even worse because you're stressed out all the time. I am sorry for my behavior." Melinda opened the box to see Lucas drew the words the cure for lupus. He colored and decorated the letters.

Melinda hugs her son and gives him his gift; she says, "I love you, Lucas! If I could give you anything, it would be a healthy me. (Inside the box she wrote a whole and healed mother.) It's not fair that you have to make so many sacrifices because of my illness. Lucas, I know your circumstances are not fair. You have a sick mother and an absent father from whom you inherited ADHD, and your big sister is not a reliable source of support. That's a lot for anyone to handle, but neither is an excuse for the stuff you do."

Lucas says, "You're right, Mom!" Melinda says, "Son, I've told you one hundred times that lupus can take my life at any time, and I can't rest if you are not headed in the right direction. Is it fair that you must grow up faster than you should? No, but Son, this is where we are in life. We all have crosses to bear. These are our crosses. Now, what are we going to do differently, and don't tell me the same old same: I'm going to stay out of trouble. I'm not going to fight. I don't want to hear those lines again because you haven't attempted to keep true to either of them. Son, what can we do differently?"

Lucas says, "I'll go to that school you want me to go to and I'll take my medication."

Melinda asks, "Every day?"

Lucas answers, "Every day!"

Melinda says, "No one wants to be different. I know it's not easy for you just like it's not easy for me to have lupus. Son, this is the right thing to do. The staff at that school is better equipped to handle your condition, and the medication will help you control your impulsive tendencies. Son, I'm trying to prepare you to be an independent person. When I'm gone, you'll be on your own."

Lucas says, "I know that; I just don't want to think about it."

Melinda says, "Every day we are moving closer to the inevitable reality. You must be prepared. Son, I need you to grow from a boy to a man in less than six months. Are you up for that?"

Lucas says, "I got you!"

Melinda says, "If you mean that, you'll be the first man in my life to ever say that and mean it."

Lucas says, "Momma, I got you!"

Melinda hugs her son and says, "Lucas, we've got this!"

Xander and Nia smile at each other as Xander gives Nia her gift; she says, "Well, Xan, what do you have for me?" Nia opens the box to see a little boy. Xander says, "Momma, if I could give you anything, I would give you a better son. I would replace me with a son that makes you proud because all I do is give you a headache."

Nia says, "I don't need a new son. I love the son I have. I need my son to act like the son I raised. You go to school, and you do what you see not what you know to do. That is not how you were raised, correct?"

Xander says, "Correct!"

Nia says, "I'm not sure what happened. One day all my kids were perfect. The next day, one of my perfect sons decided to wage a mutiny and disturb my whole household. Your behavior disrupts my life and the lives of your father, your brother and your sisters.

"I know you are a child and children make mistakes, but I taught you not to be selfish. Your behavior says I don't care about anyone in this house other than myself. Selfishness is not indicative of a family that will survive. Survival requires everyone to do what's best for the whole. For the good of the group, I need my son to be the person I carried for nine and a half months and laid in pain for thirty-six and a half hours. Do you hear me, Xander?"

Xander says, "I hear you."

Nia gives Xander his gift. Xander opens the box to see a red heart with a picture of Nia and Xander in the center. Nia says, "If I could give you anything, I would give you courage to comfortably and consistently be who you are. You are a wonderful person Xander, and you don't have to hide behind this rowdy, unruly façade. You are good enough as you are. You don't need this fake front you put on to impress people."

126

Xander says, "You're right, Mom!" Xander and Nia hug.

She says, "Xander, we can get through this especially if we work together."

Caleb sits across from Kelly, and he hands her the box. Kelly opens the box to see a brain and a heart inside an outline of a man and a rectangle all drawn with crayons. Kelly says, "A brain, a heart, in an outline of a man?"

Caleb says, "I am giving you what's in my power to give you: my clean, true, well-intentioned brain, heart, and soul. I'm going to high school next year. It's time for me to grow up, and carry out the plans we made in first grade. I'm going to college, and I'm going to be the best wide receiver I can be, so I can go pro. I'm going to buy a big house in the suburbs for you, and you'll never have to worry about money and scraping by to survive in Detroit."

Tears roll down her face, Kelly says, "Son, you got me. I wasn't expecting you to say that." Kelly looks in the box and sees a rectangle; she asks, "So what's the fourth thing?"

Caleb says, "A big eraser to erase that night."

Kelly grabs Caleb. Kelly says, "I got you that night, and if I had to go through that one hundred nights to have you, Caleb, I would. It's not how we got here; it's the fact that we are here. We have life and it's up to us to do something great with it. The Lord must have really wanted you here, now it's up to you to do something great.

"Don't you ever feel bad about that night. That's not on you. Don't feel any shame about that night, that's mine to deal with. I only told you because I want us to live in truth, and have an honest relationship."

Caleb says, "Mom, how can I not feel guilt and shame?"

Kelly says, "We need to go to counseling. Therapy can help us. You won't make it in life carrying around my burden and the shame of a man you never met. You can have empathy for me, but not guilt or shame. Promise me, you will go to therapy with me and really try."

Caleb says, "I promise!"

Kelly hugs Caleb and hands him his gift. Caleb opens the box to see a red heart with God written in the center. Kelly says, "If I could, I would give you faith, and an open heart to God. You don't come to church with consistency and when you do come you are on your cell phone. If you don't engage, you won't learn what you need to learn. There are things in this life I can't teach you. Since there is no earthly father, you need to turn to your heavenly father. Son, try him. Read that bible see what it says. I promise, you will love it."

Caleb says, "I will!"

Eli and Abigail exchange gifts. Abigail opens her gift first. Eli says, "If I could give you anything, I would give you back your mother and sister. I don't care how old you are; you need your mother and big sister. They took a lot from you that day."

Eli wrote Naomi and Abilyne in three-dimensional letters, the names of her mother and sister, in the color order of the rainbow in the box. He drew wings on the beginning and ending letters of the names.

Abigail says, "Eli, I still have a lot: my children. I need us to make it, but you won't on your current path." Eli puts his head down. Abigail says, "We have to do something, Eli!"

Eli says, "Yes, Mom!"

Abigail says, "I'm all in if you are!"

Eli looks up at his mom and says, "I'm all in!"

Eli opens his gift; she says, "If I could, I would give you a world free of violence and fear." Eli sees the earth drawn within a peace symbol. Abigail adds, "Son, we can't ask for peace if you are running around causing havoc and chaos. You've got to be better than your surroundings. You must demonstrate the behavior you desire in others. You can't be mad that someone killed your grandmother and aunt while you are running around beating people. You are attracting the energy you don't want. In order to get something different, we've got to do something differently. Eli, will you consider doing things differently?"

Eli says, "Yes!"

Mrs. Campbell called for the attention of the participants; she says, "The boys know I tell a story every meeting. With the last few minutes, I would like to tell a story of a little boy who went from needing help to being a hero, very much like the ten boys in the room today."

A Mother's Hero

Asher Levi Keaton was his mother's angel and her only child. After waiting to cement her career path, Marilyn Keaton struggled to conceive for years. At age forty-four, Marilyn finally got the news that she was with child. The next year, Asher was born.

Very early, Marilyn knew Asher was different. He didn't cry or fuss like other babies. Asher lived in silence, but it was evident that he could hear because he attended when spoken to and he looked in the direction of the speaker when someone called his name.

Marilyn, the supervising pediatric nurse at the best hospital in the metropolitan area, had services and support to help her foster Asher's development. Asher now seven-years-old displays an enhanced intellect with a photographic memory. He proficiently reads and writes in four languages; he taught himself just by reading books. Asher enjoys chess, plays soccer, and maintains all A's in school. Despite his reluctance to verbally communicate and his extreme shyness, Asher is otherwise a typical seven-year-old boy.

Asher loves to watch suspense and action movies with his dad. Asher and his dad love to watch movies starring Tom Cruise, Bruce Willis, Will Smith, but his favorite movie is The Equalizer with Denzel Washington.

Brent Keaton is a traveling pharmaceutical salesman who is often on the road, but when he is home, he and Asher never miss a movie date. They see every action movie during its opening weekend. They watch movies on Netflix after church every Sunday. Asher also loves to play chess with his dad. By age five, Asher played chess like an adult champion.

Asher's favorite thing to do is play with his friends. His lifelong friends understand him even without spoken words. Asher, Emily, and Kaden like to play tag on the hill behind the abandoned warehouse. Asher also likes to play soccer with Emily and Kaden. Emily and Kaden taught Asher how to play soccer, and, now, Asher is the best player on their team.

Emily and Kaden treat Asher like any other friend. Emily and Kaden tag Asher and he must chase them. Chasing Emily and Kaden is not a problem for Asher because he is the fastest runner on their soccer team. Asher silently counts while Emily and Kaden hide. After he counts to ten, he goes looking for them. Tag with Asher isn't conventional, but Emily and Kaden are used to Asher. They sincerely enjoy his company, and love him as a friend.

Friday

As they always do on Fridays after school, Emily, Kaden and Asher play tag at the foot of the hill near the abandoned warehouse. About fifteen minutes into their game, Emily tags Asher. Asher goes over to the tree and covered his eyes. Emily and Kaden run off to hide behind the trees. After counting to ten, Asher runs from behind the tree. Asher hears noises coming from the direction of the warehouse, so he goes behind the hill to look.

When Asher makes his way around the hill, he sees four black Cadillacs with tinted windows. Twelve men take a man tied up with rope into the abandoned warehouse. Asher watches in a trance. He can see the man fighting to get loose, but the twelve men has his body completely restrained with ropes. The twelve men laugh and taunt the man as they push and kick him into the warehouse.

When they make it into the warehouse, Asher hears ten shots. Asher's body jumps with each shot. Gun shots are louder in real life than Asher expected.

Asher's heart races and his curiosity makes him watch. The twelve men come out of the warehouse laughing and mocking the dead man. They imitate him as they shot him. They mocked his cries of pain.

Asher watches as the men get back in the Cadillacs and drive off. Asher runs over to the warehouse to get a closer look. Emily and Kaden come out from their hiding places to see why Asher is taking so long to find them. When they come out of hiding, they can't find him. They panic as they look through the whole lot.

They check behind the hill, but Asher is walking through the warehouse. Emily and Kaden run home to get an adult. Asher comes across the dead man. Asher sees the bullet casings on the floor. He smells the gun powder in the air of the dark, abandoned warehouse.

Asher turns and runs out the warehouse. Asher run as fast as he could toward his house. Halfway home, Asher runs into his panicked mother and friends screaming his name. They hug him and tell him they were so scared when they couldn't find him. Asher conceals the fact he saw something. Asher and his mother walk his friends home before they go home.

Asher takes a bath and washes his hair while his mother finishes cooking dinner. Asher sits in the tub and thinks about what he saw. He replays each gunshot in his mind. When his mother comes to check on him, Asher gasps and jumps. Marilyn asks, "Are you ok?" Asher nods his head yes. Marilyn tells him, "Dinner is ready. Hurry before your food gets cold." Asher nods his head again. Asher rinses off and dries off.

Asher gets to the kitchen table just as his dad comes through the door. They sit down as a family and eat dinner. Asher's quietness is peculiar. His parents feels a difference in his energy. His mom and dad probe, but Asher never lets on that he is a witness to a murder: a real murder. Asher eats dinner then watches a movie with his dad.

As the movie plays on the screen, Asher replays the murder in his mind. He wonders what happened that was so terrible that a man had to die. After the movie, his dad tucks him into his bed and reads him a bedtime story.

After reading the story, Brent turns off Asher's light and tells him goodnight. Brent and Marilyn perform their nightly ritual before going to bed. Marilyn tells Brent about the kids losing Asher for a while by the hill. She says, "I wonder if something happened because Asher seems distant." Brent thinks Asher was just frightened from being alone out there. Brent doesn't think anything major happened.

Marilyn asks, "Do you think he saw something or heard something that scared him?"

Brent says, "Eventually, he will tell us if he did. He's pretty good about keeping us aware of what goes on with him."

Marilyn said, "I hope so. Something is bothering him tonight. He had such a strange look on his face. When I checked on him in the bath tub, he gasped and jumped when I called his name."

Brent says, "I noticed the look too, but maybe it's nothing. Don't worry yourself, Honey. Asher is growing up. He will figure things out for himself. Get some sleep."

Brent kisses his wife good night and rolls over to turn his light out. Marilyn lays in the dark wondering what was bothering Asher. Asher lays in his bed thinking about the scared look on the man's face as the twelve men shoved him into the warehouse. Asher can still hear the loud ten blasts that ended the man's life as if he were standing next to the gunmen.

Saturday

Saturday as a normal Saturday in the Keaton home. Brent washes the cars while Marilyn cleans around the house. Asher helps Brent and Marilyn work in the yard. Marilyn tends to the flowers and plants in the garden while Brent cuts and trims the lawn. Marilyn makes lunch and they eat as a family on the patio. After lunch, Marilyn goes to the hospital to work the mid-day shift. Brent and Asher go to the movies.

As the Keatons went about life as usual, The Mitchell-Mason Gang gathers for a meeting in the back of their club. The leader of the gang, Richard Mitchell, asks about the hit last night. Gerald Mason, the number two in-charge, tell him Chekhov is sleep at the old warehouse. Mitchell asks, "You just left him there in the open or did you bury him?"

Mason answers, "He is on the floor."

Mitchell asks, "You thought that was a good place?"

Mason answers, "Our usual spot was hot. Construction crews were too close. I had to improvise."

Mitchell asks, "No one saw you, are you sure?"

Mason answers, "There was no one around. We scoped out the entire area."

Mitchell replies, "I'm not confident in your word."

133

Mitchell calls Rainman, a computer genius that hijacks information for the Mitchell-Mason Gang. Mitchell tells Rainman, "I need you to hack into the city surveillance footage from yesterday evening near the old, abandoned warehouse near the hill. I need all the footage you can find in the area before sunset." Rainman agreed to get the footage, and Mitchell promises him a payday worthy of his time.

Mitchell says, "The hit was to save me money, and your stupidity is costing me money. I need you to think clearly under pressure, Mason. You hold me down when I'm not around. For our relationship to work as smoothly and as successfully as possible, I need confidence in your ability to execute a plan. This must be the last mess up or we won't make it."

Mason said, "I'll make this right. I got it. I got you."

Mitchell said, "Are you sure you got me?"

Mason said, "I'm sure. It's already taken care of, no worries!"

After sunset Saturday evening, Mason sent a group of men to retrieve Chekhov's body and bury him in the wooded area near the warehouse. The men did as they were told. Mitchell has a nagging feeling that the mission was compromised because Mason and the men did not stick to the plan or the routine. Mitchell's motto is stick to the plan or abort and regroup.

This is not the time for the Mitchell-Mason Gang to have any negative publicity. Mitchell is close to legitimizing the gang by becoming major investors in a new real estate development along the riverside with Colesco Development Company.

Mitchell had been working toward accomplishing this goal for years. He has been saving and doing anything necessary to get his name in the pot of potential investment partners for years. Mitchell made it possible by operating a string of successful clubs around the city as a front for his violent crew.

The business community knows that Mitchell's name draws power, most importantly, street power. Mitchell had no beef or ill-will towards Chekhov, but Mitchell was eager to please someone who did.

With local underground crews and businessmen, who had been at odds for years, finally calling a truce to satisfy a coalition of local police forces working together to bring crime down, the criminal world in Metro-Detroit is tensed. The cooperative behavior is just for optics. Everyone still wanted what they wanted done and fast. Crooked businessmen and politicians often secretly hire the unconnected Mitchell-Mason Gang to commit illegal deeds for them.

The murder of Chekhov was just business for the Mitchell-Mason Gang, and the murdering business was lucrative. People like the way Mitchell handled himself, his crew and his business. The Mitchell-Mason Gang is cut throat, ruthless, and seemingly indestructible at times. Mitchell was a quiet storm; he kept a low profile and a clean record. The police nor the average citizen ever heard of Mitchell. Mitchell was meticulous with planning and execution to ensure to keep his low profile.

Mason is not like Mitchell at all, but Mason isn't afraid to get his hands dirty or doing whatever necessary to get the dollar. In a street king way, Mitchell and Mason balanced each other out. Mitchell is the brains and Mason is the muscle. One thing Mitchell did not tolerate is deviating from the plan. Mason thinks he can always get away with taking shortcuts and easy outs. Those two points are plagues in their relationship.

Sunday

Sunday came and the Keatons went to church as usual. Marilyn came from a family of devout Christians and devoted Southern Baptists. Her mother, Cyntria Luxenberg, migrated north in the great migration to find work in the car factories with her siblings.

Cyntria maintained her Southern-Christian ways in the big city over the years, and she passed her lifestyle, motivation, and beliefs to her children. Marilyn carried her mother's values into her own marriage and motherhood, and her family supports beliefs and follows her guidance.

Although Asher isn't a typical child, Marilyn loved being his mother. She will take his intellect and gifts over typical social development any day. Marilyn give her tithes and often fasts and prays in the hopes that one day Asher would verbally communicate with her. In the meanwhile, she loves her son, and her son loves her.

Marilyn loves Sundays because it is the one day of the week that she can dress her boys in nice suits. Father and son always look so handsome for church services. In church, Asher isn't like the other kids who play on cell phones and run around the church playing or being disobedient. Asher listens to the words of the sermon intently. He follows along with his own bible. He circles verses, and takes notes.

Asher was hungry for knowledge. Asher must learn and take in information everywhere he goes. It is an obsession for him. At this time in his life, he didn't see value in speaking. Some parents may have been ashamed of Asher, but not Mr. and Mrs. Keaton. They are proud of the genius in him. After church, the Keatons has lunch at their favorite Sunday spot: the pancake house near the hospital where Marilyn works. As they always do after church, Brent and Asher catch a movie while Marilyn runs errands and grocery shop for the upcoming week.

On Sunday night, Mrs. Keaton irons clothes for Asher's school week and packs Mr. Keaton's luggage for his business trip, while father and son watch their favorite movie, and read books before Asher bedtime. Marilyn comes to Asher's room to watch Asher say his nightly prayers. Marilyn tucks Asher into his bed. He snuggles with his blanket and drifts into a deep sleep. Sunday goes by, and Asher still hadn't told his parents what he saw.

Neither of the Keatons are aware that the breaking news on the eleven o'clock news on every station: the case of a missing person, Adolph Chekhov is connected to their son. Adolph's wife and children are on the news begging for his safe return home. The Chekhov family has no idea that their husband/father has been murdered because he didn't want to sell property he owned for a cheap price. Chekhov was the one hold-out stopping the Colesco Development Company from owning the entire block where the CEO wanted to build a strip mall and riverside condos and apartments.

Monday

Brent Keaton unsuspectingly leave his beloved wife and child alone as he travels state to state to promote sales for a new drug. Mrs. Keaton drops Asher off at school before going to the hospital to work her shift. The school social worker and the speech therapist have their weekly sessions with Asher. He doesn't reveal his secret to either of them.

They try to get Asher to talk or use the PEC System, but he refuses to do either. No one ever pushes the issue because Asher is the brightest kid in his whole school. His quarterly test scores are well above all the other students. The school social worker, Mrs. Parker always says, "I believe Asher can talk; he's just too bored to talk to us."

After school, Asher and Kaden ride to soccer practice with Emily and her mother. After practice, Emily's mother feed them and let them go to their favorite spot to play. When Emily and Kaden aren't paying attention, Asher hurries over to the warehouse to see if the body is still there. Emily and Kaden follow Asher. As Asher stands looking at the blood stains, Emily and Kaden walk up.

Emily said, "Asher what are you looking at?" As she comes to stand next to him, she gasps and says, "That's blood! Let's get out of here." Emily takes both Asher's and Kaden's hand and run out of the warehouse. Emily says, "That was a lot of blood!"

Kaden says, "That much blood means someone died."

Emily says, "Did you see the news? I wonder if it's that man's blood, you know the man that's missing."

Kaden says, "It does look like something recently happened in there."

Emily said, "Let's go tell my mom." Emily and Kaden take off toward Emily's house.

Asher stops them. Asher has seen enough movies to know the murderers murder witnesses and if the men find out he knows something, they will surely come after him. Asher gestures to them to shh. He makes the trigger finger gesture to his head.

Kaden tells Emily, "Asher has a point. If anyone thinks we know something, they will come for us."

Emily says, "Let's just stay away from there for a while. When the police solve the case, we can come back." The three of them run back to Emily's house.

The kids hang out in Emily's backyard for a while. Asher did not reveal his secret even though Emily and Kaden were curiously asking him questions

137

like what made you go over there; did you see anything or anyone; did you know that blood was there already and if so, how did you know. Eventually, Kaden's mom and Marilyn come to pick up Kaden and Asher. Now all three of the kids carry a secret to bed.

That night while the kids were sleeping, Mitchell receives the surveillance footage from Rainman. Mitchell watches the video alone in his office. He knocks the bottles and glasses from his desk when he notices a little boy watching the scene standing by hill. Mitchell is livid to say the least. He calls Mason in to view the video. Mason isn't bothered much. Mason says, "He's a little boy. He probably doesn't know what happened inside the warehouse."

Mitchell replies, "That might've been true until he went in the warehouse. Watch! Look how he runs out of the warehouse; he saw the body. You messed up, so it's your job to clean up."

Mason says, "You want me to kill a little boy."

Mitchell answers, "Right now, we have too much on the line for you to play nice. I need you to be the street sweeper and clean up all the litter that can cause an ugly scene." Mitchell adds, "All of our money is on the line. Unless you want to be broke, handle this situation accordingly."

Mason says, "It's already done."

Mitchell says, "You need to find out who that boy is and everyone he told. You need this done A.S.A.P."

Tuesday

The kids never mention their secret to anyone. After school, they have a soccer game. All three moms cheer them on from the bleachers. The kids play an awesome game, so it was no surprise when their team won.

After the game, the team, coaches and moms go out for pizza. Marilyn is still curious about Asher's distant behavior, but she doesn't press him to share what's on his mind. Her mother's intuition tells her he's keeping something from her.

Wednesday

Wednesday is Marilyn's day to pick up the kids from school and take them to soccer practice. The kids have fun at soccer practice. Marilyn smiles as she watches Asher enjoys his friends and favorite sport. Asher is great with the soccer ball. His moves make his mother proud. The other mothers sitting on the bleachers looking at Asher as if he was broken. Marilyn knows how the other moms look at Asher, but she isn't ashamed of her son.

After practice, Marilyn drops Emily and Kaden off at their homes. Marilyn takes Asher to his favorite restaurant Marselle's Italian Restaurant, so he could get his favorite dish: chicken alfredo and for dessert vanilla ice cream over a warm chocolate brownie with chopped walnuts topped with strawberries and fudge. Asher is so happy to be at Marselle's with his mother.

When they joyously leave the restaurant hand in hand walking to Marilyn's car, they are spotted by Mason's goons. As Marilyn drives, a set of headlights appear out of nowhere in her rearview mirror. At first Marilyn thinks it's just someone wanting to pass by, but the lights get closer and closer to intimidate her. Marilyn tries to get over, but the lights follow her. She tries to sway to the other side, and the lights follow her again. Now Marilyn is paranoid.

The lights back off, but continued to follow Marilyn's car. Marilyn drives cautiously, she keeps an eye on the car in her rearview mirror. Marilyn knows something is wrong, but she stays composed for Asher's sake. Marilyn calmly keeps her eyes on the road. Boom! Marilyn and Asher suddenly jerk forward from the car ramming into Marilyn's car. Marilyn tries to speed up, but the car follows closely. The car catches up to Marilyn's car and rams into her twice more.

The car rides Marilyn's bumper, so she drives faster and faster while trying to assure Asher sitting in the back seat that everything is okay. Marilyn turned down Sailen Hwy where a police car was sitting on the side of the road. The car following Marilyn sped off as she approached the police car.

Marilyn pulls over behind a cop's car standing observing traffic. She excitedly hops exits her vehicle. The officer sees the panic on her face. He gets out of the car to meet her. She tells the officer of how the car came out of nowhere and smashed into hers three times. The officer writes a report and follows her home. The officer thinks it is a simple road rage incident, and ensures Marilyn that the incident is over. The officer leaves Marilyn and Asher in their driveway.

Marilyn walks Asher into the house and locks the door. Asher is frightened, but he still doesn't tell his mother what he saw. Marilyn is afraid, but she holds it together for Asher's sake.

Marilyn runs a bath for Asher and calls her husband. She tells Brent what happened and like the officer, Brent think it's a road rage incident. Brent asks to speak to Asher. Brent tells Asher that he loves him and wishes him a good night.

As Marilyn and Asher carry out their nightly routine, two of Mason's goons watch their house. The goons know where they lived because all day Tuesday, Mason and his goons canvased the neighborhood trying to find Asher. Tuesday evening, they saw Asher and Marilyn getting out of the car after they came home from the pizza parlor with the team.

Mason wants to play this just right, so he wants time to plan how he is going to get rid of the boy. Mason leaves his goons to watch the house all night. He says, "Learn their routine. I want to know everything they do and when they do it."

Thursday

The goons follow Marilyn to drop Asher off at school. One car follows Marilyn to the hospital. One car stays at the school until Kaden's mom picked up kids, and take them to soccer practice.

Now, Mason's goons can guess who was near the hill with Asher on the night of the murder. They follow the kids back to Kaden's house where Emily's mother picks her up and Marilyn picks up Asher.

That night, Emily watches the news with her mother, and there is still no trace of Chekhov. Emily tells her mother that she has a secret. Emily's mother thinking it was some childhood crush, tells Emily she can be trusted with all of Emily's secrets. Emily explodes with the story of the blood in the warehouse and how she thinks Asher saw something. Emily speaks so quickly her mother tells her to slow down and start over. Emily explains that she and

Kaden Asher into the warehouse and saw blood days after Mr. Chekhov went missing.

Asher, who was supposed to be sleeping, goes to his window where he sees Mason standing in his backyard. Asher and Mason stared at each other. It's in that moment that Asher knows either he kills Mason or Mason will kill him.

While his mother slept, Asher tiptoes into her room and got his dad's gun. Asher sits at the door ready to shoot all night. What isn't going to happen is someone hurting his mother. He isn't going to allow that. Just before his mom woke up, Asher rushes to put the gun away.

Marilyn makes breakfast oblivious of the danger lurking. Just as Marilyn and Asher are about to walk out of the door, Emily and her mother ring the bell. Marilyn lets them in; she says, "Gale, Emily is everything ok?"

Gale replies, "I'm afraid not, Marilyn. We have a problem, and we need to get to the police fast."

Marilyn asks, "What? What's going on Gale?"

Gale answers, "I had a talk with Emily last night, and I think Asher may have seen something he shouldn't have."

Marilyn turns to Asher, she says, "Is this true?" Asher puts his head down and nods yes.

Marilyn says, "Oh my God!" She asks Asher, "What did you see?"

Asher put his head down and doesn't answer. Marilyn grabs him to hug him. Gale says, "Emily and I think he saw a murder. We need to get to the police, now."

Emily says, "There was a ton of blood in the old warehouse. Asher was just standing there looking at it. When I asked how did he know it was there, he swore me to secrecy. Sorry Asher, but the man's family needs to know if he is dead or alive." Marilyn loads Asher in her car. Gale puts Emily in her car, and they speed to the police station.

No one at the police station take their concerns seriously. The police treat them as two hysterical soccer moms with no credible evidence.

Marilyn tries to explain that her son wouldn't lie. She says, "If he says he saw something, he saw something." Since Asher won't speak, the police doubt he saw anything. No one in the station care to hear what Gale or Marilyn have to say, but they both persist that they need to talk to a detective.

In the commotion of Gale and Marilyn demanding to talk to a detective, Det. Monaco hears them and comes over. Det. Monaco tells the desk sergeant that he will talk to the mothers and their children. Gale tell Det. Monaco about the conversation she and Emily had. Emily tells Det. Monaco how she followed Asher into the warehouse and saw blood. Emily says, "It seemed like Asher knew something that he wasn't telling us. Even though he doesn't talk to me, he knows how to communicate with me, and I always know exactly what he's saying. We've been friends all our lives."

Det. Monaco asks Asher, "Did you see something?" Asher reluctantly nods yes. Det. Monaco asks, "What did you see?" Asher holds out his hand.

Emily says, "He needs paper."

Det. Monaco said, "Alright!" and handed Asher a pad and a pen.

Asher wrote:

On Friday, we played hide and seek. I went around the hill while Emily and Kaden were hiding. I watched twelve men take a man wrapped in ropes into the warehouse. The man was struggling and fighting. He did not want to go in the building. He looked scared and hurt. It was the man that was on the news. He was beaten and bloody. I didn't say anything because I didn't want the men to kill me too, but I heard ten gun shots, and I knew the man was dead. The man that was holding the gun when they walked out of the warehouse was standing outside my house last night. I looked him in his eyes, and he looked at me in my eyes. I know he wants to kill me.

Det. Monaco read what Asher wrote. He asks, "Does Asher make up stories? You know, create stories to entertain people."

Emily says, "Never! He is a very literal kid. He think in facts."

Marilyn says, "My son knows better than to make up lies. Besides, that would explain why someone tried to run us off the road on Wednesday night."

Det. Monaco asked, "Did you file a police report?"

Marilyn explains how she pulled behind a police cruiser and talked to a cop who told her it was probably just a road rage incident. Marilyn gives Det. Monaco Officer Ronald's badge number 312. She says, He works at the fifth precinct. He followed her home and gave her a report number for her insurance company.

Det. Monaco says, "I need you all to stay here. I'm going to the warehouse to see if there's blood. In the meantime, I need Asher to look at mugshots to see if he recognizes anyone. Asher, if you recognize anyone you saw that night just let the officer know."

Det. Monaco explains to Marilyn and Gale that he was taking a few CSI technicians to the warehouse to process the scene. He says, "If Asher saw what I think he saw, this is a big deal."

Marilyn, Gale and Emily sit with Asher as he flips through the mugshot books. Det. Monaco and the CSI techs go into the rear of the warehouse facing the hill. They immediately see the bloodstains Emily told him about. They search the area around the bloodstain and found a bullet casing.

Det. Monaco calls his Sgt. to tell him, "I think the kids are telling the truth."

Saturday night, Mason was in such a rush that he failed to realize he was leaving one bullet casing behind. Mason took the body and nine of the ten casings to bury. He didn't think to cover up the blood.

The CSI techs rush the evidence to the lab. Det. Monaco goes back to the station. When Det. Monaco sits down to talk to Asher, Asher shows him ten mugshots of people who were there when the man was shot. Asher points to Mason. Det. Monaco asks, "Was he the one holding the gun?"

Asher nods his head. Det. Monaco, turns to Marilyn and Gale; he says, "This is way more serious than you two have imagined. These are all members of the notoriously secretive and very dangerous Mitchell-Mason Gang."

Det. Monaco empathetically says, "You all are in danger. I cannot in good conscious let you go home until we sort through some things."

Emily shouts, "What about Kaden? He was at the warehouse with us. What about Kaden's mom and our dads? Are they safe?"

Det. Monaco answers, "We are going to put you in a hotel until we can sort things out. We will get Kaden and his mom now."

Gale says, "I'll call my husband and ask him to come down here now."

Det. Monaco asks Marilyn about her husband. She tells him Brent is out of town.

In about twenty minutes, two uniform officers escort Kaden and his mother in the room. Det. Monaco informs Kaden's mother about Saturday night. He says, "We want to ensure you and Kaden stay safe while we plan our next move."

Twenty minutes later, Kaden's and Emily's dads join the group. Det. Monaco explains what happened Saturday night to the dads. With everyone in the interview room, Det. Monaco and Sgt. De'Anthony, explain what needs to happen next.

Det. Monaco says, "The human blood we found at the warehouse matches the blood type of the missing man: Adolph Chekhov." He added, "Along with the blood, we found one casing. We believe, Asher witnessed a murder, and your children are in danger because they were there with Asher."

Asher pulls Det. Monaco's sleeve. Det. Monaco hands him the pen and notepad. Asher writes:

When the men left the warehouse, I went into the warehouse. I saw the man's body. He was dead with ten bullet holes in his head and chest. The man was wearing a nice business suit, Italian cut, I know because my dad has a suit just like it. He had on a navy tie, white button-up shirt with diamond cufflinks, navy pants and navy leather shoes. He had a mole on the side of his forehead. He was going bald in the crown of his head and on his forehead. He has a gold band, like a wedding band on his ring finger of his left hand. He was about your height, about six feet two-inches tall.

Det. Monaco reads Asher's note. He hands the note to Sgt. De'Anthony. Sgt. De'Anthony asks Asher, "Is there anything else you know that you haven't told us?"

Asher grabs the pad back, and writes:

The man who was holding the gun was driving the car that rammed into my mom and I on Wednesday night. De'Anthony reads what Asher wrote, he asks, "Anything else?" Asher gestures with his head no.

Sgt. De'Anthony tells the adults in the room: "Based on what Asher wrote, your children are the only living witnesses to a Mitchell-Mason Gang crime. We have never been given this much detail to a crime committed by a Mitchell-Mason Gang member. We must keep you safe. We will take you to your homes. You will have fifteen minutes to pack essential items, and get back in the police car. We have no time to waste. Does anyone have family out of state?"

Gale and her husband raise their hands. Kaden's parents raise their hands. Gale says, "We have family all over America."

Kaden's dad says, "We have family all over the Midwest and in the Southeast region."

Sgt. De'Anthony says, "You two pick a place and we will get you tickets to fly out on the first flight available. Mrs. Keaton and Asher, we can put you in a hotel until we figure things out. We will contact your husband. Don't call or contact anyone."

Gale and Bree (Kaden's mother) hug Marilyn. They tell her and Asher to be safe. Officers escort the three families to their homes to quickly pack. Emily's and Kaden's families go straight to the airport. Marilyn and Asher are taken to the new hotel: Blue Moon Inn located on the service drive of the interstate outside the county line. As they drive to the hotel, Marilyn tries to comfort and console Asher.

Asher sits on the bed thinking about the possibilities of what Mason could be planning. Asher thinks by now, Mason knows he talked to the police. Asher says to himself: Mason crossed the line first. Mason came to my home where my innocent mother was sleeping. I had to snitch to protect his mother. Mason is well beyond dangerous and capable. The police can't protect us. It's up to me to protect my mother.

While Asher is thinking, Mason and his men are watching the hotel waiting on sundown to make their move. Mason's goons saw the police at the warehouse, so they know Asher told what he saw. Mason isn't discouraged.

Mason's motto is if there's no witness to testify, the district attorney won't press charges. He also knows that because District Attorney Eve Graylin is on the Mitchell-Mason's payroll. In fact, Eve Graylin is Mitchell's cousin, a fact no one else knows.

The officers bring fast food for Asher and Marilyn. Asher and Marilyn eat the food sitting on the bed together watching television as the sun set. As soon as the sky is taken over by darkness, Marilyn and Asher hear a succession of powerful gunshots from two different guns.

Marilyn run to the window. She sees two men shooting into the police car and the two officers occupying the car. Marilyn rushes over to Asher; she whispered to Asher, "Go to the bathroom and climb out the window. Run, baby, and don't stop. Go now!" Asher looks at his mother and pulls her to the bathroom. He thinks they both can get away.

Asher climbs out the window and gestures for his mother to come. Marilyn hears the men crashing through the hotel room door. She jumps out the window. She and Asher take off running down the alley. Asher pulls his mother between two buildings. They run as fast as they can through the narrow pathway to a parking lot.

In the parking lot is a running car. Asher points to the car and pulls his mother toward the car. Marilyn says, "You want me to steal a car!" Asher pushes his mother toward the car. She says, "Okay! Okay!" They hop into the car, and drive away just as Mason and his goons pull in the parking lot shooting.

Marilyn drives frantically to the freeway while bullets hit and bounce off the car. Mason hangs out the window shooting at Marilyn and Asher. Mason's car rams into the back of the car driven by Marilyn. Asher gestures for his mom to drive faster and faster. Marilyn drives fast as she can until she is stopped by a traffic backup on the freeway due to a car accident.

She sees Mason's car coming behind her, so she instinctively drives onto the shoulder just before three emergency vehicles followed by a police cruiser blazing up the shoulder. Mason's car can't follow, so Marilyn is able to get away.

Marilyn asks herself where to go as she exits the freeway. Asher turns to his mother and gestures: gun. Marilyn asks, "A gun, where are we going to get a gun?" Asher gestures: home. Marilyn says, "Home is too dangerous. They are probably watching our house. Maybe, we should go back to the police station."

Asher insists no police station. Marilyn says, "Mommy! We can go to Granny's house and get Papa's gun. Ash! Baby! I don't even know how to use a gun." Asher touches his chest. Marilyn asks, "You know how to shoot a gun?" Asher nods yes. Marilyn says, "Of course! You literally know how to do everything. I don't even know why I asked."

Marilyn drives toward Cyntria's house. They park a few blocks away from Cyntria's street. They run down the side street and across the alley to jump the fence to get to Cyntria's backdoor. Marilyn lightly knocks whispering, "Mommy, it's me." Asher taps on the window of the den. Marilyn comes to the window; she whispered, "Mommy, it's me. Come open the backdoor."

A startled Cyntria rushes to the back door. She opens the door; she said, "What are you two doing back here?" Asher rushes in and take off running upstairs to the gun cabinet. Asher grabs two small handguns from the cabinet and bullets. Cyntria asks, "Did Asher have to use the restroom?"

Marilyn answers, "Mommy, it's a long, very long story. We just need a favor and then we need to go."

Cyntria asks, "What is it that you need, and why are you in a rush?"

Marilyn answers, "I don't have time to tell you, but I promise to explain later." Asher runs back to his mother with two guns and bullets. Cyntria asks, "Guns! Why does my daughter and grandson need guns?"

Marilyn says, "Mommy, we need daddy's old car, too. I will explain later."

Cyntria, very confused, went to the drawer to retrieve her deceased husband's keys. She hands them to Marilyn. Cyntria says, "You will call me as soon as you get where you are going? You two have me very nervous."

Marilyn replies, "Mommy, I will explain, but we have to go now."

Asher and Marilyn run out the door and to her dad's old car in the garage. They get into the car, pull out the garage and take off. Marilyn asks herself: where can we hide.

As Marilyn drives, she thinks maybe somewhere public with plenty of potential witnesses. They will be hesitant to shoot. Marilyn says, "I think we should call Det. Monaco. We can tell him to meet us Downtown. I think he is the only one we can trust."

As Marilyn drives down a quiet side street, heading toward Downtown, a car comes out of nowhere and crashes into her and Asher making them crash into a light pole. The sparking light pole tilts and fells onto the car that hit them electrocuting all the passengers in the car. Caught between the pole and the car, Asher and Marilyn climb out of the car through the passenger side window in a panic, Asher grabs the guns, and they take off running.

In a desolated area with many abandoned, rundown structures, Asher and Marilyn try to conceal themselves. They run as fast as they could as long as

they can. They come to a coney island restaurant near the freeway. Marilyn asks to use the phone. She calls Det. Monaco and tells him what happened and where they were. Det. Monaco tells her to stay there.

Marilyn and Asher try to blend in with the dining guests in the back of the restaurant when two men came in blindly shooting. The workers and patrons scrambled to get out of harm's way. Marilyn and Asher rush out of the backdoor, and down the alley.

They come to an intersection, they pause to see if anyone is coming, Asher prepares the guns to shoot. Marilyn peeks around a building. Asher steadies his grip on the gun in his hands and makes sure the second gun is securely tucked into his waistband. The pushed the bullets all the way into his pocket. Asher made up his mind to shoot back the next Mason or his goons approach.

Marilyn doesn't see anyone, so they run. Before they can get across the street a car pulls around the corner with a man hanging out the window pointing a gun. Before the man can shoot, Asher shoots him in the chest. The man falls out of the window and the car runs him over. Marilyn pulls Asher to run. The driver backs up to try to hit them, and Asher doesn't flinch.

Asher aims the gun to shoot the man in his face. The man slumps over letting go of the steering wheel. The car veers to the side and into a gas station crashing into a gas pump causing a huge explosion. Marilyn is shocked. She stares at Asher as they watch the fire.

Marilyn asks, "Son, how do you know how to do that?" Asher shrugs his shoulders. They take off running. He pulls his mother to a church. The doors are unlocked, so they quietly go in and hide in a closet all night.

When the sun comes up, Marilyn wakes Asher and they take off running. Marilyn sees a nice house with a for sale sign in the yard. She looks in the window; the house looks as if no one lived there. She and Asher climbs in a rear window. "We can hide here until we think of what to do," Marilyn says.

They sit on the floor of the dining room. Marilyn turns to Asher and embraces him; she says, "Asher, I am so sorry you've seen all you've seen over the last few days. This is not the life I intended or wanted for you. A seven-year-old boy should not have to use a gun to protect his mother, but I am so happy and thankful that you are my hero."

Asher hugs his mom and pats her back. Asher thinks to himself: I will kill them all before I let one of them hurt my mother.

They sit in the furnished, abandoned house until hunger pangs showed themselves. Marilyn has no money or idea how she was going to feed her son. She wrecks her brain contemplating the next best move. She says to Asher, "Maybe, we can make it home just long enough to eat, clean ourselves, get a car, get some money and a change their clothes. Do you think you can make it home?" Asher nodded yes. They run home unbothered.

Marilyn is so relieved to make it home. While Asher takes a bath, Marilyn calls her husband who is excitedly driving home as fast as possible. She explains what happened last night. Brent tells her to go back to the police, but she explains, "Every time the police know where we are the Mitchell-Mason Gang magically appears."

She promises to do her best to hide until he gets home. He promises he is driving home as fast as he can. He tells her he loves her, and Asher and he needs them to be safe. Brent suggests Marilyn take Asher to his parents' old, abandoned house. He says that the keys are in the top drawer of his desk. Brent says, "When you make it there, hide the car, lock all the doors and cover all the windows."

After the call, she showers, puts on fresh clothes, she and Asher eat, and get money out of her hidden stash. Marilyn packs bags of food, clothes and personal essentials. Asher gets his dad's gun. He loads it and get extra bullets. Marilyn pulls her husband's prized, classic Impala out of the garage.

Asher has the guns loaded and ready to fire hidden under the passenger seat. Marilyn tells Asher to buckle up and sit low in the back seat.

Marilyn and Asher make it to Brent's parents' old house. Marilyn parks the car three doors down in the garage of another abandoned house. Majority of the block was dilapidated and evacuated many years ago.

Marilyn and Asher run through the alley to Brent's parents' old house with all their bags and two of the three guns. When they make it to the house, Marilyn is shocked to see the house is still in fair condition. She locks all the doors and makes sure the windows are locked and the curtains closed.

Asher walks around the house creating an escape plan in his mind. Asher mentally maps all the entrances and exits. His dad always told him to know his surroundings. His dad also told him to always get to know his surroundings so well that he can move around in the dark. Marilyn lights candles. Marilyn prays for her and her son's safety, survival, and protection.

She sits close to Asher as he plays a handheld video game. She tells Asher that his dad is on his way home and that they are going to stay in his grandparents' old house until his dad gets back to Detroit in the morning. Marilyn says, "We just have to make it to the morning," as she hugs him and kisses his forehead. She has faith that God will keep them safe, but she feels fear that she can't hide from her son.

Asher and Marilyn sit quietly as the sun sets and a sinister mood creeps over the horizon. Marilyn has anxiety about surviving the night. Asher, on the other hand, is as solid as a stone as he waited to hear tires or footsteps. Asher puts his game away because he knows Mason and his goons are coming.

Marilyn lays her head in Asher's lap. Asher clutches his gun as he watches his mother rest. Asher can feel the energy of Mason and his goons close.

As Asher expected, car doors slammed. Asher nudges his mother. When she opens her eyes, Asher puts his finger over his lips. Asher covers his eyes, which means hide. He points to the closet. Marilyn tries to pull him with her into the closet, but Asher refuses to go. Asher puts his mother in the closet, closes the door.

Marilyn opens the door and whispers for Asher to come back. Asher puts his finger over his lips. Marilyn crawls out the closet calling Asher to come into the closet with her.

The front door crashes to the floor. The boom makes Marilyn jump. She begs Asher to come to her. Asher points to the closet then takes off running. Marilyn hears footsteps coming toward her, so she quietly crawls back into the closet. Marilyn is frightened out of her mind. Tears flow from her eyes as she panics.

Asher runs to the kitchen and hides in the milk chute. Mason and Mitchell walk through the front door with two of their goons. Three more goons come through the back door. Mitchell is beyond angry with Mason and everyone.

Mitchell yells, "Five minutes, find that kid and this is done. You all have let this go too far. We are all hot, and this is not the time for this. Go!"

Mason encourages the other man to solve the problem as they walk toward the dining room. Asher sit in the milk chute prepared to shoot. When one of the goons opens the door of the chute, Asher shoots him in the center of his forehead. The man falls to the floor, stunning the other two men in the kitchen.

Asher goes out the back of the chute to the rear of the house. The two surviving men shoot repeatedly into the wall tearing through the plaster, paint, installation and brick, but Asher is too quick. Asher runs as fast as he can and hides in the backyard.

Hiding behind the big tree in the backyard, Asher is ready to shoot the first person to come out the backdoor. The surviving two goons run out the backdoor to search the backyard for Asher. Asher peeks around the tree and sees a man. Asher aims and shoots him before he takes off running.

The third man chase after him while shooting. Asher runs behind the garage. Mason and his men run toward the gun shots.

Asher climbs on top of the garage, but the man thinks he ran between the garage and the fence through the bushes. The man slowly walks crouch low through the bushes causing a rustling sound.

Mason and the two goons quietly standing in the backyard hear the sound. They position themselves to ambush whoever is coming through the bushes. When the man makes it through the bushes, Mason and his two goons shoot every part of his body in less than five seconds.

In a matter of three minutes, three of the seven men are gone. Mitchell comes to the backdoor; he yells, "One kid is out thinking six adults. In three minutes, three men are gone. Do you think the three of you can manage to find one kid before another one of us is dead?"

Marilyn hears the gunshots in the back of the house, and thinks she can escape out the front of the house. Mitchell goes back into the house to search for Asher and his mom. Hearing Mitchell's footsteps, Marilyn hides in the front closet.

The few neighbors left on the block are frightened by the gunshots, so they call the police. Det. Monaco hears of the call, and instinct tells him the Mitchell-Mason Gang is after Asher and Marilyn. Det. Monaco gathers some officers, and they head to the scene of the gunshots.

Mason sends the two goons around to the back of the garage. When they get to the back of the garage, Asher shoots them both. With the last two goons down Mitchell and Mason are the only two still standing.

Mason standing in front of the garage rapidly shot up the roof of the garage. Asher climbs down the back of the garage and runs down the alley. Mason chases him. Asher, small and agile, quickly disappears. Mason walks down the alley searching neighboring properties with no luck.

Mason decides to go back to the house. Before Mason makes it up the walk way, the police are surrounding him. Mason in a panic aims his gun at the police car. Mason empties his gun into the car. The police strategically exit their vehicles and take cover behind the ajar doors of their vehicles. With no hesitation, they eliminate Mason.

Now, Mitchell is the last man standing. Mason couldn't find Asher because he quietly ran back into the house to protect his mother. Asher knows Mitchell is the only one left. Asher hears the police call for emergency medical services as he quietly made his way back into the house.

Mitchell finds Marilyn hiding in the closet. Mitchell pulls her out the closet by her hair. Marilyn is terrified, but more concerned about her son.

Mitchell asks, "Where is the boy?"

Marilyn answers, "You don't have to do this, my son doesn't talk. He can't tell anything. He doesn't talk."

Mitchell asks, "What does that mean, he doesn't talk?"

Marilyn says, "He has autism. He has never spoken a word. He won't tell if he saw something because he doesn't talk."

Mitchell says, "Call him so I can see for myself."

Marilyn says, "Asher, baby! Come to Momma! Asher! Sweetie! It's okay, Honey, come here!"

Mitchell notices the police cars outside, so he shields himself with Marilyn. Mitchell pulls Marilyn's hair tighter and harder. Marilyn screams in pain. The police storm through the front door. Mitchell pulling Marilyn's hair with one hand and holding a gun to her head with the other hand cowards behind Marilyn and taunts the police.

Asher slowly creeps up behind Mitchell. Mitchell tells the police either put the guns down or he is going to shoot Marilyn. Mitchell says, "It doesn't matter how it goes down to him. One more dead body is nothing to me, so fellas what's it going to be, huh Mr. Officer?" Every officer is stunned by Asher's bravery.

Just as he finished the sentence, Asher shoots him in the back of the head. Mitchell falls to the ground and that is the finale of the Mitchell-Mason Gang.

Marilyn rushes over to Asher and hugs him. Asher says to his mother, "Mommy, you're safe now."

Marilyn says, "Asher! (Shocked that he spoke.) Baby! You talked to me." Marilyn, in tears, adds, "I love you so much!"

Asher says, "I love you so much!"

Det. Monaco is overwhelmed by a child killing the most notorious gangster in the city in the last five decades. He take the guns from Asher; he says, "Please come with me," he escorts Asher and Marilyn to the first responders. He says to Marilyn, "They are only going to check your vitals, check for any bumps, bruises; if all is well, you two can go home."

The first responders check Marilyn and Asher. They both are cleared to go home. Det. Monaco says, "I have to keep the guns Asher used for evidence." Marilyn says, "Whatever you need. I'm so happy we are safe, and we can go home."

Marilyn puts her son in the Impala with Brent's gun still hidden under the passenger seat. Marilyn calls Brent when she gets home to tell him how Asher bravely defended her. Brent is so relieved that his family is safe and at home. He praises Asher for protecting Marilyn. Brent makes it home in the morning. He hugs his family. He tells his son, "Thank you, Son, I am so proud of you. You are so brave and so strong. You saved my wife, and I can't thank you enough!"

Soon, Emily and Kaden's family return home, but when they come home life is a little different. Asher carries a conversation like a typical seven-year-old boy. The three families have a big bar-b-que to celebrate Asher's milestone and their safety.

The End

Mrs. Campbell says, "We would like to thank each one of you for your great work and participation today. We hope day four, Bridge Day, was insightful and helpful for each one of you. We'll see you next Saturday."

Everyone claps as they ended the meeting. After everyone leaves, Mrs. Campbell and Mrs. Miller talk about the success of Bridge Day as they clean and prepare for Service Day.

Mrs. Miller says, "I don't think we had a Bridge Day with that many tears."

Mrs. Campbell says, "Our boys and mothers were wonderful today. I was so impressed by how serious the boys took it. I heard some powerful testimony."

Mrs. Miller says, "Did you see Jace?"

Mrs. Campbell says, "I saw Jace; I'm so proud of him!"

Mrs. Miller says, "This group will make for a great Service Day."

Mrs. Campbell says, "This is one of my most favorite groups ever."

Mrs. Miller says, "Mine, too! This is why we do it!"

Fifth Saturday: Day of Service

When the participants begin to arrive, Mrs. Miller leads the mothers to the atrium. Mrs. Campbell leads the boys to their usual room. Mrs. Miller and Mrs. Campbell explain the importance of service and volunteering to the participants.

Mrs. Miller explains to the mothers the benefits of their sons serving and volunteering in the community. Mrs. Miller says, "Doing something to help someone else is the best way to forget your problems and feel better about yourself.

"Additionally, the boys will also gain essential social and communication skills as they interact with ours on these occasions. Volunteering and community service look great on college applications. Most importantly, it helps young men develop a sense of responsibility to themselves, their families, and the community."

Mrs. Campbell explains to the boys that today's session is all about service. Tucker asks, "Like you want fries with that?" The other boys laugh.

Mrs. Campbell says, "No, that's customer service. I'm talking about service as in serving our Lord. Service is about doing something positive for someone and not asking for or expecting anything in return. Volunteering, donating, and caring for others are examples of service. We are going to examine the benefits we can reap from serving the ones we love and the community."

Mrs. Campbell asks the boys if they could think of needs people have in their families or neighborhoods. The boys list: money, food, homes, safety, medicine, protection, education, love, and happiness. Mrs. Campbell asks, "What are some ways people help meet those needs?"

They answer: people donate food and money; people carry old people groceries from the store.

Mrs. Campbell asks, "Is it fair to say we all need help sometimes?"

They agree that people all need help sometimes. Mrs. Campbell asks, "Does it feel good when we are in need and can't help ourselves?" The boys all say no. Mrs. Campbell asks, "How does it feel when you help other people?"

Jace says, "You feel like a hero."

Mrs. Campbell smiles. She says, "A hero, and who wouldn't want to be a hero."

Mrs. Campbell adds, "I want you to think about all the people you know. Think about some of the things that bother them, things they need, things that they want, and things they should stop. Then, I want you to think about solutions. Think of ways you can help."

Mrs. Campbell gives the boys a moment to think. Mrs. Campbell says, "Imagine what life would be like for them if someone came into their offering help and expecting nothing in return. Imagine how their lives will improve and how much happier they will be. It's important that each one of you learn how necessary it is for each of you to be giving, kind, and thoughtful.

"Yes, the person you help will benefit, but you will also benefit. You benefit socially, spiritually, and mentally. You'll feel better about yourself, your social and interpersonal skills will improve, and when you do for others expecting nothing in return you will bring goodness to yourself.

"Think about one day loving a wife and kids, caring for your aging loved ones, being active in the church, and being active in the community. All of that is service, and all of those will help you grow as a person, as a man."

Eli asks, "So, you're saying the best way to help myself is to help someone else?"

Mrs. Campbell says, "That's exactly what I am saying."

Mrs. Campbell says, "Before we move out of the circle, I want each of us to think about the people in our lives. Think about their hurts, fears, and needs. Pick one person and think of a way you can help that person that won't cost money."

She gives everyone a sheet of paper; she says, "It doesn't have to happen now, but write down one small thing you can do to help that person and keep it until you can do it. When it's done, I want you to bury the paper and never think or speak of it again."

Jace asks, "Do you think this will really help us?"

Mrs. Campbell says, "I do!"

Jace says, "Then, we will do it."

Mrs. Campbell says, "It doesn't have to be a big thing. It doesn't have to take a lot of time. The smallest, most simple thing you can do for someone could have the biggest impact on their life."

Caleb says, "When Niko beat up that bully for his friend was that service?"

Mrs. Campbell says, "He had good intentions, but service shouldn't result in violence. No one should get hit or hurt when you serve the community or your family. Just to clarify, when you perform your act of service, please, do not hurt anyone or plan any violence. Your act of service should be kind and caring. Is that clear, everyone?"

The boys say yes.

Mrs. Campbell says, "Boys, promise no violence or trouble!" The boys promise.

Niko asks, "If we can't do the one thing we know how to do, what can we do? We don't have money or a car. We can't help people."

Mrs. Campbell says, "Niko, you can think of non-violent ways to help someone. You are a very intelligent, caring young man. I have faith in you."

Mega says, "This is going to be hard."

Mrs. Campbell says, "Mega, service is something you do all the time without thinking about it. Being nice to someone or being considerate of someone is not hard. Mega, we're human and it's part of the human experience."

Tucker asks, "I don't think I've ever done anything nice for someone."

Mrs. Campbell says, "It's time to change that. Being generous and kind to others can be as simple as praying for someone or sharing your snack with someone who is hungry."

Levi asks, "So, praying for someone counts as service?"

Mrs. Campbell says, "Yes, Levi, prayers can be service. Sometimes, praying for someone is all you can do."

Lucas says, "Let me guess, Mrs. Campbell, you have a story for us."

Mrs. Campbell says, "Exactly, Lucas!"

A Brother's Hero

On a bright sunny, scorching hot summer Saturday in Detroit, Robby (age nine) and Timmy (age eleven) play with their friends at Maheras Memorial Playground.

Robby suddenly begins to feel sick. He sits under a big tree facing the Detroit River to get some shade thinking he was overheating.

Timmy comes over and asks if Robby wants to play tag. Robby says, "I am too hot. I'm going to sit here for a minute to cool off." Timmy runs over to his dad's cooler that his mom insisted they take and grabs a water for Robby. Timmy takes the water to Robby. Robby says thank you and begins to drink the water.

Timmy runs off to play tag with his friends for a while. He soon notices Robby looks tired and sweating profusely. Timmy grabs his dad's cooler and runs over to Robby and says, "Robby, I think we should go home."

Robby gets up looking like he has the flu. Timmy wraps Robby's arm around his neck, so Timmy can help support Robby as they walk home. It's a hot day, but Timmy knows Robby shouldn't be this hot. To Timmy, Robby feels like he just stepped out of a fire.

Robby makes it to the end of the first block and he says, "I can't walk any further." Robby's head falls back, and his body goes limp. Timmy lays him on the ground and runs to the nearest house.

He knocks on the door, screaming, "Help! Help! My brother needs help!"

An elderly lady comes to the door; she asks, "What's wrong young man?"

Timmy answers, "My little brother fainted please call 9-1-1 and my mother." The lady grabs her phone in a panic and calls 9-1-1. Other neighbors hearing the screams come running to help.

"Oh God, help us! It's a little boy," says one neighbor. Another neighbor gives Timmy her cell phone to call his mother. Vivian is at home doing her typical Saturday routine. Saturday is her one day of the week to enjoy her home. Her husband works the day shift at the plant on Saturdays to earn extra money. Vivian stays busy working as a social worker at the guidance center Monday to Friday 8am until 5pm.

Vivian answers the unknown call suspiciously. When she hears her son's panicked voice, her heart stops for a second. Timmy sounding scared and sad tells his mother Robby fainted a block away from the park. Vivian grabs her purse, runs to her car and pulls off.

Within minutes Timmy's mother, Vivian Culver, and an ambulance arrive. Vivian is a nervous wreck. She rushes over as the first responders attend to Robby. Timmy hurries to embrace Vivian as she looks at her son on the ground. Timmy and Vivian are distraught. Timmy says, "Momma, I tried to get him home, but he passed out. They don't know what's wrong with him, but he has a fever. I could feel it."

Vivian responds to Timmy, "Son, you did all you could do. You did a good thing for your brother. God will take care of the rest," tears roll down her face holding one son and watching the other as he is rolled into an ambulance.

The emergency worker turns to Vivian, "Mrs. Culver, you can ride with us or follow us to the hospital."

Vivian gathers herself, she says, "I'll follow you."

Vivian and Timmy run to her car. As Vivian drives, Timmy uses her cell phone to text and call his dad, but his dad inadvertently locked his phone in his car. When they arrive at the emergency room reception area, the reception nurse tells Vivian, "Have a seat, and when Robby is put into a room she will be called to the back."

Vivian and Timmy wait for an hour before they hear anything. The nurse leads them to a room housing an unconscious and unwell Robby.

161

When Franklin goes on break, he reaches in his back pocket for his phone. He panics when he realizes he doesn't have his phone. Franklin rushes to his car to find his phone. He sees the message from Timmy and rushes to the hospital.

Robby is connected to fluids intravenously, a heart monitor, and a urinary catheter. Robby heart beats normally. He looks as if he was in a peaceful sleep. The chill of the hospital and the hydration from the IV help improve his appearance.

Vivian touches her son and prays over him just as her husband walks in the room. He walks up behind Vivian to look closely at his unconscious son; he asks, "Vivian, what did they say?" Vivian answers bursting in tears, "No one has said anything."

Timmy is sad for his parents. He has never seen either of them cry. As his heart breaks for his parents and his brother, a doctor finally walks in, but he has no answers. He tells the family we are running tests, but have yet find a definite cause.

The Culver family sits by Robby's bedside waiting on someone to ensure them that their life together will go on as normal. They desperately want someone to tell them that Robby will wake up soon and they can take him home. Eventually, a word comes, but it's not the message they want to hear.

A doctor comes into the room at midnight to tell the Culver family that Robby's kidneys are struggling to properly function, and they are running test to find out why. He also says Robby would benefit from a dialysis treatment while we await test results. He also informs them that Robby will be hospitalized for a while.

Mr. Culver says, "Whatever my son needs. We have good insurance, so it should cover whatever you need to do." The doctor has Mr. Culver sign a consent form. Mrs. Culver stands over her son to pray for a miracle. She prays for a complete healing and restoration of her son's health. She prays her son will live a long life full of prosperity.

Mr. Culver tells his wife to take their son home and get some rest, but they refuse to leave. The nurse assigned to Robby brings the family pillows and blankets. Vivian and Timmy get comfortable in the empty bed next to

Robby. Franklin sits in the leather-cushioned window sill watching a machine pump, beep, and chart his son's lifeline.

In the morning, Mr. and Mrs. Culver along with Timmy watch the medical team wheel Robby out for a dialysis treatment. Timmy is sad that his little brother is so sick. Robby is the good son; he never causes his parents pain or problems. Timmy is the one always in trouble. Timmy is the one his parents are always stressing about. Timmy wants so badly to fix this for his family's sake. His parents have suffered enough from his behavior; they do not deserve this.

Mr. Culver goes to grab the family something to eat while they wait on Robby to return from the dialysis treatment. When he returns with the food, the top nephrologist of the hospital, Dr. Kenny comes into the room to tell the family what the medical team has discovered thus far.

Dr. Kenny explains Robby's kidneys have stop functioning, which is causing his whole body to shut down. He further explains Robby will be connected to a dialysis machine, transported to Children's Hospital and his name will be added to the donor's list.

Vivian breaks into an overflow of tears. Mr. Culver and Timmy held in their pain to comfort Vivian. The doctor goes on to urge the family members to all get screened to see if anyone is a match. Dr. Kenny says, "If a family member is a match, the process can be much quicker.

Mr. and Mrs. Culver agree to the test. Timmy says, "I'll get tested too! I want to help."

Franklin tells his son, "You're just a boy, my boy and I couldn't handle both of my boys…"

His wife cuts him off because Franklin who had been so strong begins to break. Vivian says, "Mom and Dad will go first. If we aren't a match, you can take the test." Timmy puts his head down and reluctantly agrees.

The nurse comes in the room to get Vivian and Franklin. Before they leave the room, Vivian tells Timmy to keep an eye on his brother. Timmy closer to talk to his brother. He says, "Little Brother, I hope you wake up soon. It's so scary to see you like this. I know you are going to be okay because I'm going to give you one of my kidneys. Mom and Dad are scared about it, but I know it will be okay."

Timmy talks to Robby until his parents come back. Timmy asks his parents what happened. Vivian says, "We both took two blood tests."

Timmy asks, "Are you a match? Is it my turn?"

Vivian says, "We have to wait for the results."

Timmy says, "We can't keep waiting Robby is sick and he needs help now."

Vivian hugs Timmy. She says, "I know, Son. I know."

Just then they hear a little voice saying, "Mom! Dad!" They all rush over to Robby. They are so happy he is awake. Vivian squeezes his hand and tells Robby they all are so happy he woke up.

Franklin asks, "How do you feel, Son?"

Robby asks, "What is wrong with me?"

Vivian tells Robby he needs an operation because his kidneys aren't working as they should. Robby asks, "Why aren't they working?"

Franklin says, "They don't know. The doctor want to give you a new one."

Robby asks, "Where is the kidney coming from? Will the doctor make it?"

Timmy says, "I'm going to give you one of mine."

Vivian says, "Your dad and I took some tests to see if one of us can give you one."

Robby looks at his dad; he asks, "Am I going to be okay?"

Franklin answers, "Son, you're going to be fine. You have the best doctors and nurses working for you."

Vivian adds, "And, God is on your side. He is working through the doctors and nurses to heal you."

Robby asks, "Momma, we just have to pray?"

Vivian answers, "Yes, Son, we all have to pray!"

That night, as Franklin prepares to go spend the night at the hospital, Franklin and Vivian talk about the possibility of Timmy being a donor. Franklin is against

it; he says, "We could possibly lose both sons."

Vivian says, "It's a pretty safe surgery, and both boys can live a long healthy life with one kidney."

Franklin says, "I will give my son what he needs."

Vivian says, "I just think we should be open and explore all possibilities."

Franklin says, "We will cross that bridge if we get there. You and Timmy have a good night sleep, and I'll see you in the morning."

Vivian responds, "Okay, Franklin! Call me if you hear anything."

Franklin says, "I will!" Franklin leaves the house. Vivian tucks Timmy in and she lays down, but she doesn't sleep much.

The next morning, Vivian and Timmy arrive at the hospital to find out that Vivian nor Franklin are a perfect match. The doctor explains to Vivian and Franklin that siblings have a higher chance of being a match than a parent. The doctor says it will be worth it to see if Timothy is a match.

Franklin asks, "What's the long-term risks for Timothy if he does this?"

The doctor explains, "Timothy will need healthy eating patterns and habits because African Americans are at higher risk of developing diabetes and high blood pressure. Non-contact sports, so no football. Basketball, golf, track and baseball are all fine." The doctor looks at Timmy and asks, "Are those sacrifices worth saving your brother's life, Timothy?"

Timmy says, "I want to save my brother. Whatever I need to do, I will do."

The doctor turns to Vivian and Franklin; he says, "Mom and Dad, I think he has made up his mind."

Vivian asks Timmy, "Are you sure, Son?"

Timmy says, "I was born to do this. I can do this!" Timmy turns to his brother and says, "Don't worry, Little Brother. I know I am a match. You are going to be fine."

The doctor tells Mr. and Mrs. Culver, "If Timothy is a match, both boys will be sent to Children's Hospital. Don't worry Children's has the facilities and staff to support both boys." He assures them that Timothy will be fine, and that the surgery is safe.

The doctor leads Timmy to the nurse who takes him for the tissue typing and crossmatching tests. Vivian and Franklin pray with Robby. Robby tells his parents he's scared, but they try to comfort his fears. They explain he or Timmy would feel pain during the surgery. They may be sore afterwards for a while, but once the pain goes away life will be normal for both of you.

Robby says, "I hope Tim is a match, so he can save me."

Vivian says, "I hope so too, Son! I hope so too!"

That night, Vivian stays with Robby and Franklin goes home with Timmy. Everyone prays silently all night that Timothy would be a match for Robby. It's a night that seems like it will never end.

The sunrise is a symbol of relief; the results of the test will be available soon. Timmy is convinced he will be a match. Mr. and Mrs. Culver know if Timmy isn't a match, things can be complicated for Robby and the wait to find a match will be long and gruesome. Timmy and Franklin get up and get dressed to go back to the hospital.

Franklin and Timmy stop to get breakfast. When they get to the hospital, Vivian is in the bed with Robby laughing at cartoons. Vivian, Timmy, and Franklin sit and eat laughing at the cartoons trying to pretend like life is normal. Their nerves fill the room as they await the results of Timmy's tests. Everyone is nervous except Timmy. Timmy is a rock; his faith has already told him he is a match. The smell of the food makes Robby want to eat, but Robby can't have solid food.

Soon the doctor walks in with the results. Dr. Kenny says, Mr. and Mrs. Culver, Timothy is a perfect match. We must run some more test to make sure

Timothy is healthy enough to withstand the surgery, but I think he will be cleared. Once Timothy is cleared, the boys will be transferred to Children's Hospital where the surgery will happen.

"Dr. Monroe, the head of the nephrology department at Children's, along with his team will perform the procedure. They are the best team in the Midwest, your boys will be in good hands."

Vivian says, "I hope they are blessed hands." Franklin agrees as he and Vivian sign the consent form for Timmy to have more test to confirm he is healthy.

By Wednesday, both Culver boys are at Children's Hospital and are ready for surgery. Timmy tells his father, "For all the silly things I've done and all the stress I've caused you and Mom, this is the least that I can do to repent for my childish behavior. Almost losing your little brother makes you grow up fast."

Franklin says, "Son, I greatly appreciate your sacrifice, but I don't want you to do this because you think you owe us."

Timmy responds, "I am doing this because it is the right thing to do, and Robby deserves to live."

Robby and Timmy both have successful surgeries. They both go on to live long, healthy lives thanks to Timmy sacrifice.

The End

Mrs. Campbell says, "I'm not saying you need to give a body part away to be of service; all that is required is that you think of someone other than yourself. Give a little of your time and attention to someone else, be kind even if they are undeserving of your kindness, and don't expect anything in return.

"I know you all think you are super tough and pretend you don't care about things, but I know neither are true. I know there has been times in each of your lives when you looked out for someone without using violence. Does anyone want to share?"

The boys are quiet for a while. They look around the circle waiting for someone to speak. Mrs. Campbell says, "Well, what about being helped. Can anyone think of a time someone helped you? Especially think of a time someone was there for you and you didn't deserve it."

Xander breaks the silence; he says, "Mrs. Campbell, I know that my behavior has ruined my family. My family is always unhappy and stressed out because of my behavior. I know I need to change, and I can't explain why I haven't. Despite all that I do at home and at school, my parents continue to love me, and I know I don't deserve it. They encourage me to behave. As much as I want to give them what they want, I manage to fail."

Mrs. Campbell says, "Maybe your service is to ask for help; go find out what's going on in there (She points to his head.). It could be more complicated than you think, or it could be a simple easy fix. Either way, it's worth your life and your future to put in the work, now. Waiting until you get older, will only make it more difficult."

While the boys discuss the benefits of therapy and counseling, Mrs. Miller and the mothers discuss supporting their young sons as future fathers, husbands, and productive and contributing members of society who are career-oriented people.

Mrs. Miller says, "We look at our young sons and we see our babies. It's hard to imagine them as men, fathers, and husbands. Being a man isn't something that just happens on your eighteenth birthday. Every day of your son's young life is practice for his manhood. As mothers, we must purposely cultivate conditions that grow our sons from boys to men.

"When you think about the behavioral and mental expectations we have for men, you realize how much stamina, motivation, self-control, resilience, and strength that is required to be a man. Those are characteristics that take a lifetime to cultivate.

"We can't just expect our son to wake up on his eighteenth birthday with the resiliency of a man. We need to start during his childhood exposing him to experiences that will develop resiliency, a sense of responsibility, and a commitment to the people, places, and things he loves.

"Since the boys in the program are exhibiting behaviors that are counter-productive to our goal and they are making defiant choices, we must be even more diligent. We should purposely give them responsibility and hold them accountable. They need to understand that there are lasting consequences to their behavior. As good as they are in causing havoc and flourishing in chaos, they need to be just as thorough and committed to service, family, community, and profession."

Mrs. Miller and Mrs. Campbell bring the mothers and sons together in pairs. They spread the groups all over the building to give them as much privacy as possible. Mrs. Miller instructs each mother to wash her son's face and brush his hair while she tells him about the best memory she has of him. Mrs. Miller hands each mother a brush, comb, a white towel, and a white bowl of warm water.

Mega sits while Megan brushes his hair and tells him about the day, he first said Mama to her. Megan looks so happy as she tells the story. Megan says, "We were so happy back then. You were so cute. When I would come home from work you would run up to me saying, 'Mama, Mama!'"

Megan washes his face as she talks about the bond she thought they were going to have; she says, "When I picked you up and held you in my arms, I never thought we would end up here. Mega, how did we end up here, barely talking? I thought I was holding my lifelong best friend; a person who was going to love me more than anyone else for the rest of my life." Mega looks disappointed in himself; he has no response.

Abigail washes Eli's face as she tells him about the day he was born; she says, "Having you hurt like you couldn't imagine, but when the nurse laid you in my arms, I was the happiest woman in the world. You were so cute. You wrapped your little hand around my finger, and you opened your eyes. When I looked into your eyes, I knew I was going to love you forever."

Abigail brushes Eli's hair. She says, "Then you needed me for everything, and it made me feel like a mother. You cried and I fed you for the first time. In that moment, I thought we were creating a mother-son bond to never be broken, and somehow here we are broken. It's not too late to get that back, Eli, if you want it."

Rita stands behind Niko's chair brushing his hair. Rita says, "Remember those days when we did this all the time. You were such a fussy baby, but I loved you so much. There was this one day that I will always remember. Granddad brought you a football, and we were playing with it in the backyard.

"Granddad had you running around with that football in your arms like a running back. It was adorable. We laughed and laughed. We took pictures and videos. We had a really good time. Even you were smiling and laughing."

Rita gently washes Niko's face. "After Granddad died, you just didn't smile anymore. Niko, we all would love to see you happy again," she says.

Kelly sits face to face with Caleb as she tells him about his first night at home. Kelly says, "The house was quiet. I rocked you in the rocking chair. Your eyes were wide open. You were so alert to only be a few days old. You were looking at me. You moved your hands around until you touched my face. When I was talking to you, it was like you were listening to every word I said, and out of nowhere you smiled at me. I knew in that moment we would love each other forever."

Kelly starts to brush Caleb's hair, and continues her story. "I had just given you a bath, so you smelled so good like baby wash and baby oil. I held you against my chest until you fell asleep. You only slept for a few hours before you wanted a bottle, but I didn't mind because I had a precious, beautiful son. I was happy to feed you."

Xander sits in the chair while Nia stands behind him brushing his hair. Nia says, "Xander, when you were a baby, you were so cute. One day, you reached for me and said, 'Mama! Mama! Mama!' I couldn't believe I was really a mother and you loved me. You have no idea how it feels to be a mother with a son that loves you. "When I picked you up, you just kept saying, 'Mama, Mama Mama!' You hugged me so tightly. My heart melted."

Nia comes around to the front of the chair to wash Xander's face; she continues her story, "That day, I thought you loved me so much," Tears poured from Nia's eyes. "I love you so much, Xander."

Lucas sits quietly as Melinda washes his face and tells him her favorite memory. Melinda says, "My very favorite memory is of our very first Christmas together. You were six months old.

(Melinda starts to brush his hair.) You had these fat cheeks and this curly hair. You were the cutest baby I had ever seen.

"One of your gifts was a t-shirt that said my first Christmas. I let you taste a candy cane. At first, you made this face like you didn't like it, but you reached for another taste. We went to Great-Granny's house and the family just loved on you the whole day. You were so sweet the whole day. I knew that day I had someone to love forever."

Mecia says to Jace, "I know stuff like this isn't easy for you, so I want you to know I appreciate you for trying."

Jace says, "Thank you!"

As she brushes Jace's hair, Mecia says, "After you and the boys came to stay with us, you were distant and quiet for a long time. I remember the first time you smiled. It was a Friday night. We were eating pizza and watching movies. You and the boys were playing on the floor. We were laughing like a happy family.

"For that one moment, I thought we had a break through. I thought this was it. This is the moment that I will have three sons. Finally, Jace is coming around, I thought. And even though, it only lasted one night, I so appreciated that moment."

Mecia gently wipes Jace's face. She says, "Jace, I'm not sure how you feel about me, but I love you and I am happy you and your brothers are my sons."

Lea brushes Levi's hair as she tells him her favorite memory. She says, "Remember, we went to the carnival when you were little. You rode every ride. You ate some of everything. I remember how your face lit up when you saw the horses. That's when you fell in love with horses. I don't know why, but I love that day. Both my boys were whole and happy." She wipes his face with the cloth, and says, "I will never forget that day."

Tucker sits as Inga washes his face. She walks behind the chair to brush his hair. Inga says, "I miss you needing me like this. You are all grown up and independent now, which is a good thing. I'm glad you can take care of yourself. I just miss how close we used to be. Do you ever miss that, Tucker?"

171

Tucker says, "I do!"

Inga says, "Remember when we all would snuggle on the floor and watch movies. Every Saturday night, we would have junk food and watch movies for hours until you decided hanging with your friends was more important. I loved those nights. I missed those nights, but I have accepted my little man is growing up. I'm giving you space to do that, but that doesn't mean cut me out. I'm here for you, Tucker."

Brad sits as Stephanie brushes his hair, she says, "I can remember your first haircut. You were going to start kindergarten the next day. Those were good times.

I was so nervous. I was sure you were going to cut up, but I remembered something that made me feel better.

"After your father died, I was holding you in my arms one night. You were cooing and making noises. I started crying. You put your hands on my face wiping my tears as if you were saying it's going to be alright, Momma.

"In my deepest sadness, you had a way of keeping me sane. It's like you knew something was wrong and you were there for me when I needed someone and something. I'll always be grateful to you for that," she says as she wipes his face.

Mrs. Miller and Mrs. Campbell remove the old bowls and towels and replace them with new bowls with fresh warm water and clean white towels. Mrs. Campbell instructs each boy to wash his mother's feet as he tells his mother about a moment or a time, he greatly appreciated her presence or her service.

Mrs. Campbell tells the boys that if they are fortunate enough to care for their mothers they will be blessed for their service. Look at this exercise as a glimpse into what it's like to be of service to your mother when she needs you.

Rita sits in the chair as Niko removes her shoes to rinse and wipe her feet. Niko says, "Ma, my eighth birthday you made sure I got everything I wanted. You worked so hard to get all the stuff, to decorate, and to make sure everyone had a good time.

Every birthday, holiday, and family day you go out of your way. I appreciate all you do even though I don't deserve it. You are a good mother, and one day I will pay you back." Niko dries his mother's feet and slips back on her shoes.

Xander helps Nia sit in the chair. He takes off her shoes and socks; he says, "You deserve to be cared for because you do so much for us. I appreciate how you are always there for us. (Xander takes one of the towels and dips it in the bowl of water. He wipes her feet with the towel as he talks.) I especially appreciate how you provide for us every Christmas.

"You go all out every Christmas from the food to the decorations to the gifts under the tree. I can remember the year you gave me my PlayStation and X-Box. I begged for those gaming systems all year. When I woke up and saw them under the tree, I flipped out. I was so happy. Even when I act up, you still look out for me."

Xander takes the other towel to dry her feet. He slips her socks and shoes back on her feet. He says, "Mom, if the time comes, I can take care of you."

Mega sits on the floor before Megan. Mega says, "Mom, I never say thank you to you. I just expect you to do everything and give me anything I want. You never ask much of me but to behave in school, and I don't even do that right.

"I am thankful for all that you do, but I especially appreciate the day you saved our dog, Scuba. I thought Scuba was going to die, but you came and rushed him to the vet. You found the money to pay the bill. I was so happy when the vet said we could take Scuba home. If you wouldn't have got him to the vet, he would have died. But that's you, Mom, you always save the day without anyone saying thank you or help."

Jace sits at Mecia's feet. He takes off her shoes; he says, "I know I am not easy to take, but I do appreciate you. After my parents died, we barely had food and clothes. My little brothers didn't get love or hugs. When we came to stay with you, you hugged my little brothers with so much love that I got peace. I knew with you my brothers would be good. I knew from the moment we met that you would be good to them.

173

"Our first Christmas with you, you got everything on my brothers' lists no matter how big or how small. After all we had been through, we needed that day. We needed to know someone still loved us. I'm so grateful to you for showing us that. The last thing I want to do is to cause my brothers to lose another mother, I'm going to get myself together."

Mecia says, "I believe in you, Son!"

Kelly sits in the chair watching Caleb take her shoes off. She says, "Son, this is really sweet of you."

Caleb says, "Mom, I can take care of you. Remember, I made you soup when you had the flu."

Kelly smiles and says, "Yes, Caleb! I remember."

Caleb says, "I washed your car before, too!"

Kelly says, "Yes, you did, Son!"

As Caleb takes a towel to dip it in the water, he says, "See, I can take care of you."

Caleb wipes Kelly's feet with the towel; he says, "Mom, I remember the time we went to the water park when I was little. I had so much fun. Did you have fun?"

Kelly answers, "Yes, I did!"

Caleb asks, "Remember, the first pair of Jordan's you brought me. I still have them even though I can't fit them. Remember when I fell and needed stitches. After we left the hospital you took me to get pizza. There are so many great memories that I can't choose just one. You're a great mother and you do so much. I may not say it, but I really do appreciate you." Caleb dries Kelly's feet.

Lucas sits at Melinda's feet. He says, "You're usually the one that cares for everyone." Lucas takes off her shoes; he says, "Someone needs to take better care of you."

Melinda asks, "Is that your way of saying you will help more around the house?"

174

Lucas says, "You don't think I will do it. Do you?"

Melinda says, "Son, that's not true. You know you have a hard time finishing tasks. You start out perfectly and about five minutes in you give up."

Lucas washes his mother's feet as he says, "You think I'm lazy."

Melinda holding in her laugh, says, "Not lazy, Son, just energy conservative, you know like the washer and dryer. You do any and every thing you can to do the least amount of work as possible."

Lucas dries his mother's feet; he laughs and says, "This is the moment I'll remember because this is the moment I'm going to change. I'm going to do my part." Lucas put back on her shoes.

Lea says, "This is weird, huh, Son?" as Levi takes off her shoes.

Levi says, "It is weird."

Lea says, "So, Son, I can count on you if I ever need you?"

Levi says, "Of course," as he washes his mother's feet.

Lea asks, "Levi, have you thought of a memory, something that made you happy?"

Levi says, "I have a bunch of good memories, but the go-kart you got me was the best memory. We had so much fun riding it at the park. Remember the time we all went to the park. We took turns riding it. We had so much fun. It was so funny when Dad crashed into that tree. We laughed for days after that." Levi dried his mother's feet; he says, "I will always remember that day."

Lea says, "Son, I'm so happy that you really enjoyed it."

Tucker washes Inga's feet as he says, "I have a lot of good memories. You and dad have given us a good life. I loved when we lived at our old house, and we would have bonfires in the backyard. Our whole family came over. We still had Cousin back then. Life was good back then. You would cook gumbo.

"You never make gumbo anymore. Remember the cookout when all the kids got water guns. We had that big water fight that day. That night, we sat by the fire and made s'mores. Since Cousin died, we don't have fun like that anymore."

Tucker dries Inga's feet as she says, "Son, I'm so sorry. I hadn't even realized you missed that. Tell you what, I will get your father to build a firepit in our new backyard when summer gets here, and I will make gumbo this weekend. You can eat as much as you want." Tucker puts Inga's shoes on her feet.

Brad washes Stephanie's feet as he tells her his favorite memory. Brad says, "Six summers ago, we went on vacation with Auntie and Grandmother. We drove through Ohio, West Virginia, the Carolinas to get to Georgia than Florida and Texas than all the way back home. I had the time of my life.

"We had a good time. We saw a bunch of places. We were a big happy family without worries or cares. Everything was all good until I went back to school. I wish things would have stayed that way, but I just couldn't keep it together. I let us down. I let you down."

Stephanie says, "Bradley, it's never too late to make it up to me. We can always be that happy again. If you really want too, Son. It's all up to you."

Brad dries his mother's feet. Brad says, "I hear you, Ma."

Abigail sits looking at Eli taking off her shoes; she asks, "Son, are you okay with this?"

Eli says, "Momma, I'm good. I need to do something nice for you."

Abigail says, "I appreciate this. Not just this, but the fact that you are really participating in this program. I feel like you're finally getting it, and I see a change in you."

Eli says, "I think I feel changed," as he washes his mother feet.

Eli says, "Holidays, birthdays and summers are always great with you. You always try to make the best of them, but I love when we go fishing and have picnics at the park. It's always so quiet and peaceful at the park. One time, we were sitting on a blanket on the grass while dad was fishing.

He didn't catch anything that day, but sitting there with you, him and Ethan just made me feel good.

"The sun was shining on the river. It was hot, but the shade from the tree kept us cool. Most important thing that happens when we are at the park is you smile the whole time. You are so happy, and it makes me happy."

When the boys are done, Mrs. Campbell and Mrs. Miller gather everyone in the atrium. Seated in a circle, each boy sitting next to his mother with a renewed feeling of connectedness. Mrs. Miller and Mrs. Campbell take turns calling the boys up one by one to get their medal of service.

The medal of service is inscribed with the words Medal of Service at the top, around the edge are the words Servant Leader, and in the middle of the medal is the boy's name. Mrs. Campbell and Mrs. Miller presents each mother with a Certificate of Servitude for being an excellent mother and servant leader of her family.

At the conclusion of the service presentation, Mrs. Miller and Mrs. Campbell conclude the day. They congratulate and thank the participants for a great day of participation. When everyone leaves, Mrs. Miller and Mrs. Campbell clean up and set up for the Day of Planning and Preparation.

Sixth Saturday

When the participants begin to arrive, Mrs. Campbell directs the boys to their room, and Mrs. Miller directs the mothers to their room. When all the boys are sitting in the circle, Mrs. Campbell welcomes them to Day Six: Planning and Preparation Day. Today we will brainstorm ways to achieve our goals and the things we will need to do to be ready. To help you get ready, we are going to start our day with a story."

Mission: Impossible (Code: Black)

The Proposition

Special Agent Connor Black of the FBI wants a promotion to Special Agent in Charge, and it's no secret. His stellar work since joining the FBI has made him a star and darling of the agency.

Agent (Agt.) Black grew up studying martial arts and boxing; he trained his wife and his kids to defend themselves in hostile or violent situations. His physical capabilities and streets smarts are the keys to his success in the Bureau.

Connor started as an officer of the law in the DPD working his way up to S.W.A.T. Team Leader where he spent ten years before transitioning to the FBI stationed in San Diego, California where his wife was born.

Agt. Black promised to take his wife and children on a Caribbean vacation as soon as he finished the current case, so his family was looking forward to a conclusion of the bank robbery case he was working.

On the night he accomplishes that mission, he is approached by the Security Department Associate Manager (Sec. Dept. Assoc. M.) Kirk Meier and the Special Detective Unit Associated Manager (SDU Assoc. M.) Ronald Reynolds with a thick file folder.

Sec. Dept. Assoc. M. Meier congratulates him on the capture of every member of a bank robbing gang. Sec. Dept. Assoc. M. Meier also tells him his work was greatly appreciated.

SDU Assoc. M. Reynolds mentions that everyone is aware of his ambitions within the Bureau. SDU Assoc. M. Reynolds tells Agt.

Black that his help on a very important case could guarantee him the promotion he wants. Curious, Agt. Black asks about the case. In the back of his mind, he sees his wife will killing him if he cancels their family vacation.

SDU Assoc. M. Reynolds explains that the Bureau just secretly captured Braze "Dough Boy" Mercer, who is a major trafficker on the west coast. They pull out pictures of Braze Mercer. SDU Assoc. M. Reynolds says, "As we were talking to him, we realized the striking resemblance he has to you. No one knows we have him, and we want to keep it that way. That's where you come in, we can maintain our cover if you go undercover as Mercer and complete just one deal."

Agt. Black says, "I promised to take my family on vacation. My wife will kill me if I take on another case."

SDU Assoc. M. Reynolds says, "It'll take eight hours to complete this mission, and most of that is travel time."

Sec. Dept. Assoc. M. Meier says, "You wouldn't need to cancel your vacation just delay it or meet your family there. A small personal inconvenience could be a huge favor in the Bureau's eye with a great professional benefit."

SDU Assoc. M. Reynolds says, "All you have to do is deliver money to the distributor."

Sec. Dept. Assoc. M. Meier says, "You're in and out and back with your wife on the same day; she will never know."

SDU Assoc. M. Reynolds says, "Black, this mission is top secret, so no one, I mean no one can know what you are doing."

Sec. Dept. Assoc. M. Meier says, "Take the file; memorize it. You need to know everything about Mercer."

SDU Assoc. M. Reynolds says, "You need to look, smell, talk, think, move, walk like him by Wednesday."

Agt. Black says, "That's only two days."

SDU Assoc. M. Reynolds says, "You're smart! You will figure it out!"

Sec. Dept. Assoc. M. Meier says, "Your country, your fellow Americans are counting on you."

Agt. Black says, "I'll do it."

SDU Assoc. M. Reynolds says, "We are keeping Mercer off the books until we take down the bigger fish. We have him in a safe house. In the morning, we will pick you up and take you to meet him."

Agt. Black asks, "Where exactly is the drop and who is the plug targeted in the operation?"

SDU Assoc. M. Reynolds says, "LA!"

Sec. Dept. Assoc. M. Meier adds, "Juan Cruz, Jimmy Nunez, and Maddux Rushmore are the targets."

Agt. Black's bottom lip drops: he says, "Cruz, Nunez and Rushmore of the WC3 Connection? They are the most dangerous gang anywhere. Essentially, you are giving me three days to single-handedly take down the biggest, most dangerous drug crew on US soil, while keeping my family vacation plans on track.

That's impossible!"

SDU Assoc. M. Reynolds says, "That's why it's called Mission: Impossible!"

Sec. Dept. Assoc. M. Meier adds, "Code: Black!"

SDU Assoc. M. Reynolds asks, "So we will see you here, o six hundred hours?"

Sec. Dept. Assoc. M. Meier adds, "Don't forget this is a top-secret mission. You tell no one."

The Preparation

SDU Assoc. M. Reynolds and Sec. Dept. Assoc. M. Meier drive Agt. Black to the safe house to meet Mercer. Mercer and Black stare at each other in shock.

It's like they are identical twins that were separated at birth. Mercer and Black are rendered speechless by their physical resemblance.

Mercer says, "You stole my face!"

Agt. Black responds, "I'm two years older, so I'm the original." Mercer laughs. Agt. Black records how Mercer talks and laughs, so he can study him.

SDU Assoc. M. Reynolds and Sec. Dept. Assoc. M. Meier tell Mercer to explain the organization and how the deal will go. Mercer explains how he interacts with the Connection, "I'm sort of an extension cord. I purchase merchandise from the WC3 to resell for profit to various local dealers." Mercer explains the dos and don'ts of dealing with the WC3 Connection: always go alone, no cell phones, no guns, no sunglasses, dress nice, but don't look suspicious.

Mercer says, "Never flirt with or look at their women. Don't ask any questions. Don't rush! Make sure you have enough money; Nunez will check it to make sure. Don't make small talk. Speak when spoken to! Don't stare! Don't appear nervous. Don't appear to be watching anyone or anything. They don't like that. Get in and get out as fast as possible. I drop off the money, the product magically appears at my spot when the sun goes down. They have delivery guys, and only their guys touch their product. Make sure you drive my Impala. They won't let any car they don't recognize anywhere near their spot."

After meeting with Mercer, Connor went home to explain things to his wife, Kelsey. He tells Kelsey that he needs to take a flight the next day to do one thing for work and he would meet the family on the island. Kelsey is not happy; she says, "We're supposed to be together as a family. And, we all know you. One day will turn into two days, which will lead to you not coming at all."

Agt. Black says, "I'm not. (Kelsey gives him a look of disbelief.) No. (Kelsey lowers her head.) Don't look like that. I'm not going to miss this vacation."

Kelsey says, "You have broken more promises than I can count. You put your work first, and we never complain."

Agt. Black says, "I know, and I appreciate you all. I'm going to make it. I'm just taking a different flight."

Kelsey says, "Let's just put this conversation to the side."

Agt. Black says, "You're mad. Don't be mad."

Kelsey, sounding mad, says, "I'm not mad. I'm disappointed."

Agt. Black says, "That's even worse."

Agt. Black stays up all night studying and acting as Mercer. He needs to pull this off, so there's nothing to stop him from meeting his family. Agt. Black feels an immense amount of pressure to complete the mission and satisfy his family. Despite his nervousness, he knows he must remain cool. He goes over Mercer's files and listens to his recording of Mercer speaking. He imitates Mercer's voice.

The Meeting

Agt. Black drops his family off at the airport and he drives to Mercer's house. He dresses in Mercer's clothes. He goes in Mercer's garage intended to get Mercer's Impala. Agt. Black sees two identical Impalas one black and one navy, and he is confused. Mercer didn't mention having two Impalas, and he didn't mention color. Agt. Black goes on a hunch and drives Mercer's black Impala to LA with a black bag full of money in the passenger seat.

Agt. Black makes his way to a warehouse. Everything is just as Mercer described it. Agt. Black does everything Mercer told him to do. After dropping off the money, he drives to Mercer's business house to wait for the shipment to arrive. When dark covers the city, two guys pull up, unload the contents of their trunk into the house, and drive away. Agt. Black leaves to maintain his cover. He drives Mercer's car back to his house.

Two agents in plain clothes, go in Mercer's business house to confiscate the shipment. Agt. Black gets in his own car and drives to the office to debrief with SDU Assoc. M. Reynolds and Sec. Dept. Assoc. M. Meier.

Agt. Black tells them everything that happened. He wants to know the next move, but they told him to go vacation with his family and they would fill him in when he returns.

Agt. Black drives home. When he opens the door, he sees his family's luggage at the door. He calls for his wife with a confused voice. She walks in the living room from the kitchen. Agt. Black says, "What…"

Kelsey cuts him off; she says, "The airline offered a nice piece of change for anyone willing to change their flight until tomorrow. The kids and I took the offer because we want to fly out with you."

Agt. Black says, "Kelsey, I swear, I was keeping my word this time."

Kelsey says, "Don't be so self-righteous, Kalley and I wanted new designer handbags."

Agt. Black says, "A new purse makes everything better."

Kelsey says, "Only if a pair of shoes comes with it."

Agt. Black says, "So, you and Kalley used my card to buy a pair of shoes to match your new purses."

Kelsey says, "Expensive shoes!"

Agt. Black asks, "How expensive?"

Kelsey just makes a face; she says, "Dinner is in the kitchen. I'm going to bed." Agt. Black sits and eats. He is happy the day is over. He made it out completing the task, and now he can go on the vacation his family wanted.

The Chaos

Agt. Black and Kelsey are sleeping when their son, Colton, wearing his emergency headset, leans over and whispers to his father the secret code word the family chose to alert each other if danger is near: Code: Black. Agt. Black jumps.

Colton whispers, "There are men surrounding the house."

Agt. Black asks, "Where is your sister?"

Colton says, "I hid her. The cameras are on the targets."

Agt. Black says, "Good! You know what to do."

Colton turns to run out the room. Agt. Black says, "Colt, Son, I'm proud of you. Don't be scared. We will be alright."

Agt. Black whispers in Kelsey's ear, "Code: Black!" She opens her eyes to see him telling her to shh. He says, "Go to the panic room! The kids are already in there." Kelsey hops out of bed and quickly makes her way to the panic room with Kalley and Colton.

Agt. Black peeks out the rear windows of his bedroom to see cars full of men in the alley behind his house. He grabs his cell phone and the stash of weapons from the closet in his bedroom. He calls the agency for help as he runs to prepare for the upcoming fight.

Colton, Kalley, and Kelsey anxiously sit in the panic room watching the men on the video feed from the night-vision equipped hidden cameras Colton put around the exterior and interior of the house. Agt. Black builds a bunker in his front room. He pushes down shelves, flips over couches, and bunkers down under a window awaiting the men to get closer to the house. Agt. Black and Colton communicate through the emergency headsets.

Colton watches twelve masked men dressed in all black standing on the perimeter of the house outside the fence. The men survey the house to determine the best entry point. Kalley and Kelsey are frightened, but Colton's nerves are as solid as steel. Colton and his dad have booby trapped the backyard and practiced what to do if anyone ever broke into their house. Colton's dad taught him to manage his fear, so he can think clearly in high-pressured situations.

The men cut through the fence and cautiously approach the house. Colton counts the seconds between their steps. He needs one of them to step on the perfect spot between the bushes. When one of the men steps on the spot between the bushes, they inadvertently step on a string that releases two thick planks of wood with sharp nail sticking out of it.

The nails go into the stomachs and arms of four of the six men walking toward the rear of the house. The other two men in the rear of the house look shock as the four men are impaled by the sticks. The four men are stuck because the nails are too far into their bodies to be easily pulled out.

With no time to help their injured comrades, the two men proceed toward the house. Colton watches them hoping they walk under the big tree. The two men take cover under the big tree to conceal their presence just as Colton hoped they would.

Before the men could take one more step, a huge net falls over their heads and entangles with the net under their feet. The men tried to run, but the nets have them trapped. Either of them have a knife to cut the nets, so they are stuck hanging from the tree. Kalley and Kelsey hug Colton because he has the back of the house handled. Now, it is up to Agt. Black to handle the six men in the front.

Connor watches the men in the front of the house separate. They split into two groups of three and approach each side of the house. They quietly look for easy access to the house. One of the men discovers a small window is weak. He knocks the edges of the window out of the wall. He slides in head first, and hits his head on a brick knocking himself unconscious. His friends pull him out the window and lay him on the ground.

On the other side of the house, the men search for an entry point without success. Sounds of sirens and fast cars approaching scare the remaining five men away. They quickly pile into their cars and drive away.

FBI agents swarm the house collecting evidence, the seven men, and the cars left behind. Colton makes a copy of the video footage he recorded for the FBI agents. The agents tell Connor to take his family to a hotel for the night to give them a chance to process the scene.

SDU Assoc. M. Reynolds and Sec. Dept. Assoc. M. Meier arrive on scene, and they insist the Black family go to a hotel for the night with police protection. SDU Assoc. M. Reynolds promises the family will be escorted to the airport before the sun comes up. They believe the Black Family will be safer on an island than in the states for a week while they try to wrap up the Mercer case.

Connor and his family pile up with their luggage in the back of FBI's SUVs. The agent drives the Black family to a small hotel behind the airport. The agent tells the Black family to be ready to roll out to the airport in four hours. Two agents park in the parking lot outside the family's room.

As they enter the dingy hotel room, Kalley and Kelsey are shaken by the events from earlier that night. They ask Connor what did he do yesterday to make men come after them. Connor explains how he posed as Mercer for a huge meeting with three of the worst men in California.

Kalley and Kelsey fuss at Connor for an hour for making such a dangerous and risky move. Kelsey says, "I know you want a promotion, but to risk your life is a bit much. What about us? You, this family is all I have. I can't lose any part of that."

Kalley says, "Dad, we could have all been killed. I'm not an FBI agent. I don't want to be shot or murdered because you want to chase criminals." Connor puts his head down. He is speechless as his wife and daughter blame him for the chaos they experienced.

When the girls finally settle down, Connor sits in a chair by the window rotating his gaze from his wife and two kids to the parking lot. Connor is fighting his sleep because something tells him the WC3 connection wouldn't give up so easily.

An hour before they're slated to leave for the airport, two cars rush into the parking lot. The speed of the cars entering the lot puts Connor on high alert. Silenced gunshots ring out, as bullets flick off and fill up the two FBI cars.

Connor wakes up Colton; he says, "Son, I need you to take care of your mom and sister. Get them to the airport and call for help. Son, all you need to do is cross the alley, and run into the terminal." Connor hands his son a small gun; he says, "You know what to do if anyone gets close."

Connor runs out of the room. Colton wakes up his mother and sister; he says, "We need to go now! Now!" Kalley and Kelsey hop up oblivious to the silent gunshots happening in the parking lot.

As they run out the room, Kalley asks, "Where's dad?"

Kelsey says, "You know your father."

Colton leads them out of the backdoor; he says, "Dad said get to the airport and call for help. We just need to cross the alley and get into the terminal."

187

As Colton, Kalley and Kelsey run across the alley, Connor braces for a fight; he flips over the lobby furniture and bunkers down with perfect aim at the door. As four men approach the hotel's front door, Connor start shooting. He shoots two of the men before they can return fire.

Connor knows he only has one gun, so he hides to conserve his bullets. The men walk into the hotel; they walk around the lobby looking for him.

Colton, Kalley and Kelsey are running through the airport's parking lot almost near the terminal's door when a man hops out and grabs Kalley. Kalley elbows him in the ribs and kicks him as Kelsey kicks him making him lean over while Colton aims the gun at him.

The man lets Kalley go, and she falls on the ground giving Colton enough room to shoot him. Colton, Kelsey, and Kalley make it into the airport and rush over to an TSA officer. They explain what happened. The TSA officer places an emergency call to the airport authority alerting federal agents.

At the hotel, one of the men walks in the janitors' closet where Agt. Black is hiding behind a shelf. When the man slowly walks around the shelf, Agt. Black hits him with his fist and elbow knocking the man out. Agt. Black uses a rope to tie the man up.

Agt. Black notices there's a backdoor in the closet. He opens the door that leads him to the rear where the dumpsters are kept. Agt. Black quietly and cautiously walks around to the front to check the mutilated FBI vehicles.

In the first vehicle, there is a wounded agent, but he's alive and conscious. The agent in the passenger seat is dead. Connor applies pressure to the wound as he moves the agent to the other FBI vehicle. Black puts the bleeding agent in the back seat. The agent in the second vehicle behind the wheel is wounded, but alive and conscious. The other agent in the second vehicle is dead.

Agt. Black lays him on the ground. Agt. Black moves the wounded agent to the passenger seat. Connor tells the bleeding agents, "We need to get to the airport." Connor starts the car and pulls out the parking lot at full speed. A car pulls out behind them and closely follows them. Connor says, "Hang on!"

Agt. Black puts the car in second and pushes the pedal to the floor. The car speeds up to keep up with them. The car bumps into them. The metal of the cars clings as they make contact.

The car crashes into them twice more breaking the rear axle pushing them into a tree. Agt. Black is stunned when he hits his head in the crash. Cruz walks up and smashes the window. The shattering glass splashes all over Agt. Black. Cruz pulls Agt. Black out of the car and lays him on the pavement of the street.

Cruz holds Agt. Black by his collar; he says, "You know, you almost had us fooled. You looked like Mercer. You sounded like Mercer, but the black Impala made us think something wasn't right. Mercer never drives the black Impala to drop offs."

Cruz asks Agt. Black, "We couldn't stop thinking about that black Impala, so we drove to Mercer's to see what was going on and there you were. We immediately realized you weren't Mercer. We want our product, or you must pay the value of our high-quality product."

Agt. Black listens to Cruz as he tries to gain his awareness and normalize his spinning head. Before Agt. Black could speak, one of the agents shoots Cruz in the back of his knee knocking him to the ground. The other wounded agent shoots the gun out of Cruz's hand. Wounded, but alive, Cruz is taken into custody. Agt. Black says to Cruz, "I would love to talk, but I have a plane to catch."

Police cars pull up and take over the scene. Emergency Medical Service vehicles take the two wounded agents and Cruz to the hospital. A police cruiser takes Agt. Black to the hotel to get his family's luggage and drops him off at the airport with his family. Connor says, "I told you, I was not missing the plane."

Kalley says, "Dad, your head. Maybe we shouldn't go."

Agt. Black says, "We are getting on that plane, and we are going to enjoy our vacation." The Black family hugs and walks to the gate to wait to board their flight. They enjoy a week in the Caribbean even with the knot on Connor Black's forehead.

The End
189

While Mrs. Campbell tells the boys the story, Mrs. Miller welcomes the mothers to Day Six: The Day of Planning and Preparation. She says, "Today we are going to talk about supporting our sons by holding them accountable. When they grow up, they will be someone's father and husband. They need to start preparing for manhood." Mrs. Miller leads the group in ways to promote a sense of responsibility in the boys.

Mrs. Miller says, "Give them choices letting them know upfront the consequences. Giving choices alleviates arguing and promotes independence. Choices and consequences are things adults struggle with every day, all day. Go to work or don't get paid, do your chores or have a dirty home, pay the bills or have no utilities, pay your rent or be homeless, abide by the laws nor go to jail. Those are all choices adults filter through daily. There's no one standing over adults making them commit to a choice or guiding through the decision-making process. Adults makes decisions and are left on their own to deal with the consequences.

"However, the lesson of choices and consequences will not work if you protect him from the consequences. Life will not protect or buffer anyone from consequences. Simply say, Son, you can do this or not, and you have given him a choice.

"If he chooses not to comply or perform the task, he will lose a privilege, but we don't argue. Whatever rules you set initially is it. Don't change or lighten the consequences. Be consistent with your fidelity to the process, and the process will really help you with discipline issues.

"You give the choices and state the consequences one time. Don't negotiate or debate. Don't repeat yourself because he heard you the first time. Just as faithful as you are with handing out consequences, be faithful in rewarding.

"Also, let the past be the past and trust him. If you hover over him guiding him to make good decisions, you negate the purpose of the process. If you keep reminding him of past failures, you'll kill his confidence. To monitor his progress set deadlines, schedule meetings, and ask for updates or evidence of progress. It is solely on him to do his part."

Mrs. Miller leads the mothers through some examples of recent incidents with their sons. Mrs. Miller coaches the mothers in moving away from the punishment–discipline model. To a choice and consequence or reward model. They discuss recent incidents and brainstorm ways they could have addressed the incidents differently.

Next, they discuss creating plans and contracts, using if-then statements, and daily or weekly check-ins. Mrs. Miller gives an example of a mother and son sitting down together and creating a plan which includes a schedule for check-ins and rewards, if-then statements to reinforce the concept of giving choices and stating the consequence upfront, and distinguishing desired and undesired behaviors.

When Mrs. Campbell is done with the story, Mrs. Campbell and the boys discuss how the family was able to survive. Mrs. Campbell asks, "What did the family have to their advantage?"

Jace says, "They had a plan."

Eli says, "They practiced!"

Mrs. Campbell asks, "What is the advantages of planning and practicing?"

Levi says, "You're prepared when whatever you practiced happens for real."

Mrs. Campbell says, "I like all of those answers and they were exactly what I was looking for to make my point."

She continues, "When we want to change our behavior or adopt new habits, it is a good idea to not only have a plan but to also practice the behavior we want to adopt. The more you practice, the more natural the habit becomes eventually becoming a part of your routine.

"Just like good basketball and football players practice, people who make good decisions and think quickly under pressure practice. Each of you are going to have to set goals, plan your steps and practice the changes you want to make.

"Additionally, each of you will have to practice following the rules in school. That means replacing undesirable behaviors with desirable behaviors. Instead of hitting and fighting, try walking away, talking things out calmly, and ignoring some things. Instead of lying, try to communicate your needs or wants to your mother. Instead of following the crowd, be a leader of your own movement.

"Focus your excess energy on something positive you love to do. When faced with difficult choices, stop and think through the options, consequences and possible outcomes." The boys listen to Mrs. Campbell's every word. They think about the behaviors they need to replace and the behaviors they need to adopt.

Mrs. Campbell asks the circle, "Is there anything in the story someone can relate to in their own life?"

Caleb says, "When I was little, my mom and I were eating dinner and watching tv when bullets from high-powered assault weapons came through the windows and wall. We had to dive on the floor and lay under the table. The sound of the bullets ripping through the windows and walls was so scary. The hot metal, wood, and glass fragments cut us up.

"We couldn't move because the bullets were coming from all directions. We were so scared. It seemed like we were under the table forever, but it was probably less than five minutes."

Mrs. Campbell says, "Caleb, I am so glad you and your mom weren't hurt, such a blessing."

Tucker asks, "Who was shooting?"

Caleb says, "Five men were shooting at my neighbor, so they shot up all the apartments in the unit."

Tucker says, "That was messed up."

Lucas asks, "Were the men caught?"

Caleb says, "I don't know. We never asked anyone about that night. The police came, but since no one was shot they did not do much investigating."

Niko asks, "Do you still live there?"

Caleb says, "We moved the very next day. My mom said she just couldn't stay in an apartment with so many bullet holes."

Mega asks, "Did you move with your dad?"

Caleb says, "I don't have a dad; it's just my mother and I."

Xander says, "Everyone is made by a woman and a man, so you have a dad."

Caleb says, "A stranger did something horrible to my mother, but he went to jail. I never met him. I only saw a picture of him." When Caleb said that, everyone knew what he meant.

Eli asks, "Do you think you will ever want to meet him?"

Caleb says, "I don't know that I want to meet him. It would be so awkward. He hurt my mother, but he is fifty percent of me. His ancestors are my ancestors.

There are things about myself I wonder if I inherited from him. I wonder why would he hurt a good woman, and will I ever think to do that to somebody? Is it in my DNA? I kind of want to talk to him, but I also don't want to talk to him."

Jace says, "Mrs. Campbell don't you think he needs to face him and get his questions answered? It may be good for him to know."

Mrs. Campbell says, "It's an option he should explore when he is mentally mature and capable to handle those answers. It won't be an easy or comfortable conversation. It could be helpful, but it could cause even more trauma depending on how the conversation goes.

"If the man is resistant and defensive, it could be hurtful to Caleb. If the man is honest and remorseful, it could be a revealing conversation."

Eli says, "I think he owes you some answers. I will go with you, if you want me to go with you for support."

Brad says, "Write him a letter first. If he writes you back, you will know if it is safe to visit him face-to-face. I will go with you, too."

Mrs. Campbell says, "Brad, that is a great suggestion. You write him. He writes you back. You can have your mother read it first to make sure it is beneficial to you. Talk to your mother to see how she feels about you contacting him. Remember, she experienced a great trauma, so contacting him will be a big emotional step for her."

Caleb says, "I will talk to her when this is over to see how she feels about writing him."

Mrs. Campbell says, "Caleb, that is brave of you. If you need some support, let me know."

Mrs. Campbell and Mrs. Miller bring the mothers and sons together. Mrs. Miller tells the group, "We are going to create a simple behavior plan, which is a contract agreeing to terms between mother and son, so that everyone is clear on expectations and desired outcomes."

Mrs. Campbell says, "The key to a successful plan is starting simple. We will be working on three components today. After you have successfully navigated through this initial plan, you can add more details later. For now, each component should have no more than three items. The goal is to make it easy to understand and memorable for both of you."

Mrs. Miller says, "The three components we are working on today are: desired behaviors, consequences & rewards, and a schedule."

Mrs. Miller explains, "First, mother and son should pick one to three new or replacement behaviors, for example: remaining calm and talking through disputes, always complying with school rules, or being a leader or individual despite the majority. The key in this section is to pick the biggest three behaviors that disrupt the functioning of the family unit."

Mrs. Campbell says, "Keep your behaviors simple, concise and clear so everyone is on the same page."

Mrs. Miller says, "Section two is consequences and rewards."

Mrs. Campbell says, "This section should plainly state what will happen based on section one. If-Then statements are a great way to state your thoughts in this section. For example, if John Doe fights in school, he will lose video game privileges for thirty days.

"Each day John Doe doesn't fight, he earns 30 minutes of video game time. If John Doe completes his chores, he will get an allowance. If John Doe doesn't complete his chores, his allowance will go into a savings account to pay for college."

Mrs. Miller says, "The final component we will be working on today is a schedule. This section simply states when the rewards and consequences will happen, and when you will meet or talk to discuss progress. Lastly, this section is also appropriate for deadlines.

"For example, Johnny has seventy-two hours to complete his assigned duties or Johnny chores must be completed by Wednesday night before bedtime every week. Also, be sure to schedule rewards. So, if one of the rewards is an extra snack after dinner for a good day at school then specify that Johnny will receive his extra snack every night after dinner."

Mrs. Campbell gives each mother a notepad and two pens. Mrs. Campbell says, "We encourage each contract to include some form of service. It can be a replacement behavior or a consequence. For example, If Joe Blow fails to complete daily tasks, Joe Blow will volunteer for two hours at the soup kitchen in our neighborhood."

Mrs. Campbell and Mrs. Miller circulate the room as the mother/son pairs begin working on their behavior contract.

Abigail and Eli agree that Eli must stop fighting and disrupting class. Abigail says, "Son, the rowdy behavior at school. The yelling out, talking while the teacher is talking stop today. And, you must keep your hands to yourself and mind your business.

"Son, you love music. Every day you don't get in trouble at school, you can download one song. Every day you get in trouble equals an hour that you will volunteer at church. And we sit down to talk, just you and I every Friday."

Eli asks, "What if I have a good week?"

195

Abigail says, "I will personally take you to the video game store after church on Sunday. If you get in trouble more than two times in one week, you will serve as an usher on Sunday, cut the grass, wash the cars, and I get to keep your allowance to do whatever I want."

Eli says, "Let's shake on it!" Abigail writes out the plan. They both sign it.

Mrs. Campbell puts the contract in a bronze frame; and says, "Put this somewhere in your home where it is visually accessible to you both." Mrs. Campbell wishes Eli luck, and tells Abigail and Eli to enjoy the rest of the day."

Kelly and Caleb start working on their plan. Kelly says, "Son, if your grades and behavior don't improve after this program, you will give up football. Also, I want you to join academic games and the debate team. If you can comply, I will get you tickets to a professional football game next season."

Caleb, still stunned by Kelly's first remark, says, "Give up football?"

Kelly says, "I can't allow you to openly defy me and let you have what you want. You have until your next progress report to improve your grades. The first time you get suspended for behavior, no more football."

Caleb's mouth drops. He says, "Mom, no more football?"

Kelly continues with the terms of their contract, "We will check in every Saturday night. If your chores aren't done by Saturday night 8pm, no football, no allowance, and you will be grounded for the week. Also, you will volunteer at the soup kitchen two to three times per week. If you continue fighting and disrupting class, you are going to a boarding school."

Caleb says, "Boarding school?"

Kelly says, "I'm not playing with you. When this program is over, you need to show me improvement or no more football and you're going to boarding school." Kelly and Caleb sign their contract.

Mrs. Campbell puts the contract in a silver frame; she says, "Put this somewhere in your home where it is visually accessible to you both." Mrs. Campbell wishes Caleb luck, and tells Kelly and Caleb to have a good week."

Xander tells Nia, "Ma, another one of my favorite memories is you and I working in grandma's garden. I liked the idea of growing life to give life. I thought it was fun even though we were dirty. We got a chance to talk. I still remember how Grandma taught me how to plant seeds. She let me till the soil and plant seeds. Watching the garden grow, knowing I helped, made me feel like I could do something good. Like that garden, I can do something good."

Nia says, "I know you can, Son, that's why I haven't given up on you."

Nia says, "We've got to replace some current behaviors with some new ones. Instead of fighting, you should seek a better solution. You can talk to your teacher or counselor. You can also ignore some things; you don't have to react to everything. Acting up in class is unacceptable. If you need stimulation or fun, you should try sports, find a hobby or join a club. You must be more responsible, adhere to rules and expectations at home and at school like a mature teenager."

Xander says, "Those are simple, I can do all that."

Nia says, "Xander, it doesn't take much to make changes. Small steps combine to make one big leap forward. If you take small steps, I can work with that. If you can't get it together in school, Xander, we are moving. I refuse to let my son fall victim to the streets."

Xander says, "Move?"

Nia says, "You have until the end of the semester to show improvement, at that time your dad and I will decide if we should move or stay. Check in with me every Monday, Wednesday and Friday.

"You must bring a progress report home daily. If you forget it or lose it, I will count that as a bad day. You need to make this a priority, and be committed or it won't work. You will volunteer at both the community center and the church at least one day each per week. Every night you will read a page in the bible.

"You will take the garbage out every night and wash the cars on the weekends. Xander, these are non-negotiables. If they are not done as scheduled, you will not have any privileges, you will not receive an allowance, and you will not participate in any activities or outings. For every good week, I will double your allowance. If you have an excellent week, I will triple your allowance."

Xander says, "Double my allowance, triple my allowance, okay!"

Nia and Xander sign their contract. Mrs. Campbell puts the contract in a wooden frame, and says, "Put this somewhere in your home where it is visually accessible to you both." Mrs. Campbell wishes Xander luck, and tells Nia and Xander to have a good day."

Lucas and Melinda agree to terms for their contract. Lucas says, "I will take my medicine. I will go to that new school. I will do my best. I will not fight and act out in class. I will take my education seriously."

Melinda says, "You will also go to church, actively listen to the sermon, and volunteer after services with the youth ministry. You will take out the trash every night. We will meet every Thursday during dinner time to discuss your progress." Lucas says, "If I do everything I am supposed to can I get a car magazine at the end of the week?"

Melinda says, "We can also go to auto shows." Lucas is excited about going to auto shows.

Melinda asks, "Is there any other reward you would like?"

Lucas thinks for a moment. He says, "A bigger allowance!"

Melinda asks, "How big?"

Lucas smiles. He says, "Double!"

Melinda says, "Okay!"

Melinda writes out their contract. Melinda says, "Son, a good man keeps his word."

Lucas says, "I will keep my word."

Mrs. Campbell puts the contract in a glitter coated frame; she says, "Put this somewhere in your home where it is visually accessible to you both." Mrs. Campbell wishes Lucas luck, and she tells Melinda and Lucas to have a good day.

Melinda and Lucas happily walk out the door to their car. As Lucas gets in the car, he says, "I should have put a new pair of Jordan's in the contract."

Melinda says, "I am willing to consider a new pair of Jordan's after you show you are dedicated to the plan."

Lucas says, "You'll buy new shoes for me?"

Melinda says, "Whatever it takes, Son!"

Lucas says, "I can't wait!"

Mecia and Jace sit negotiating the terms of their contract. Jace says, "I should get a small reward every day, and a big reward every week."

Mecia says, "What kind of rewards interest you?"

Jace says, "Food and money! I like snacks like chips, cookies, and candy."

Mecia says, "So, snacks will be your daily reward, and how much money for your weekly reward?"

Jace says, "Twenty dollars!"

Mecia says, "A good week is well worth twenty dollars."

Jace says, "Deal!"

Mecia says, "You agree to no fighting, no disruptive behavior in school, and you must volunteer at the community center and at church at least one day per week at each."

Jace says, "That's doable!"

Mecia says, "If your obligations aren't fulfilled every Saturday by dinner time, there will be no weekly reward."

Jace says, "That's fair!"

Mecia says, "Jace, I need you to really take this seriously. You are modeling the behavior your brothers will learn. If you continue down this road, your brothers will follow you. Do you want that?"

Jace says, "No, Ma'am!"

Mecia says, "You really have to set a better example."

Jace says, "You're right! I don't want my brothers behaving like me."

Mecia makes Jace pinky promise that he is committed to the plan before she finishes writing out the plan. Mrs. Campbell puts the contract in a bronze frame. Mrs. Campbell says, "Put this somewhere in your home where it is visually accessible to you both." Mrs. Campbell wishes Jace luck, as she winks at him. She tells Mecia and Jace to have a good week!"

Lea and Levi come to an agreement. Lea lists the desired behaviors: 1) Display behaviors compliant with school expectations every day the entire school day. 2) Attend and fully participate in family therapy. 3) You will help Mr. Haughton at barber shop after school at least twice per week. Does that sound good, Son?"

Levi says, "Sounds good, Mom! Do you think my reward can be a visit to Granddad's?"

Lea pauses for a moment before she says, "Why don't we just move to Granddad's? He's been begging us to come for years."

Levi says, "Really, Mom?"

Lea says, "Yes, Son! Let's just go, a change of environment may be good for you."

Levi says, "Mom are you sure you can leave work?"

Lea says, "I will work it out for you, Son!"

Levi says, "Mom, you're the best!"

Lea says, "Son, you're the best!"

Lea rewrites their contract to reflect their new plan. They will move with Lea's father who lives in the south and owns a horse ranch.

Levi will work the stables and have access to the horses. Levi will maintain his grades and he will stay out of trouble. They will meet weekly to review Levi's progress. Levi and Leah the sign contract.

Mrs. Campbell puts the contract in a wooden frame; she tells them, "Put this somewhere in your home where it is visually accessible to you both." Mrs. Campbell wishes Levi luck, and tells Lea and Levi to have a good day.

Tucker and Inga brainstorm the desired behaviors Inga wants Tucker to display. Inga says, "Tucker, I want you to play football because everyone needs a passion, but it's a privilege. You can't keep taking my kindness for weakness. I'm supporting you because I want this for you not because I have to let you play. If you want to keep playing, you are going to have to make some changes."

Tucker says, "I will make those changes. I'm serious this time."

Inga says, "If you don't, no more football! I will need weekly check-ins where you show me evidence, not limited to but including: completed homework, completed chores, graded papers, or a progress report from school. That means no phone calls about you acting out and disrupting the class. No suspensions! No fights!

"After practice, you come straight home. You must earn privileges to go anywhere else. Sundays, we go to church as a family, and you need to find a role to serve in at church. You have until the end of the month to pick a position. Deal?"

Inga and Tucker shake hands, as Tucker agrees to the terms. Inga writes out the details of the three components of their contract. When Inga finishes writing, Inga and Tucker sign their contract.

Mrs. Campbell sees they are finished and walks over to put their contract in a bronze frame; she says, "Put this somewhere in your home where it is visually accessible to you both," as she hands the contract to Inga. Mrs. Campbell wishes Tucker luck, and tells Inga and Tucker to have a good week."

Brad and Stephanie agree on the things Brad needs to change. Stephanie writes out the contract as they talk. Stephanie asks, "Brad, what do you want for yourself when you are thirty or forty years old?"

Brad says, "I want a home, a family, a company that designs video games, and to provide for myself and my family."

Stephanie says, "Are you doing anything right now to prepare for that life?"

Brad says, "No!"

Stephanie says, "You are on track for jail or to be one of those dudes that just runs through the hood doing nothing. Is that what you want for yourself?"

Brad says, "No!"

Stephanie says, "You're a smart kid, Bradley, but without an education the chances are highly stacked against you. An education at least gets you a chance at an open door. I just want what's best for you, but you've got to want it for yourself. Do you?"

Brad says, "I do!"

Stephanie says, "Bradley, you need to act like you are working toward something. You need to study more and improve your grades to A's or B's nothing less. No suspensions, not one, Bradley.

"And, you need to learn to interact with people like a normal human. You can't keep using your fists to make people do what you want. I know you love video games, but you need to expand your mind. You will read one three-hundred-page novel every month, rotating between fiction and non-fiction.

"You will write a five-paragraph report summarizing and analyzing the book, which is due on the first day of the next month. Smart men are well-read and well spoken, and they can walk into any room with any mix of people and hold an intelligent, interesting conversation. It's very important that you expose yourself to new and different things. Reading books can take you all over the world and expose you to diverse experiences.

"If you do everything I ask you to do, you can play all the video games you want. Just remember, you do what you have to do, so you can do what you want to do. Do you understand, Bradley?"

Bradley indicates that he understands. Bradley and Stephanie agree to the terms, and sign the contract. Mrs. Campbell puts the contract in a black frame;

she says, "Put this somewhere in your home where it is visually accessible to you both." Mrs. Campbell wishes Brad luck, and tells Stephanie and Brad, "I'll see you next week."

Rita and Niko discuss the three components of their contract. Rita says, "I know you love clothes and shoes, so if you give me what I want, I will give you what you want."

Niko says, "Okay! Let me see what you are talking about." Rita writes the desired behaviors: Niko will learn to better handle conflict by attending and fully participating in therapy and counseling. Niko will pick somewhere in the community to volunteer twice per week. Niko will behave in accordance with school policy while anywhere on school grounds or during events. Niko will do his daily chores at the time they are expected to be done as stated on the chore chart in the kitchen. Lastly, Niko will improve his grades by increasing the amount of effort and time he invests in school.

If Niko effectively demonstrates the above five behaviors for seven consecutive days, he will earn a weekly reward of ten dollars. If Niko fails to demonstrate any of the listed behaviors, he will not receive any allowance. If Niko effectively demonstrates the five behaviors for a full month, he will be rewarded with a shopping trip with a limit of one hundred dollars.

Rita says, "How does this sound?"

Niko says, "It's cool!"

Rita says, "So, we have a deal?"

Niko reaches out his hand; and says, "Deal!"

Niko and Rita shake hands, sign their contract and give the contract to Mrs. Campbell. Mrs. Campbell puts their contract in a white frame; she says, "Put this somewhere in your home where it is visually accessible to you both." Mrs. Campbell wishes Niko luck, and tells Rita and Niko she'll see them next week."

Mega and Megan agree that Mega will take his education more seriously by studying more and completing assignments on time, and he will continue to participate in basketball. Megan convinces Mega to agree to volunteer at the soup kitchen near their home one day of each week that he doesn't have practice.

Megan asks Mega if he can commit to cleaning his room every Sunday after church.

Mega says, "If I improve my grades, volunteer and keep my room clean, will you send me to basketball camp in the summer and pay for me to join the teen basketball gym? It will really help improve my chances to get a scholarship to a private high school, which will be my ticket to get into a good college."

After pleading his case so well, Megan couldn't help but agree to the terms. Megan says, "Son, I cannot argue with that!"

Megan and Mega signs their contract. Mrs. Campbell sees they're done, and walks over to them. Megan tells Mrs. Campbell, "I'm so grateful for this exercise because we needed to come to this understanding."

Mrs. Campbell says, "I'm glad it was helpful." Megan hands Mrs. Campbell the contract. Mrs. Campbell puts the contract in a glass frame; she says, "Put this somewhere in your home where it is visually accessible to you both." Mrs. Campbell wishes Mega luck, and tells Megan and Mega to enjoy the rest of their day."

Mrs. Campbell and Mrs. Miller talk as they clean up and prepare for completion day. Mrs. Miller says, "We have a good group this session. Each person seems committed to the process."

Mrs. Campbell says, "The mothers' faces and body language has changed drastically from day one. Today, they look so much happier as if a heavy burden has been lifted off their shoulders."

Mrs. Miller says, "Even Jace and Mecia seem to have had a breakthrough."

Mrs. Campbell says, "Amen!"

Seventh Saturday

Day of Completion

Mrs. Campbell and Mrs. Miller enthusiastically greet the mothers and sons as they walk through the door for the last day. The boys go to their circle and the mothers go to their circle. Everyone is excited and ready for the day. When all the participants are present, Mrs. Campbell and Mrs. Miller start their presentations.

Mrs. Miller talks to the mothers about forgiveness, building trust, and moving forward. She explains that the mother-son relationships won't grow if the sons are held hostage to the memories of their past.

Mrs. Miller says, "The journey on this road leading to the future starts with forgiveness. I know saying it is easier than actually doing it, but it is the absolute necessary first step." Mrs. Miller gives each mother a yellow legal pad; she says, "I want you to write the deepest hurts and embarrassments your son or sons have caused you. Take a minute and think deeply and purge it on the paper."

The mothers silently write. Some faces fill with tears, but each mother sticks with the process. Mrs. Miller lights a low-burning candle in a coffee can. She calls each mother to the candle to burn the paper. She tells the mother to exhale as her paper burns. She says, "As the paper burn, let go of the pain and anger you hold against your son." Each mother burns the paper and exhale the negativity of the past.

Mrs. Miller says, "Next on the road is building trust. I know they are growing boys, but they need to know you trust them. They will make mistakes and deal with the consequences, but that's healthy. It helps prepare them for adulthood. It's okay to let them bump their heads and to make them clean up their own mess.

"You should have conversations about trust. Discuss how you and he define trust, how your trust is earned, and make sure it is clear how your trust can be lost or broken. Most importantly, after today, the boys should know they have a clean slate, and the trust you're giving is not impeded by the past because we are moving forward."

Mrs. Miller hands each mother a white piece of blank paper. She tells each mother to write down the good qualities and characteristics of her son. She says, "Sometimes, we focus on the faults and flaws of our children especially when we are overwhelmed by their behavior, but it's good to remember the good in everyone. Let's celebrate and cherish the good things he does and the personality traits that make us smile."

Mrs. Miller adds, "We know we are here for their behavior. We know everything they did in the past. Their behavior has been discussed a million times. Moving forward requires discontinuing negative conversations.

"Also, we move forward by planning for the future. Talk about college; talk about the upcoming football or soccer season. Provoke hopefulness and excitement about the future. Set goals: both long term and short-term goals are important. Celebrate every little step toward accomplishing the goal."

As Mrs. Miller talks to the mothers, Mrs. Campbell talks to the boys about having a plan to achieve their goals. Mrs. Campbell says, "When we set a goal, we need to logically think how we will achieve the goal. The best way to attack a goal is one step at a time. Take small steps if necessary.

"It's important not to overwhelm or pressure yourself. It's okay to pace yourself especially if you set multiple goals, but I beg you to press yourself when things get tough.

"There are going to be times when the plan needs to be re-evaluated. Don't look at those times as failures; think of them as moments of self-reflection. You may not have the whole picture when you start the plan, so you may have to plan it one step at a time."

Niko says, "Mrs. Campbell, I bet you have a story for us about kids who had a plan to accomplish their goals."

Mrs. Campbell says, "You boys know me so well!"

Mega says, "I like your stories, Mrs. Campbell, I can relate to them and they are interesting!" Xander, Caleb, and Jace admit they like the stories too. The rest of the boys also say they enjoy the stories.

Niko asks, "Do you tell the same stories to every group?"

Mrs. Campbell says, "No! The stories are inspired by the conversation of the day."

Caleb asks, "Are the stories real?"

Mrs. Campbell says, "They are real. They are based on people or events that I encountered in twenty years of working as a social worker."

Xander says, "Well, start the story, I can't wait any longer!"

Mrs. Campbell starts the story and the boys listen intently, hanging on her every word.

Sister Bloggers: Deadline Detroit

On a dark, cool spring night in Detroit on a desolate block with plenty of trees, bushes and no street lights, Sylvia Brock walks alone without a destination. Sylvia is lost; she knows her location, but she fails to understand her life's purpose. With no direction in life and no obligation of her time, Sylvia roams the streets at night.

Sylvia walks pass an overgrown row of bushes growing over a fence between a vacant lot and a dilapidated vacant home. As Sylvia passes the bushes, a hand reaches out and wraps around Sylvia's mouth and quickly pulls her into the bushes.

The next morning, Rueben, the golden retriever from across the street, is out walking with his owner, Kevin Krouse. Rueben runs into the bushes and comes out with blood on his coat. Kevin gets closer to Rueben and sees the blood stains before searching the bushes.

When Kevin gets to the fence, he sees Sylvia eyes open, but lifeless leaning against the fence. Kevin just moved into the city from the suburbs, so Kevin isn't accustomed to handling violence. Kevin panics.

Kevin runs out of the thick, overgrown bushes to call the police on his smart phone. In his panic, Kevin trips over Reuben and falls, getting his sweatpants dirty in the dirt and scraping his hand on the concrete.

The police wrap the yellow tape around the bushes and barricade the block with police cruisers. The police hold back on lookers and news reporters while the crime scene investigators process the scene and Reuben. Detectives question Kevin and the neighbors. Kevin is nervous and overwhelmed fear and freight as he stumbles through the story of finding the body.

News reporters and news vans from all the local news outlets are on the scene at each corner. The reporters speculate that she's the latest victim of the Detroit Grand Reaper, growing the possible list of victims to ten. Police have yet to confirm that the ten crimes are linked, nor have they identified a person of interest. Police are urging women to be vigilant and aware of their surroundings always. They, also, ask women not to be alone at night.

All the residents in the neighborhood know Sylvia as a homeless woman that was harmless. She never bothered anyone. They describe her pattern of behavior as roaming the neighborhood talking lowly to herself. Not one neighbor can think of any reason someone would have to hurt her.

The detectives talk to Sylvia's family. The family says she struggled with mental illness her whole life. She never had friends or typical childhood experiences. Reporters go live from the scene and report Sylvia lived a sad life and met a tragic end.

The Sylvia Brock story is on the front page of the newspaper and the leading story of every local news broadcast, so the students in Mrs. Liman's business class at Jefferson High are talking about the story before class starts.

Mrs. Liman starts class with a discussion on opportunity, demand, and supply. She talks about businesses that started with people taking an opportunity to supply a demand or need. She explains that the best business plans start with an idea to provide a product or service people need or making an existing product or service more convenient and readily available to more customers.

Mrs. Liman explains how technology is opening more doors for people to take a chance to make their own opportunities. She adds that the most successful business people are those who can convince people that they need a convenience, product or service.

She ends with, "But, the happiest business people are those who have figured out how to make their passion their profit." The class discuss business ideas that would require a low cost to start, but would supply a need or service.

Mrs. Liman tells the class they have two weeks to create, write and produce a project that includes a written business plan with projected cost and profits and two visuals. She gives them a layout for the business plan and a list of ideas for visuals.

All three of the Toms sisters are in Mrs. Liman's class. At dinner, they tell their mother about the assignment and brainstorm ideas for businesses based on their interests and their talents and how they can make them profitable. The news comes on and the Detroit Grand Reaper is the lead story.

Tamrah, the eldest triplet, says, "I got it. People need information. We love to provide information."

Their mother laughs, she says, "You mean, you love to gossip!"

The girls look at her, Tamryn says, "We are girls!"

Tamrah continues, "We can work cameras, computers, and we are active social media users."

Tamla says, "You mean, we can create our own news outlet like a blog."

Tamrah says, "Exactly!"

Tamryn, the youngest triplet, asks, "How do we make money? How will we make it profitable?"

Tamrah says, "People make money as bloggers all the time by attracting advertisers."

Tamla says, "We can research profitability of blogging include the data in our business plan."

Tamryn says, "We can create a page on different social media outlets to post stories and that will be our visuals."

Tamla says, "Our Mac, iPhones and iPads will help us record, edit, and upload videos."

Tamryn says, "I'm seeing your vision. I think we can do this."

Tamrah says, "Our first big story can be the Detroit Grand Reaper. Ten people are dead in nearly a month; I think it's more to this story than a single serial killer. There's something big that's someone is not seeing or saying."

Tamla says, "This project has three parts that need to be done in the first week: 1) researching and creating the actual plan; 2) researching the murders and writing the story and 3) creating the platforms on social media to host our stories that will serve as our visuals. The second week will be production and launch. Who wants to do what?"

Tamryn says, "I'll research and write the plan."

Tamrah says, "I'll research the Reaper murders."

Tamla says, "I'll start working on creating our pages."

Their mother, Tamil Toms, just listens and watches the girls talk as she eats. The girls get up from the table and run upstairs. Tamryn comes back down to say to her mother, "Mom, I can clean the table for you."

Tamil says, "Go, do your homework! I can handle the kitchen."

Tamryn says, "Thanks, Mom!" Tamryn runs back up the stairs and the girls start on their project.

The girls work diligently for a week on their project. In that week, two more victims are linked to the Detroit Grand Reaper. The Toms sisters are suspicious of the media's assumption that there's one killer, and they are determined to find out who is the real Detroit Grand Reaper.

With all the preparation for the blog and their business plan complete, they are now ready to go out into the neighborhood and investigate the Detroit Grand Reaper Murders. The first thing they do is go to the scene of each murder. They record footage of the scenes and the surrounding areas.

Next, they talk to homeless people and other kids to see if they have anything to add to the story. Lastly, they create a map and mark the location of each of the murders. Those killed with a knife are marked with a green marker, and those killed with a gun are marked with a red marker.

Early Saturday morning the girls are looking at the map. Tamrah says, "Five of the twelve suspected Grand Reaper murders fit a pattern: the victims were all homeless females, the locations of the murder were streets near the train tracks between the plant and the freeway, and the manner of murder was a combination of strangulation and stabbing. Sylvia Brock, Mattie Murdock, Red Harris, Shayna Miller, and Talitha Lakes all fit the same pattern."

Tamla says, "Do you think someone is traveling on the train to Detroit to kill people?"

Tamryn says, "We need to go to the train tracks and see what is out there."

The girls hurry to get dress, eat breakfast, brush their teeth, and gather their equipment. They ride their bikes to the train tracks. They pull out their phones to record houses, buildings, and landmarks along the train tracks.

They start at the plant and ride their bikes along the tracks and stop at the freeway. They stand on the service drive thinking.

Tamryn says, "Did anything stick out as strange, suspicious or awkward?"

Tamla says, "Behind the hills near the plant, there was an old, wooden barn looking building. It has a strange vibe; maybe we should get a closer look."

Tamrah says, "Let's go!"

The girls ride their bikes to the old red barn behind the hills. The barn has no glass in the windows or doors. They document the entire building and the surrounding land. They go into a creepy, dark back corner.

Tamrah says, "Someone has been living here."

Tamla uses the flashlight on her phone to light up the barn; she says, "Creepy! Look at these drawings!"

Tamryn says, "It's like someone has drew the murders. Look, it's exactly five pictures."

Tamla says, "Tamrah, you've got to report your theory."

Tamrah asks, "Do I look okay?"

Tamla says, "You look great!"

Tamla and Tamryn record Tamrah explaining her theory that five of the twelve murders are related. Tamrah talks about the five drawings depicting the related murders. Tamrah talks to people who live near the old, red barn. Every person reports that a mysterious man that goes in the barn very late and comes out the barn very early.

They explain it is always dark when he travels, so none of the neighbors have seen his face. A few neighbors report seeing a man carrying a bag, dressed in all black with a hat near the barn, but it is too dark to tell exactly what he is wearing.

The Toms Triplets go to the scenes of the other four murders they think are related. Tamrah explains why she thinks the Detroit Grand Reaper is responsible for only five of the murders. Tamrah interviews a few neighbors to each of the four scenes.

Again, Tamrah is told that a man dressed in all black carrying a bag roaming the neighborhood near the times of the murders, but no one could identify him because he travels only when it is very the dark. Several neighbors report seeing the women walking alone just before the murders, and no one saw anything suspicious around the of the murder reported times of death.

The triplets go home to edit their videos and write the article. Tamla posts the videos and article on all social media outlets. The posts are an immediate hit. With a convincing theory, the triplets convince people that multiple murderers are freely killing in the City of Detroit. Victims' family members comment and thank them for exposing a possible suspect.

After church, the sisters break down the details of the other seven murders. The girls discover there are two possible shooters. Four girls died from close contact wounds from a small caliber gun. Three girls were shot several times with a large caliber weapon in random parts of their bodies from about three to five feet away. There's no foreseeable pattern in the location of these homicides. Sunday night before going to bed, the girls post their theory that there are possibly three killers, two shooters and the Detroit Grand Reaper.

The darkness of the night brings a chill that covers the city while the girls sleep. Natalie Lopes leaves out the Coney Island with her friends at 2 a.m. An older model all black Crown Victoria with tinted windows pulls into the parking lot. Natalie and her friends are startled by the slow-moving car following them. They slow up and watch as the back window rolls down.

Natalie and her friends feel afraid of the unknown behind that window, but they keep moving. When Natalie and her friends reach their vehicle, the Crown Victoria stops. As Natalie and her friends are about to get in their car. A long barrel of a gun slowly sticks out the window and shoots Natalie and her friends. Her friends are only superficially injured, but Natalie is gravely injured leaning in the back seat of the car.

On the opposite side of town near the train tracks, Belle Wilmer walks alone with no place to go. The breeze pushes the grass and ruffles the bushes as Belle walks down a poorly lit street. The sound of nothingness in the night echoes through the atmosphere as Belle bravely walks lonely, slowly, and cautiously through the dark going nowhere. When Belle reaches the corner, she looks around to see if she sees anyone. Belle sees no one, so she turns the corner.

When she passes the garage of the corner house, darkness swoops her up and pulls her in the alley. Belle is thrown to the ground with the strength of an ox. Belle inhales to screams, but the blade impaling her chest impedes her ability to scream. As quickly as darkness snatched Belle is as quick as it left her there to die.

When the triplets awake, Belle and Natalie's murders are breaking news. The sisters' news articles and videos are so popular that they are featured on all the local morning news broadcast. The kids at school talk about the sisters' posts all day. Tamla and Tamryn even talk to relatives of victims that are students at Jefferson High and willing to go on record with their thoughts on the case.

The family members say the police are telling the family nothing, and most of what the families have heard came from people in the neighborhood. Each person the sisters talk to thank them for getting the truth out and possibly saving people by making them aware of the two additional killers.

While eating dinner with their mother the girls convince their mother to take them around after dark to the new crime scenes. Tamrah says, "Mom, we will be in a car the whole time. All the victims were on foot or getting in or out the car."

Tamla says, "Mom, it's homework. We wouldn't ask unless it was important." Tamil doesn't think it's safe, but the girls beg and plead until Tamil gives in and agrees to take the girls to the crime scenes after sundown.

Sitting in the car with Tamil, the girls discuss the new cases. Tamrah says, "Natalie went to a jazz club Sunday night with her friends, and they stopped at the twenty-four-hour Coney Island afterward. Natalie, like Donna Fleming, Annette Sims, and Raychelle Newman, was a professional woman, no criminal history, no ties to any criminal offenders."

Tamla says, "They were not victims of convenience. And, it is unlikely that they were victims by coincidence."

Tamryn says, "Notice, Natalie was with other women, but was the only one killed. The shooters had ample time and access to kill all the women, but only chose to kill one."

The sisters and their mother look around the parking lot. Tamil says, "Logistically, there is no reason that only Natalie was killed. There wasn't anything blocking the other women."

Tamrah rolls down the back window of her mother's Charger; she says, "I have a clear view of everything. All sides of every car."

Tamryn says, "A professional murderer for hire would make sense for those four women because there's no other logical connection."

Next, the Toms family drives by the Belle Wilmer crime scene. Tamil says, "It's really creepy back there."

Tamryn says, "The brush gives the perfect cover for a predator lying in wake."

Tamla says, "Mom, go down a block and make a right." Tamil drives towards the old, wooden red barn. When the car gets near the barn, a dark figure carrying a duffle bag bursts out of the darkness, runs across the street back into the darkness. All three girls shout, "That's him!"

Tamil shouts, "Call the police," as she drives away as fast as she can.

Tamryn says, "We don't need the police, I got him running on video." Tamla and Tamrah celebrate.

Tamil takes the girls home; she says, "Girls, this is way too deep, way too dangerous. You all cannot go near that barn again." The girls agree to stay away from the barn. They go in their room and post the video of the dark figure running.

They also post their theory that a professional murderer for hire was responsible for the deaths of Natalie Lopes, Donna Fleming, Annette Sims, and Raychelle Newman. They explain the similarities between the murders and how the murder cases were different from the murder cases of Nikita Walsh, Prea Cole, Dana Motts, and Blaire Bunch. The new posts immediately go viral. The sisters make national news for their thorough investigation.

Although the sisters did nothing illegal, the police knock on the Toms front door early the next morning. Their father, Tariq Toms, answers the door. The police ask Mr. Toms to stop his daughters from posting about the murders.

They warn the family that their posts put their family in danger. The girls plead with their dad that they did nothing wrong and they have a right to speak as free United States citizens. Mr. Toms asks the police if the girls had violated a law. The police reiterate that the posts are dangerous. Mr. Toms vows to talk to the girls after school. The girls have no intention on stopping their blog.

The sisters' blog, Deadline Detroit, and their social media pages are so popular that Mrs. Liman congratulates them for finding a niche and using their passion to supply a need in the community to make the community better.

Mrs. Liman says, "This is exactly how happy, successful business owners start."

Mrs. Liman's comment only fuels the sisters' determination even more. At lunch, the sisters plan their next move with their blog and brainstorm ideas

216

to convince their father to let them continue their blog. They know whatever they come up with must be good and big.

The sisters decide to take an in-depth look at the Nikita Walsh, Prea Cole, Dana Motts, and Blaire Bunch murder cases to prove three separate killers are responsible for terrorizing the city. As they eat, some kids came over to their table yelling, "They got'em! They got'em!"

Tamrah asks, "Who!"

One boy says, "Check your phone. The police got the Detroit Grand Reaper, or at least the guy from your video." The sisters all hurry to pull out their phones to check the news.

The breaking news headline on every media outlet in Detroit reads Teen Bloggers Help Find Detroit Serial Killer. The boy says, "The news said you all will get the ten-thousand-dollar reward if he is the killer."

Tamla says, "This is big! Dad can't argue with us solving crime and bringing people to justice."

Tamryn says, "Getting that reward, identifying the other two killers, and getting rewards for solving those two cases will make our business legitimate."

Tamrah says, "Who in Detroit could possibly be a hitman with actual skills to always hit their target. I know people shoot all the time in Detroit, but who could be that efficient to be sure to kill a specific person in a group of people."

Tamla says, "Police officers!"

Tamryn says, "Military"

Tamrah says, "That still leaves a lot of people."

Tamla says, "Not if we can find the cars. An all-black Crown Victoria in perfect condition with tinted windows doesn't ride down the street every day. When you think about it, it's a rare car these days."

Tamryn says, "We have to go back over the other seven shootings to see what kind of cars were seen in the area around the time of the shootings."

Tamrah says, "There has to be a way to find those cars."

Tamla says, "People with rare cars show their cars off on Belle Isle, on social media, or car clubs. If we point out what cars to be on the lookout for someone will report suspicious cars that fit the profile."

Tamryn says, "Good plan, Tamla!" After school, the sisters work hard to produce a detailed analysis of all the cars near each of the eight shootings. They find pictures of similar cars and post the time and location witnesses report seeing the suspicious vehicles.

An hour after posting about the cars possibly involved, a follower who happens to live near the Donna Fleming and Annette Sims' murder scenes, Sharee Noble, comments that an all-black Crown Victoria with tinted windows was in the neighborhood around the times of both Donna Fleming and Annette Sims' slayings. Many followers post they agree with the sisters' theory that a professional murderer for hire may have caused the death of Natalie Lopes, Donna Fleming, Annette Sims, and Raychelle Newman.

With their posts and videos trending, the sisters sit at the table in the kitchen to talk with their father after dinner. Their father, who was totally oblivious of what is going on and why, is awaiting a good explanation. They explain their project and how they only have a few more days to present it to Mrs. Liman. The also point out all the ways their project helps the community, which is what Mrs. Liman said a good business does.

Tamla points out, "Mrs. Liman said to use our talent and passion to make the world a better place. If that guy is really the reaper, we just saved lives." Mr. Toms listens to his daughters go on and on. Tamryn asks their mother to support them, but Tamil refuses to take sides.

Tamil says, "I'm not in this."

Mr. Toms looks to his wife, but she continues eating her dessert. Tariq Toms tells his daughter their research is okay, but they must stay away from the red barn and crime scenes. Mr. Toms says, "It's just too dangerous for such young girls to be hanging around or looking around a crime scene. No posting pictures or videos. I don't want anyone trying to get revenge or silence you. I just can't risk that even for the good of the world. You four are my priority. Is that a good deal?"

Tamryn says, "Yes, Daddy!"

Tamla says, "It's reasonable!"

Tamrah says, "That's not investigative reporting. Dad no pictures, no videos equal boring posts! No one will want to follow our pages."

Mr. Toms says, "That's the deal, take it or leave it!"

Tamrah yells, "Mom!"

Tamil says, "Tamrah, meet your father, Tariq! Tariq meet your daughter, Tamrah! You all must learn to deal with each other, communicate with each other, and stop putting me in the middle to solve your disagreements and be the peace maker. Girls, he is the man of this house, he is your father, his word has to mean something."

Tariq says, "Thank you!"

Tamil says, "Tamrah is your daughter, and all girls want is for their fathers to hear them and really listen."

Tamrah says, "Thank you!"

Tamil says, "T2 and T3, let's go! These two need to talk. Neither of you can get up until you talk it out."

With Tamil and the other two sisters gone, Tariq feels comfortable to talk. He explains how the thought of someone harming his daughter is inconceivable. He says, "If someone hurts you, I will kill them or die trying. I wouldn't survive, and when you become a parent you will see life differently. All I want is for you to grow up safely and happily. I want to support you but you're a tenth grader and that's too young to be investigating crime scenes.

"Just because I am asking you to stop, doesn't mean I'm not proud of what you have accomplished. I am extremely proud and concerned. We live in a very dangerous city, so what you're doing makes me nervous especially sense I work all the time. I hate that I'm missing so much of your life, but I'm working overtime six days per week to make this a good life for us.

I will agree to any pictures and videos not related to murder scenes and murderers. Investigate something else and I will drive you myself."

Tamrah smiles at her dad, she says, "I'm sorry, I yelled. Everything you said was logical and reasonable. You work very hard to provide a great life for us, and we never say thank you. Daddy, I love you too. And, if someone hurt you, I wouldn't survive."

Mr. Toms hugs his daughter; he says, "Thank you, Tamrah."

Tamrah says, "Thanks for really opening up and talking to me, and I do respect you. I'm sorry if it seemed like I didn't."

Tariq says, "We're good, always have been and always will be."

Tamrah asks, "Since it's all good now, can we get up from the table."

Tariq says, "Your mom was serious!"

Tamrah says, "Tell me about it." They both call Tamil wanting permission to get up from the table.

Tamrah shouts, "Mom!"

Tariq yells, "Tamil, Honey!"

Wednesday morning, breaking news and newspaper headlines read: Confession in the Reaper Case Thanks to Teen Bloggers. The city is buzzing with energy that the sisters' video of the dark figure led to the capture of Fletcher Trod also known as The Detroit Grand Reaper because he always used a knife to end the lives of his victims.

With the confession, police officials announce that the creators of the blog, Deadline Detroit will receive the ten-thousand-dollar reward for the capture of Fletcher Trod. The sisters discuss finalizing their project. The news of the reward produces an extra profit outside the projected earnings.

Tamla says, "Mrs. Liman has to give us an A. We have done exactly what she said to do to make a great business."

Tamrah says, "I feel like we don't have to stop when this project is done. We can just choose stories with a different subject matter."

Tamryn says, "Water! We can investigate water next."

Tamla says, "Great idea! I like it!"

Tamrah says, "In the meantime, we have forty-eight hours to identify two shooters."

Tamryn says, "Sister, let's do it!"

At lunch, the sisters talk to some friends about the confession and how the community is responding. They watch news clips of women thanking the sisters for helping catch the reaper. They read comments on their detail analysis of the cars.

Several people comment that a black Charger was near the Nikita Walsh, Prea Cole, Dana Motts, and Blaire Bunch murder scenes. Notably, several people mention the Charger had expensive rims with a red, green, and white emblem in the center of the rim.

One of the students is related to a detective, so he tags him; he says, "My Uncle Ray is a homicide detective. I'll tag him and text him to go check it." The sisters thank him for his help. They think about the profit and gain of murdering Nikita Walsh, Prea Cole, Dana Motts, and Blaire Bunch could the murders be for financial gain or self-gratification.

Tamla says, "We need to look at those cases to see if they have anything in common."

Tamryn says, "I'll check their social media pages."

Tamrah says, "Great idea, Tamryn!"

Before bed, Tamryn calls Tamla and Tamrah to her room. Tamryn says, "I found something. It's huge! Big! Big! Big!"

Tamla asks, "What did you find?"

Tamryn says, "Each girl posted about going on a date with a new guy between one and three days before they were shot." Tamryn shows Tamla and Tamrah the posts.

Tamla says, "Tamryn, you have to post this now."

Tamrah says, "This has got to be the clue."

Tamryn posts that there is a possible link between Nikita Walsh, Prea Cole, Dana Motts, and Blaire Bunch. Tamryn explains that the women had a date within days before their demise.

Within minutes, the victims' friends leave comments on the post noting a common thread. Each of the victims met a mysterious man on a new free dating app, The Beholder's Eye.

No one knows the name of the man, but Nikita Walsh's best friend, Lana McGhee, knows the username of the man Nikita went on a date with because Nikita showed her the man's profile. Lana comments that Nikita went on a date with KnightRyder89.

Tamla texts their friend to tell him to forward the tip to his uncle the homicide detective. The sisters celebrate a possible break in the shooting cases: the black Charger and the username on the dating app. They go to sleep excited, hopeful that a resolution is coming soon to both shooting cases.

Thursday morning, Tamryn wakes up and goes straight for her phone. She discovers she is tagged in a story by a girl who claims to have had an experience with a creepy man using the handle KnightRyder89 on The Beholder's Eye dating app. Several other girls post a similar experience. The girls are sure this is the lead they were hoping would come.

Tamrah is sitting in fifth period when a group of students come to the door shouting, "Turn on the news!" Mrs. Browning turns on the news. It's a live action video of an active police chase.

In broad daylight, a black Charger with luxury Italian rims and all tinted windows flees several police cruisers down the interstate at speeds over 120 m.p.h. The entire school watches the intense chase wondering who is the driver of the Charger. The Charger increases speed as it zooms pass cars and weaves through traffic.

Nervous drivers dodge the speeding car and the approaching police cruisers. The sound of helicopters and sirens blaze through the television. The news helicopters hover over the chase as news casters give commentary of the erratic movement of the cars. Police cruisers block all entrance ramps of the interstate. The approaching police cruisers coordinate their movements to keep civilians safe.

When the police clear the interstate of civilians, they strategically position themselves to surround the Charger. The Charger tries to evade police in a construction zone. Construction crew members rapidly scatter to the side of the road to escape from the oncoming speeding car. As the road narrows to one lane, the police cruisers form a single file line behind the black Charger. The chief of the Detroit Police Department gives the order to stop the Charger when it passes through the construction zone.

S.W.A.T Team members have the spike strips in place at the end of the one-lane construction zone. The Charger approaches the spike strips at full speed. The police cruisers follow slowly to give the S.W.A.T. Team a chance to remove the strips once the Charger has rolled over them.

The reporters in the helicopter explains what is going on as the students are captivated by the action-packed images on the television. The students watch the Charger roll over the spike strips at full speed. The explosion from all four tires releases so much pressure that the Charger lifts from the ground. The students gasp as the Charger becomes airborne and soars into the embankment. The pressure of the impact sends the Charger into a spiral rolling over twelve times before landing on its roof.

The students are amazed and on the edge of their seats as they wonder who is driving the car. Police cruisers come to a stop. Police officers storm from their cars with weapons aimed and surround the flipped Charger. Police officers stand on guard as two officers approach the car to open the driver's side door.

The students watch in suspense as the police pulls out the driver, a masked man dressed in all black. Another masked man crawls out of the back-passenger's side window. Police siege on the man who has his face in the grass and his hands and legs spread out.

The students shout at the television, "Take off the mask! I want to see who it is!" The curious students watch as the police officers search and cuff the two men.

The suspense holds the students' attention as they anticipate the officers removing the mask. The police lift the men off the ground and onto their feet. As the police walk the men towards police cruisers, an officer snatches off the masks.

The students gasp again, "OMG! OMG," the students say in a moment of shock.

One student yells, "That's Hakim and Khalid!"

Another student yells, "Those are the Golden boys! Their father is the rich guy on those car and boat commercials."

The students are shocked. One student says, "I didn't expect this at all."

The news reporters express shock when they recognize the men in custody. Police put the men in the back of two separate cruisers, and the cruisers pull off. One helicopter follows the cruisers to the precinct, and one stays on scene.

Cameras record every second of police searching the vehicle. Police find weapons, money and disguises stashed all over the car. The students watch every second of the search. Students question if Hakim and Khalid are professional hitmen.

The Golden Boys are known for partying and spending money on expensive clothes, but no one ever questioned where they got their money. Everyone assumed they got their money from their dad.

The sisters spend Thursday evening finalizing their project and preparing their final presentation. Tamrah says, "Sisters! Excellent work!"

Tamla says, "We possibly helped the police catch two serial killers. We went viral several times."

Tamryn says, "Our presentation and report have all the components Mrs. Liman said to include. The report is thorough and well-written. All we really need to do now is lead the police to the third killer."

Tamla looking at Tamrah and pointing to Tamryn says, "What she said!"

Tamrah says, "T3, I like your thinking."

Tamla asks, "What's our next move?"

Tamryn says, "Let's create a fake profile on the Beholder's Eye dating app using a profile picture that looks similar to the victims to see if KnightRyder89 will reach out to us. We can probe him for information to forward to the police. We may find out something important."

Tamla says, "Great plan!"

Tamrah says, "Let's go!"

They work vigorously to create the profile before going to bed. Tamla says, "I bet we will have a message from him by the time we wake up in the morning."

Tamrah says, "He won't be able to resist. Predators are creatures of habits and patterns."

Tamryn says, "Like a moth to a flame, he will fall right into our little trap." The sisters high-five each other.

Tamla says, "When we present tomorrow, everyone will already know most of our presentation."

Tamrah says, "We've got to convey our message in a manner that intrigues and captivates the audience."

Tamryn says, "We are going to rock it; don't worry!"

Tamryn and Tamrah are lying in bed with Tamla talking about their presentation when their mother runs into the room. Tamil excitedly says, "Turn to the news! Hurry! Hurry!" Tamrah rushes to get the remote and change the channel. The lead story on the eleven o'clock is the Golden Boys confess to being hitmen. The sisters simultaneously gasp.

The news anchor, Klein Cleats, explains how the teenaged bloggers led the police to professional murderers for hire who happen to be the sons of Wolf Gunner Welling.

Klein Cleats introduces a news conference headed by the Chief of Detroit Police Department. The chief explains that the Hakim Welling and Khalid

Welling have confessed to murdering several people including four females in Detroit for money.

The chief explains that guns found on the scene of the police chase earlier that day are the weapons that ended the life of more than twenty-five people all over the Midwest of America. Also found hidden on one of Wolf Gunner Welling's properties was the black Crown Victoria with tinted window used in the four homicides of the Detroit women.

After the chief's speech, reporters ask questions. One reporter asks if the Toms sister will get the reward because they are responsible for the tip that led to the killer. The chief says it's a possibility. The department is looking into if the Toms sisters are owed the money. The sisters watch the broadcast in awe.

Tamil says, "Ladies, you did it again! I'm so proud of you."

They hug their mom; Tamil says, "Now, go to bed!"

The girls tell their mother goodnight.

Tamil tells them, "Goodnight! I love you!"

The girls say in unison, "We love you, Mom!"

Tamryn and Tamrah go to their own rooms.

The big news Friday morning is the resignation of Mr. Welling as CEO of his own company and the swearing-in of the chief financial officer as the chief executive officer. Despite Mr. Welling swearing he knew nothing of his sons' criminal enterprise, he gave up his position to prevent damaging the reputation of the company he spent his whole adult life building and nourishing. The sisters watch the press conference as they eat breakfast.

The sisters feel bad for Mr. Welling; Tamryn says, "It's quite possible, Mr. Welling didn't know what his sons were doing."

Tamil says, "He certainly didn't profit from their crimes. He didn't need the little bit of money those boys made."

Tamryn says, "I hate he has to give up his company."

Tamil says, "The things parents have to do for their children."

Before leaving for school, the sisters check the messages on the dating app. They read ten messages before coming across a message from KnightRyder89.

The message reads: Hello, Beautiful! I would love to take you out. Tamrah replies: Why don't you tell me a little bit more about yourself. I need to know who I am going out with.

Tamla says, "Good comeback, T1!"

Tamrah says, "Thank you, T2!"

When the sisters get to school, everyone is talking about the confession. Everyone congratulates the sisters on a job well done! Tamla and Tamryn get passes so they can attend Mrs. Liman's class first hour to present their project with Tamrah.

Mrs. Liman is beyond pleased with their presentation and project. The sisters are happy with the response they receive. The students in the class encourage the sisters to keep the blog up. Some even give suggestions of topics they want to see investigated.

After school the girls check their messages, there's another message from KnightRyder89; it reads: I'm twenty-seven years old. I'm a mechanic. I live in Detroit. Tamla types: What's your real name? You know my real name, so I should know yours. I can't go out with someone and I don't know their name.

KnightRyder89 replies: My name is Gavin Bryant.

Tamla types: What do you like to do for fun?

KnightRyder89 replies: I like to listen to music, watch movies, and hunt. What about you?

Tamla replies: I play tennis and golf. I like to run and workout. I also enjoy music and movies.

KnightRyder89 responds: Maybe we can incorporate some of your hobbies in our date.

Tamla replies: Maybe! I'll consider a date when I feel more comfortable.

Tamrah says, "We've got to get the name to the police, but first let's Google Mr. Gavin Bryant."

Tamryn says, "I'll text Joey to see if he can get his uncle to contact us."

Joey calls back immediately; he says, "I'm here with my Uncle Ray now. I'll let you speak to him."

Detective Rayford Mills gets on the phone. Tamryn explains from beginning to end what the research says about the third case. After listening to everything the girls have on the third suspect, Detective Mills tell the girls to stop all communication with the suspect and to send Joey a text with the login information to that account.

While the girls eat dinner with their mother, Detective Mills and a group of detectives go over the blog Deadline Detroit and the messages on the Beholder's Eye dating app. They read what the girls wrote about the victims and the potential suspect.

Detective Rick says, "These girls did a thorough job. I mean I think he's the killer after reading all this. He likes to hunt; the victims were hunted. These girls may be onto something. We need a warrant for this dating app."

Detective Mills says, "They're just kids."

Detective Johnson (the only female detective in the group) says, "Kids who have solved two murders. Two murders we had nothing on until they gave us what we needed. They are smart young ladies with good instinct. I trust their instinct. Based on their investigation, it's worth taking a close look at KnightRyder89."

Detective Mills says, "We have nothing else to go on. Detective Johnson apply for the warrant."

Detective Johnson says, "On it!"

To celebrate a job well done on their project, Tamil takes the girls to a movie and out for dessert after dinner. When they get home, their dad is home. The sisters tell him all about their presentation.

He congratulates them on their good work; he says, "I'm so proud of you for working together like a team and accomplishing your goal. I am so proud to say I have daughters who are smart, motivated, and determined. I know you three will do something great with your lives." They hug their dad, and tell him thank you.

Mr. Toms asks, "So, does this mean you girls are done with the murder case?"

Tamrah says, "We have done all we can for that case, so I say yes. We are done with that case."

Mr. Toms asks, "So will the next story be less dangerous?"

Tamla says, "We haven't decided exactly what the topic will be, but we have a million non-violent ideas."

Mr. Toms says, "Well, I'm so glad to hear that!"

Tamryn says, "Glad enough to take us for some ice cream tomorrow?"

Mr. Toms says, "With hot fudge brownies!"

Tamryn says, "My man!"

The next day, the girls enjoy a relaxing day. Their dad takes them for hot fudge brownies and vanilla ice cream before he goes to work. The girls spend the rest of the Saturday with their mother. The sisters convince Tamil to take them to the mall to shop for spring and summer clothes and shoes. After shopping, Tamil takes the girls for dinner. Saturday ends peacefully in the city. Even the news has nothing new to report.

Sunday comes around and the Toms sisters make breakfast for their parents before the family goes to church. After church, the sisters enjoy the nice weather while riding their bikes through their neighborhood. They stop at the park to swing for a bit. They return home and prepare for the upcoming school week. They watch the evening news and again the news has nothing new to report. Monday and Tuesday are also quiet news days.

Wednesday after school, the Toms sisters eat dinner with their mother while they watch the evening news. Finally, what the Tom sisters were waiting for: Breaking news headline: City-Wide Manhunt for a Suspected Serial Killer.

Klein Cleats reports how a tip to Detective Mills from the teenaged sister bloggers lead police to the identity of the third suspect in the Detroit Grand Reaper case. Klein Cleats explains how it was thought to be one suspect until the teenaged sister bloggers analyze the case concluding there were three killers on the loose in Detroit.

Cleats says, "This is what we have learned so far. Police are looking for Garvin Gant Bryant in connection with the deaths of four local women: Nikita Walsh, Prea Cole, Dana Motts, and Blaire Bunch.

Under the username: KnightRyder89 on the Beholder's Eye dating app, Bryant went on a date with the four women and within three days after their date the women were found deceased from a single gunshot wound to the head.

A warrant for Bryant's arrest was issued at nine a.m. this morning. Police have stormed every address connected to Bryant, but have yet to find him. It is suspected that he is on the run. Police took an arsenal of weapons, several computers, and a tablet from one home."

Co-Anchor, Anita Barr, says, "Posts on social media and a blog created by a set of triplet sisters led to the capture of Fletcher Trod also known as The Detroit

Grand Reaper, Hakim and Khalid Welling (rich boys turned hitmen), and now with a tip generated by the sisters, the police are actively hunting Garvin Gant Bryant. If all three men are convicted, the sisters could be the recipients of thirty-thousand dollars in reward money. We at the evening news want to thank three brave teenaged girls for taking an interest in our city."

The sisters watch the news with their parents happy that the case is about to be resolved and the women of Detroit will be a little safer when the third killer in the Grand Reaper case is taken off the streets.

Tamla says, "I think our intel is right."

Tamrah says, "The police have to think so too or they wouldn't be looking for him."

Tamryn says, "I'll be glad when he is in custody."

Tariq Toms says, "I will feel safer with him behind bars."

Tamil says, "I hope they catch him soon."

In the early hours of Thursday morning while the Toms family sleeps, Gavin is hiding alone in a dark, quiet house with several high-powered guns. Police and dogs track him by his smell. Gavin is full of adrenaline and fear as the sound of the dogs get closer and closer. Gavin's heart is beating out of his chest. He is profusely sweating as he loads his guns. Gavin hears the back door slowly open.

Gavin is in a corner of an upstairs bedroom peeking out the window. He watches the police dressed in body armor walk toward his home in an attack formation. They quietly sneak into the dark house led by police dogs.

Gavin crawls out of the window onto a ledge and climbs onto the roof. He hides behind the chimney in the night sky highlighted by the moonlight. Gavin nervously sits waiting, but he doesn't hear anything. The dogs lead the police to the window that Gavin climbed out of. The police assumes he climbed down, so they rush out of the house to search for him.

The dogs sit outside the house because they no longer can trace his scent. The police scatter in fear that they have lost him. When the air is quiet, Gavin cautiously climbs down the back of the house.

He slowly and quietly creeps through the dark alley. He hears chatter and dogs barking behind him. The dogs smell his scent and begin to run in his direction. The dogs lead the police down the dark alley. Gavin hears the footsteps chatter getting closer. Gavin hides between two garages with his gun clutched tightly in his hand.

When a group of police officers walk pass, he shoots one cop before scurrying away quickly. The police panic seeing one of their own lying on the ground. Three officers take off behind Gavin led by a barking police dog. Another group of officers split up to surround him. Gavin runs shooting behind him hoping to keep the police away. The police, unphased by Gavin's shots, continue to pursue him down the narrow path between two houses.

When Gavin makes it to the front of the houses, he turns the corner at full speed. Running in the darkness, Gavin cannot see before or behind him. He runs blindly around another house and face first into a breaching battering ram. Gavin is knocked out instantly.

He is cuffed and put in the back of a police car. The police clear the area and speed away with the suspect and his weapons in custody. Gavin is taken Downtown to the Police Headquarters where he is booked for four counts of first-degree murder.

The Toms family wakes up to the news of Gavin's capture, which gives them all a huge amount of relief. Mr. and Mrs. Toms watch the news as they eat breakfast. Mr. Toms says, "Finally, he is caught!" Tamil calls for the sisters to turn on the news. The sisters celebrate his capture.

Friday morning, Mr. Toms answers the phone. It's the mayor. The mayor wants to give the Toms sisters the key to the city for their hard work and diligence on the case. When Mr. Toms tells the girls that they will receive the key to the city, the girls jump up and down screaming.

Mr. Toms tells his family, "The whole family is invited to breakfast before school on Monday morning. The girls can pick the place. At breakfast, the mayor will give the girls the key to the city."

The girls simultaneously say, "The Original Pancake House!" Mr. Toms laugh.

The End

When Mrs. Campbell finishes the story, she and the boys talk about what made the sisters successful. The boys list the things they think helped the sisters succeed: dedication, willingness to take risks, supportive parents, team work, effective planning, self-evaluation, and service to the community.

Mrs. Campbell was pleased that her boys were able to get every point of her story; she says, "Boys, I am so proud of you. Each of you are on a path to change. You have been open to receive the lessons, and I have such high hopes for each of you and your future."

Just as Mrs. Campbell finishes her sentence, she sees the bus pull up; she says, "Boys, it's time for a field trip." The boys get excited. They want to know where they are going, but Mrs. Campbell refuses to tell the location. Mrs. Campbell lines the boys up and leads them to the bus. Mrs. Miller and the mothers follow the boys to the bus.

None of the participants know where they are going, but the boys assume they are going somewhere fun. They ride for about fifteen minutes and pull up to a big brown building. The boys are disappointed because they don't see go-karts, video games, or a sports field or court. They all asks Mrs. Campbell, "What's this place?" and "Why are we here?"

Mrs. Campbell tells the boys, "You're going to have to come in to find out."

The boys follow Mrs. Campbell off the bus to fulfill their curiosity. Mrs. Miller and the mothers follow the curious, complaining boys who are still disappointed the trip isn't a fun one.

The mothers are left in the dark as well, but Mrs. Miller convinced them to trust the process. The mothers know Mrs. Miller and Mrs. Campbell have good intentions for their sons, so they don't question their methods.

The participants are immediately stopped at the entrance checkpoint by armed guards. Each participant walks through a metal detector before a guard waves a wand around their legs, arms and pockets. When everyone makes it through the metal detectors and checkpoint, the county sheriff and deputy-sheriff come through the door and welcome the group to the Life Development Center for Adjudicated and Emancipated Youth.

The sheriff, Sheriff Chants Terrell, and deputy-sheriff, Deputy-Sheriff Thomas O'Rourke, take the group on a tour of the facility. First, they tour the east wing that houses babies, toddlers and young children who have no parents. The sheriff and deputy-sheriff take the group in to meet some of the children. The sheriff explains that children are abandon every day at hospitals, police departments, and fire stations. The county created this center to address the issue of numerous youths with no homes or unhealthy homes.

The mothers and boys play with the children. It is heartbreaking for the boys to see the happy, naïve children smiling.

Sheriff Terrell says, "They never had a family, so they don't know any other way of life. This center is all they know. They live and are schooled here." The boys have pity on their faces as they play with the children and the toys.

Talking to the parentless children make the boys realize how fortunate they are to have mothers who love them even when they don't deserve it. The kids are clean and look healthy, but the mothers and boys see that there is something missing in the kids' eyes.

The boys had a preconceived notion that kids without parents should be sad and depressed, and somehow seeing the contrary to that belief made the severity of the situation hit the boys harder.

The boys talk among themselves about how every child needs at least one parent. The kids are very friendly and affectionate with the mothers and sons.

Mrs. Miller and Mrs. Campbell don't speak a word. They let the scene have an organic effect on the group. They observe the boys' display compassion, and it brings the social workers joy. Before this session, the boys didn't think of themselves as good people. The need of the children make them gentle, kind, and loving toward children. The boys begin to understand what Mrs. Campbell was saying about service and doing something kind for others will help yourself.

The deputy-sheriff leads the group to a big room with chairs arranged in a double circle, while the sheriff went toward the housing units of the center. The sheriff tells the group to have a seat in the outer circle. They sit quietly not knowing what to expect next.

Deputy-Sheriff O'Rourke welcomes the group to the recovery circle. He explains, in this room, teenaged addicts come to purge their demons and support each other on the road of recovery.

He says, "When Mrs. Miller and Mrs. Campbell bring a group for a visit, we invite the visitors to meet our participants and have a dialogue. Their participation in these sessions is seen as community service. As recovering teen addicts, one thing they each want is to stop another teen or child from following in their footsteps."

Sheriff Terrell walks in with five girls and twelve boys dressed in white t-shirts, gray jogging pants, and white socks with their flip-flops. None of the teen residents are allowed to have belts, strings, or anything they can use to injure themselves.

The teens walk to the inner circle to sit with every eye in the room on them. Each one of the recovering teens stand up to introduce him or herself, and to tell their addiction story.

Mrs. Miller and Mrs. Campbell again are silent, and let the stories of the teens take an organic effect on the boys and their mothers. It worked like a charm.

There is not a dry eye in the circle.

The speakers and listeners both cry like babies as each teenager tells how he or she became addicted to drugs and homeless. The stories have several common themes: unstable homes, some form of abuse, lack of direction, unsupportive family, low levels of supervision, poverty, failure in school or dropping out of school, and ruined dreams and opportunities. One by one, the teens stand up and pour their heart and truth out to complete strangers.

After each teen spoke, the sheriff allows the group to ask the teens questions. One of the boys talks about losing his football scholarship, Tucker asks the young man, what he is going to do now that playing college football is not an option. The young man burst into tears, and says he is determined to get clean and go to college to study psychology.

He says, "Since living out my dreams is probably not going to happen, I want to help other young people from experiencing what I went through with drugs. No teen should struggle with addiction. We should be living life in high school getting ready for college. I hope something one of us said will prevent each of you from taking steps down the path of drugs."

The sheriff leads the teens back to the housing unit, and he gathers the second group of twenty boys and eight girls. While the sheriff is gathering the next group, the deputy-sheriff explains that they were about to meet the adjudicated youth.

He says, "These are the residents mandated here for a certain amount of time by the court system as a result of committing a crime. They were sent here instead of jail because this was their first offense. This program has one goal: rehabilitation. Get the teens back on track, hopefully avoiding a second offense."

The sheriff leads the second group into the room; they sit in the inner circle. This group wears inmate-like uniforms. One-by-one the teens introduce themselves and talk about their life of crime. The teens explain how rough life had been for them as children, so they turned to the streets to survive. Once in the streets, they had to do cut-throat things to survive like steal, hurt people, and sell drugs or themselves.

The teens talk about life in the center with restrictions. One of the boys says, "You take your freedom for granted until one day you no longer have control of your life. At seventeen-years-old, I have a bedtime of eight o'clock. I miss my grandmother's cooking. I miss holidays with my family. I miss going to school and hanging with my friends. I am missing out on my teenage life, and I'll never get these four years back." The boys listen to the stories thinking how easily this could be them standing up their telling their stories of bad behavior.

Another teen says, "I made choices and now I suffer the consequences. At first, I had no clue that my behavior would result in me being arrested at age fourteen, going to court, and being sentenced to stay in a building all day every day until my eighteenth birthday.

"I am missing my entire high school experience. I won't get to go to any homecomings, the prom, or a graduation all because I was out in the streets wilding out when I didn't have to be. My mother gave me everything, and I took her for granted. It broke her heart when I was arrested. In the courtroom, she broke down crying. I couldn't take it. I set a bad example for my little brothers and I regret that so much."

As the young man speaks, the boys feel guilt and shame because they are just like him. They realize they can head down that same path. The sheriff takes the residents back to their housing unit.

The deputy-sheriff leads the group to the bus. The boys get on the bus in complete silence. Each boy sits next to his mother. Their heads hang low. Mrs. Campbell tells the group that they are going to head to their next stop.

No one asks where they are going because they are still dealing with the heaviness of the experience at the center. The bus pulls off, as each mother comforts her son. After the heart-wrenching visit to the center, broken places were visible in every son and mother. No one says anything, but it is clearly communicated on the bus ride that things had to change.

Soon, the bus pulls in the parking lot of a beautiful church. The group unloads and walks into the church. The boys are greeted by ten men of the church. The group is invited to have lunch with the men. The men talk to the boys and the mothers while they eat getting to know each other.

After lunch, the men of the church take the boys to the sanctuary while the women stay in the dining hall. The men talk to the boys about the importance of men praying and having a relationship with God.

Deacon John Stafford invites the boys to the altar to take a seat. He says, "The first step to building a relationship with God is learning how to pray and praise. When do we pray? Why do we pray?" None of the boys have an answer.

Deacon Stafford says, "Pray about everything! Pray before you make a decision, pray when you need strength and courage, pray for safety and health for your family every morning, pray when all is well, and pray when living is hell. Praying for and covering your family daily are duties of a man."

Brother Matthew Helms asks the boys, "Who prays?" Not one of the boys raise a hand, so Brother Helms asks, "Who knows how to pray?" Again, the boys have no response. Brother Helms says, "That's the first thing we need to work on."

Each man takes one of the boys for one-on-one coaching. The pairs spread out in the sanctuary to give the boys privacy to express their truth. Brother Helms keeps Jace at the altar.

Brother Helms always takes the boy that Mrs. Miller and Mrs. Campbell mark as the most difficult. Brother Helms knows what it is like to be a troubled youth. Brother Helms was once in the same situation, but he turned his life over to Christ.

Brother Helms asks Jace, "What's on your mind and heart? What are you thankful for? What concerns you or troubles you? What do you want for your loved ones? What do you need? What does your family need? Those are the questions I want you to answer, but not to me to Him.

"I want you to start with Heavenly Father, I come to you and from there lay your burdens at his feet, leave them at the altar and trust that he will do what's according to his plan. End with 'In Jesus name I pray.'" Jace listens with his heart as Brother Helms speaks.

Jace opens his mouth to pray; he says, "Heavenly Father, I come to you to give thanks for Mecia for adopting my brothers and I. Mecia saved us from a bad situation, maybe you sent her, so I thank you for that.

"I pray you save my little brothers from making the mistakes I made. I am so sorry for hurting Mecia's feelings and stressing her out. She didn't deserve that. I haven't been a good big brother, and I am ashamed of myself for that.

"I pray you keep Mecia safe and healthy. She deserves something nice for all she's done for us. I pray my brothers will be better sons than I have been. I hope they make her proud and happy. In Jesus name I pray."

Brother Helms asks, "Do you feel a little better, a little lighter? That's how you make it through the day, day-by-day. You have to pray day and night just to keep your sanity."

Jace says, "I do feel better."

Brother Helms says, "Just say what's on your heart and God will handle the rest." Brother Helms leads him to sit on the first pew. One-by-one the groups sit on the pews. Sitting on the pews is the cue to the others that the group has completed the prayer.

When all ten groups are seated, Deacon Stafford begins to talk about the next phase of building a relationship with God. Deacon Stafford holds up the bible, and says, "Studying the bible is also key to your relationship with God.

You will get to know who he is and what he wants from you. Does anyone read the bible regularly?" For the third time the boys have no response.

Deacon Stafford says, "When it comes to your personal journey, as a beginner you should search the bible by subject. When you get comfortable with the bible, you can move toward studying people, places and events. Eventually, you will be reading the bible book by book.

"If you feel guilty, look up guilt in the index and read all the verses listed under guilt. If you feel shame, look up the verses about shame. If you need faith or courage, look up the verses about faith and courage."

Each boy is given a bible inscribed with his name on the cover in gold letters. They break off into pairs again to practice looking up subjects in the bible.

Brother Helms takes Jace back to the altar and asks what is the biggest concern he has right now. Jace takes a minute to think. After a moment of introspection, Jace says the murder of my biological parents is something that bothers me daily.

He adds, "I don't know what to do with all the feelings and thoughts I have, and it's ruining my relationship with Mecia, my adoptive mother. I really want to stop hurting her."

Brother Helms says, "We have several things we need to look up: grief, death, anger, pain and family. Let's look up family first." Brother Helms pulls out his phone to search bible verses on family, and a list populates on his screen. He says, "This is a good one. Let's read 1 Corinthians 13: 4-8."

Brother Helms reads the verses to Jace and asks what is he trying to tell us. He says, "Let's break it apart by sentence. Let's talk about two adjectives in the first sentence: patient and kind. What do those look like to you?"

Jace says, "Being polite, not yelling or being frustrated."

Brother Helms says, "Are you any of those to Mecia, why or why not?"

Jace says, "I am not those to anyone because I don't know how to be either."

Brother Helms asks, "Do you think Mecia deserves you trying to learn how to be those things?"

Jace says, "She does!"

Brother Helms says, "You have got to heal the hurt and let her in to help you and love you or nothing will ever change. You pray about that hurt. Study the bible on those feelings and talk to someone about those feelings. Next line, let's look at the verbs envy and boast. What does those look like to you?"

Jace says, "Bragging and talking about yourself. I'm not a bragger."

Brother Helms says, "The third sentence talks about not dishonoring others, being self-seeking, or easily angered. Are you any of those towards your brothers or Mecia?"

"I am all of those things to my brothers and Mecia," Jace says with his head held low.

Brother Helms says, "The next sentence talks about disliking evil and loving the truth, and right now Jace you are telling your whole truth. That's a huge step toward making a change. The last sentence says we should protect, trust, hope and persevere.

"As a man, I know you are ready to do all of those. I hear it in your prayer, your concerns, and your spirit. Out of five lines, you are only lacking in two, that means you are closer to being the man you want to be than you realize."

The boys and men congregate and sit on the steps of the altar. One-by-one the ten men tell the boys what led them to turn away from their old lives and turn toward a life in Christ.

The boys were shocked at the admissions of acts of crime, acts of violence, spending time in prison, abandoning loved ones, drug abuse, feeling shame and guilt, needing forgiveness, searching for something and finding God was the cure. The men revealing their truth made them more relatable to the boys.

Deacon Stafford says, "We are not here as born saints. We are sinners, we have sinned a lot. We stand here as sinners trying to serve the community by saving the next generation from making the same mistakes. It's not too late for anyone of you. "Before you cross the line, please remember us.

It's not worth prison, the literal prison or the spiritual prison that will keep you a slave to guilt, anger, and shame. And that leads me to my final point of maintaining a relationship with God: ritual."

Deacon Stafford continues, "Daily, weekly you need a routine to keep you in the right mind set. Prayer in the morning, reading verses in a bible or reading a spiritual publication like Daily Bread, spending time with other people walking the path, some form of service or way to give to someone else are all very important to keep you focused and fed spiritually.

"Do we fall short? Yes! But that's why we have each other. Through fellowship and gathering, we are there to catch each other before we fall too far. We can encourage each other, learn from each other's struggles. You all are welcome back here at any time. Even if it's not us, we beg you to please get some positive, trustworthy males in your life to serve as models and leaders.

"Another thing you should do is bond with and support each other. There is no better brotherhood than the men you are standing with. Who could understand you more than someone standing in similar shoes?"

The boys listen to Deacon's advice. Before boarding the bus, the men give the boys their contact info and invite them to the church's anniversary dinner. The boys excitedly accept the invitation.

When the group gets back to the First Step Center, they sit in a big circle. Mrs. Miller calls each mother to the center of the circle to present her with a survival bag with things to comfort her during the hard times: candles, chocolate, warm socks, gift cards, an engraved bible, and two parenting books.

Mrs. Campbell calls each son to the center of the circle to present him with a certificate of completion. Mrs. Campbell and Mrs. Miller hug each person and wish them the best on their journey before they walk out the door for the last time.

Life After the First Step Program

Monday after the seventh Saturday, Lea's transfer was approved. Not only did she get the location she wanted, but she also got a promotion. Lea and Levi pack and move to her father's ranch in Louisiana.

Levi starts at a small magnet school with a diverse student body. The students are well-mannered and well behaved, so Levi has no one who encourages or supports off-task behavior. Lea insists that he gets involved at school, so Levi joins the golf, tennis, soccer, and debate team. Lea and Levi are able to heal and move forward with the guidance of a family counselor.

As promised, Lucas starts his medication and transfer to the school for boys with ADHD. Melinda signs Lucas up for tutoring at a learning center. Lucas attends tutoring for an hour twice a week to improve his reading and math skills.

Melinda and Lucas meet every Thursday to discuss Lucas' progress. Lucas keeps his word and attends church. He pays close attention to the sermons and volunteers at the church. Melinda becomes vegan and works out every day after work to stay as healthy as she can for her son.

After the First Step program, Jace asks Mecia if he could go to the African-centered school. Jace says, "The kids there know how to act, and it'll help me keep myself in order." Mecia agrees because she is happy that Jace is trying to change.

Jace says, "I, also, want to go back to that church we went to with Mrs.

Miller and Mrs. Campbell. Brother Helms and Deacon Stafford told me they'll mentor me and baptize me.

Mecia says, "Whatever it takes, Jace, I will support you."

Jace says, "Last thing, now that we are working on our relationship, can I call you Mom?"

Mecia says, "Of course you can, when you feel ready, I would love that!"

Mega works hard to uphold his part of the deal to earn the tuition to basketball camp and the membership fee to the basketball gym for teens. Megan is so impressed with Mega's improvement that she keeps her part of their deal. She even gives him a new pair of Jordan's for camp.

When Mega starts the seventh grade, he is the best basketball player in his school's league. He plays hard hoping to get a full scholarship to attend a private catholic high school.

Tucker is determined to continue playing football, so he does everything in the contract. Inga is beyond thrilled with Tuckers progress. They have their weekly meetings on Sundays after dinner to discuss Tucker's progress.

Tucker proves he is keeping up his grades with a weekly progress report. Tucker even got an after-school job babysitting for his neighbors. Showing so much progress and increased responsibility, Inga let Tucker hangout with his friends from the team after practice at least twice per week.

After the First Step program, Rita is so proud of Niko for showing an increased effort in school, staying out of trouble, and volunteering at a group home. Niko helps the leader of the group home keep the house clean and he reads books to the children who live in the group home.

Niko has changed a lot, and he is looking forward to going to high school next school year with a new attitude. Most importantly, Niko no longer makes his mother sad. Niko earns his monthly shopping trips, so he can't wait to show off his new clothes at school in the fall.

Abigail and Eli have improved their relationship so much since the First Step program. Abigail finally has the relationship with her son that she always desired.

Eli volunteers and serves at church even though he is staying out of trouble.

Eli figures serving at church is a way to pay for his past sins. Eli, also, keeps in contact with Deacon Stafford. Deacon Stafford is like a mentor to him. Deacon Stafford and Eli hang out once a week to do something fun.

Kelly and Caleb attend family counseling to deal with the past. Kelly supports Caleb with keeping his part of the contract. She helps him write a letter to his father. When his father writes him back, she takes him to meet his father. Meeting his father was life changing.

She is his biggest cheerleader at every football game. With his improved relationship with his mother and questions answered by his father, Caleb is in a better personal space, and his performance in football and academics has improved greatly. Caleb is more confident and pleasant.

Counseling has help Caleb and Kelly build a strong, healthy mother-son relationship. Caleb volunteers at the soup kitchen two days per week, and he and Kelly attend church every Sunday.

Xander, Nia, and Xander's dad, Xavier, decide as a family to move to another state. Xander and his parents talk about the improved financial opportunities they would have if they moved. Xander sees the possibilities of better jobs and increased salaries for his parents as a reason to move.

After they move, the family attends family counseling twice a month. Xander and Nia sit down for a short talk every Monday, Wednesday, and Friday. With the changes the family makes, Xander upholds his part of the contract. Attending a new school, he is staying out of trouble, improved his grades, and doing his chores.

Stephanie convinces Brad to attend anger management and grief counseling. Brad is handling his emotions as a maturing young man should. He reads books as he promised and keeps up his grades. Stephanie and Brad's relationship improved so much that Bradley walks Stephanie down the aisle in her wedding.

Bradley, Stephanie, and her new husband study the bible together as a family. It is helping to create a deeper, lasting bonds between Bradley, Stephanie, and Stephanie's new husband, Eshawn. The relationships they are building is helping keep peace in their home.

Burying the Paper and the Past

Niko walks over to Rodrick. Niko nervously starts to speak, he says, "Hey Rod!" Rodrick looks up and quietly stares at Niko. Niko says, "I was wrong to put my hands on you. I want to apologize to you. I also would like to apologize to your family. I should've broken up the fight, not jump in. I hope you can forgive me and we can be cool with each other." Rodrick reaches out his hand and Niko shakes it.

At the end of the day, Rodrick goes up to his family in the car waiting to pick him up from school. Rodrick tells his parents that Niko wants to apologize to them.

Niko goes up to the car and apologize to Rodrick's parents. Niko tells them he recognizes he was wrong. He also asks for their forgiveness.

When Niko gets home, he buries the paper in his backyard. After that day, Niko and Rodrick can put the past behind them and be cordial with one another.

Xander makes things right with his mother and he feels good about that. However, Xander feels a little guilty when he thinks about his past behavior. Wanting to make things right with his whole family, Xander writes thank you and apology cards to his family.

To heal things with everyone, Xander gets a summer job, he saves every check to purchase gifts for his family. When everyone hugs him with a huge smile on their face, Xander buries his paper. Now, Xander can move forward in life.

Mega always knew that he had to apologize to Stanley Wilford for hurting him. Mega, who has changed, is now embarrassed by his behavior.

Stanley Wilford isn't returning to school because his parents fear Mega and the boys that jumped him would hurt him again.

Mega convinces his mother to reach out to Stanley's mother, Joy Wilford. Joy agrees to give Mega a chance to talk to Stanley. Mega walks up to the Wilford's front door.

When Joy opens the door, Mega says hello to her and quickly and sincerely apologizes to her. Mega says it is unfair to Stanley that he stays home when he was the victim. Mega says it's like he is punished.

Mega says, "Every child needs to experience school, trust me, I just learned a lot about life and consequences. It's unfair that Stanley suffers consequences for my behavior. If you let Stanley comeback, I can do one of two things and I'll let you and Stanley choose. 1) I can protect him. I will not let anyone fight him again, or 2) I will transfer to a new school with my new friend, Lucas. I am the one who should have a consequence. Whichever makes you feel safe is what I'll do."

Joy appreciates Mega's apology and proposal. Joy says, "You should ask Stanley what he wants." She calls Stanley to the door. Mega apologizes to Stanley and presents his proposal.

Stanley says, "I don't think you need to go to a new school. If you're done with it, I'm done with it." The boys shake hands. Joy watches the interaction and smiles.

Mega says, "I promise neither one of you will have a problem with me again." Mega goes home to bury his paper in the back yard. Mega and Stanley are able to be friends and play at the park together, but Mega decides to go to the school with Lucas. Mega is lured by the benefits of small classes and new era school structure.

Tucker learns one lesson that really helps him get in a better emotional state: forgiveness. It was a struggle, but Tucker forgives the murderers. Tucker had to pray about it, meditate on it, attend grief counseling and do some soul-searching. Tucker's able to let go of the hate and anger. When Tucker lets go of the hate and anger, he becomes a more peaceful person.

After he forgives his cousin's murderers, he is a better friend, student, and football player. Tucker says a prayer and buries his paper in his backyard. When Mrs. Campbell assigned the task to write down someone you can help, Tucker wrote: ME. Tucker wanted to be the best Tucker he could be.

Brad was ordered to the First Step program for beating a classmate with a book. Martin Calvin was embarrassed by the fight with Brad. Martin Calvin had panic attacks for weeks when he returned to school after the incident.

Now that Brad had completed the First Step program and counseling, Bradley felt bad about Martin's suffering. The more mature and aware Brad, walks up to Martin and apologizes for his behavior. Brad tells Martin that he has changed and he doesn't want any problems with Martin.

Brad says, "You're safe Martin; you don't have to worry about me bothering you ever again." Martin and Brad shake hands and they never have a problem again. The truce helps Martin calm his anxiety.

Eli convinces his mother to let him take drum and keyboard lessons at the church. Eli practices four days per week with the music director at the church. When Eli becomes proficient with the drums and keyboard, he convinces the music director of the church to offer lessons at the Life Development Center for Adjudicated and Emancipated Youth.

Sheriff Terrell welcomed the church's involvement. Eli taught the little kids and the music director, Coleman Kyle, gave lessons to the teens. After one of the kids Eli had been working with for a while was able to play a few notes, Eli buries his paper in the backyard. Eli wanted to make a little difference in the world. Eli thought teaching kids music was the best way to heal the world.

Levi thought about the motherless/fatherless children at the Life Development Center for Adjudicated and Emancipated Youth. Levi convinced Lea to volunteer once a week with him. Lea and Levi made fast friends with Zac a toddler who was abandon at birth. Levi and Lea found themselves looking forward to seeing him every week.

One day Levi sat Lea down and presented her with a proposal. Levi said, "We have room, we have love, and you are the best mother, Zac needs all of that. We love him and he loves us. I was thinking you could adopt Zac.

I will help you with him and I'll keep my grades up and stay out of trouble, so you don't have to worry about me." Lea thinks about his proposal for a few weeks before she agrees with the proposal. It was a long process, but Zac became Levi's little brother.

Lucas is succeeding at his new school. For the first time, Lucas is learning and actively participating in school. Lucas' relationship with his mother is now as strong as ever. There was just one thing in Lucas' life that needs to be address: his sister.

Lucas convinces his sister to come to counseling with him. It took a long time, but his sister starts to respond to the counseling. LaKisha, with the support of Lucas and Melinda, changes her life. One day, LaKisha hugs and thanks him for supporting and introducing her to a new life style. After that talk, Lucas buries the paper in his backyard.

Jace owed his family for the unnecessary stress he caused. Jace wanted to make sure his brothers didn't follow in his footsteps, so Jace convinces Mecia to enroll his brothers at his new school. Jace thought the culture of the school would help his brothers.

He also convinces Mecia to let his brothers get baptize and mentored by Deacon Stafford and Brother Helms. Jace prayed for his brothers and taught them how to pray. One night before bed, Jace hears his brothers praying together. Jace knows he had accomplished his goal. Jace buried his paper in the backyard.

Caleb was able to pull off a miracle, Caleb convinces his mother to listen to his father's apology. Kelly and Inmate 272948-77 sit face to face in the visitor's area of the jail. Inmate 272948-77 looks Kelly in her face and delivers a heart-felt plea for forgiveness. Kelly, who has made peace with the situation because she didn't want to ruin her son's future, accepted his apology. Kelly and Caleb continue going to therapy and counseling to deal with what Inmate 272948-77 had done to her. Caleb buried his paper and moved on with his life.

www.ingramcontent.com/pod-product-compliance
Lightning Source LLC
Chambersburg PA
CBHW051511120626
46551CB00012B/869